# ASTRID ™

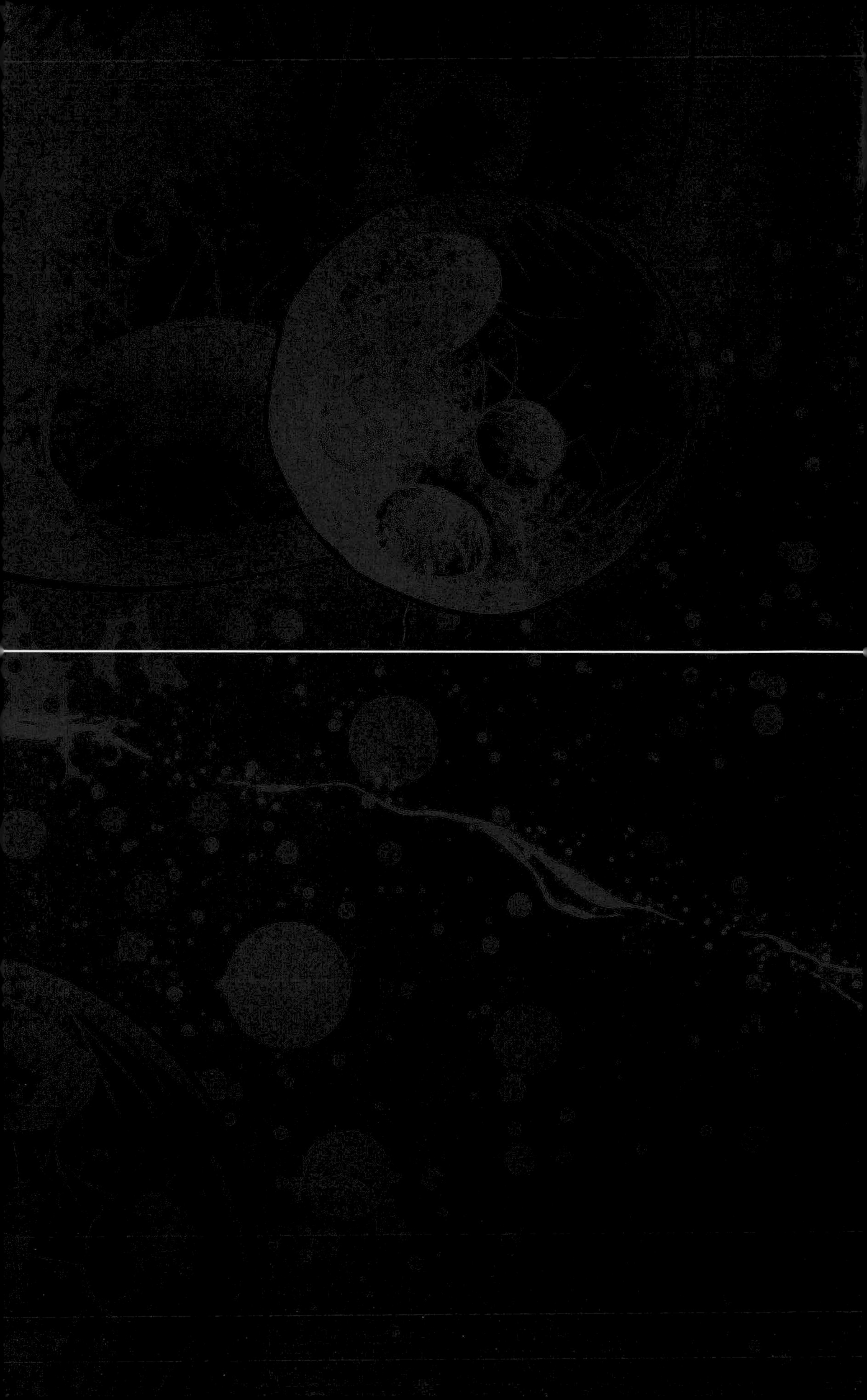

GALACTIC PEACEKEEPER

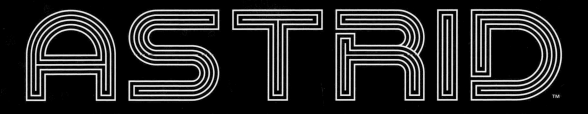

ASTRID™

CULT OF THE VOLCANIC MOON

BY KIM W. ANDERSSON

DARK HORSE BOOKS

SOUND EFFECTS LETTERING
## NATE PIEKOS OF BLAMBOT®
PRESIDENT AND PUBLISHER
## MIKE RICHARDSON
EDITORS
## SHANTEL LaROCQUE and JIM GIBBONS
ASSISTANT EDITOR
## KATII O'BRIEN
DESIGNER
## JIMMY PRESLER
DIGITAL ART TECHNICIAN
## CHRISTINA McKENZIE

NEIL HANKERSON EXECUTIVE VICE PRESIDENT • TOM WEDDLE CHIEF FINANCIAL OFFICER • RANDY STRADLEY VICE PRESIDENT OF PUBLISHING • MICHAEL MARTENS VICE PRESIDENT OF BOOK TRADE SALES • MATT PARKINSON VICE PRESIDENT OF MARKETING • DAVID SCROGGY VICE PRESIDENT OF PRODUCT DEVELOPMENT • DALE LaFOUNTAIN VICE PRESIDENT OF INFORMATION TECHNOLOGY • CARA NIECE VICE PRESIDENT OF PRODUCTION AND SCHEDULING • NICK McWHORTER VICE PRESIDENT OF MEDIA LICENSING • KEN LIZZI GENERAL COUNSEL • DAVE MARSHALL EDITOR IN CHIEF • DAVEY ESTRADA EDITORIAL DIRECTOR • SCOTT ALLIE EXECUTIVE SENIOR EDITOR • CHRIS WARNER SENIOR BOOKS EDITOR • CARY GRAZZINI DIRECTOR OF SPECIALTY PROJECTS • LIA RIBACCHI ART DIRECTOR • VANESSA TODD DIRECTOR OF PRINT PURCHASING • MATT DRYER DIRECTOR OF DIGITAL ART AND PREPRESS • MARK BERNARDI DIRECTOR OF DIGITAL PUBLISHING • SARAH ROBERTSON DIRECTOR OF PRODUCT SALES • MICHAEL GOMBOS DIRECTOR OF INTERNATIONAL PUBLISHING AND LICENSING

PUBLISHED BY DARK HORSE BOOKS
A DIVISION OF DARK HORSE COMICS, INC.
10956 SE MAIN STREET
MILWAUKIE, OR 97222

DARKHORSE.COM
KIMWANDERSSON.COM

FIRST EDITION: NOVEMBER 2016
ISBN 978-1-61655-690-7

1 3 5 7 9 10 8 6 4 2
PRINTED IN CHINA

INTERNATIONAL LICENSING: (503) 905-2377
COMIC SHOP LOCATOR SERVICE: (888) 266-4226

LIBRARY OF CONGRESS CATALOGING-IN-PUBLICATION DATA

NAMES: ANDERSSON, KIM, AUTHOR, ILLUSTRATOR.
TITLE: ASTRID : CULT OF THE VOLCANIC MOON / BY KIM W. ANDERSSON.
DESCRIPTION: FIRST EDITION. | MILWAUKIE, OR : DARK HORSE BOOKS, 2016. |
  SERIES: ASTRID ; VOLUME 1
IDENTIFIERS: LCCN 2016028982 | ISBN 9781616556907 (PAPERBACK)
SUBJECTS: LCSH: COMIC BOOKS, STRIPS, ETC. | BISAC: COMICS & GRAPHIC NOVELS /
  SCIENCE FICTION.
CLASSIFICATION: LCC PN6790.S883 A48 2016 | DDC 741.5/9485--DC23
LC RECORD AVAILABLE AT HTTPS://LCCN.LOC.GOV/2016028982

SPECIAL THANKS TO FRIDA WILLÉN,
A.M. BERGMAN, JESPER RÖNNDAHL, JOHAN KIMRIN,
KARL JOHNSSON, LISA SCOTT, MATS STRANDBERG,
AND SARA B. ELFGREN FOR ALL THEIR HELP.

THIS BOOK HAS BEEN PRODUCED WITH SUPPORT BY THE SWEDISH ARTS GRANTS COMMITTEE.

WITH THE SUPPORT OF **K**ONSTNÄRSNÄMNDEN

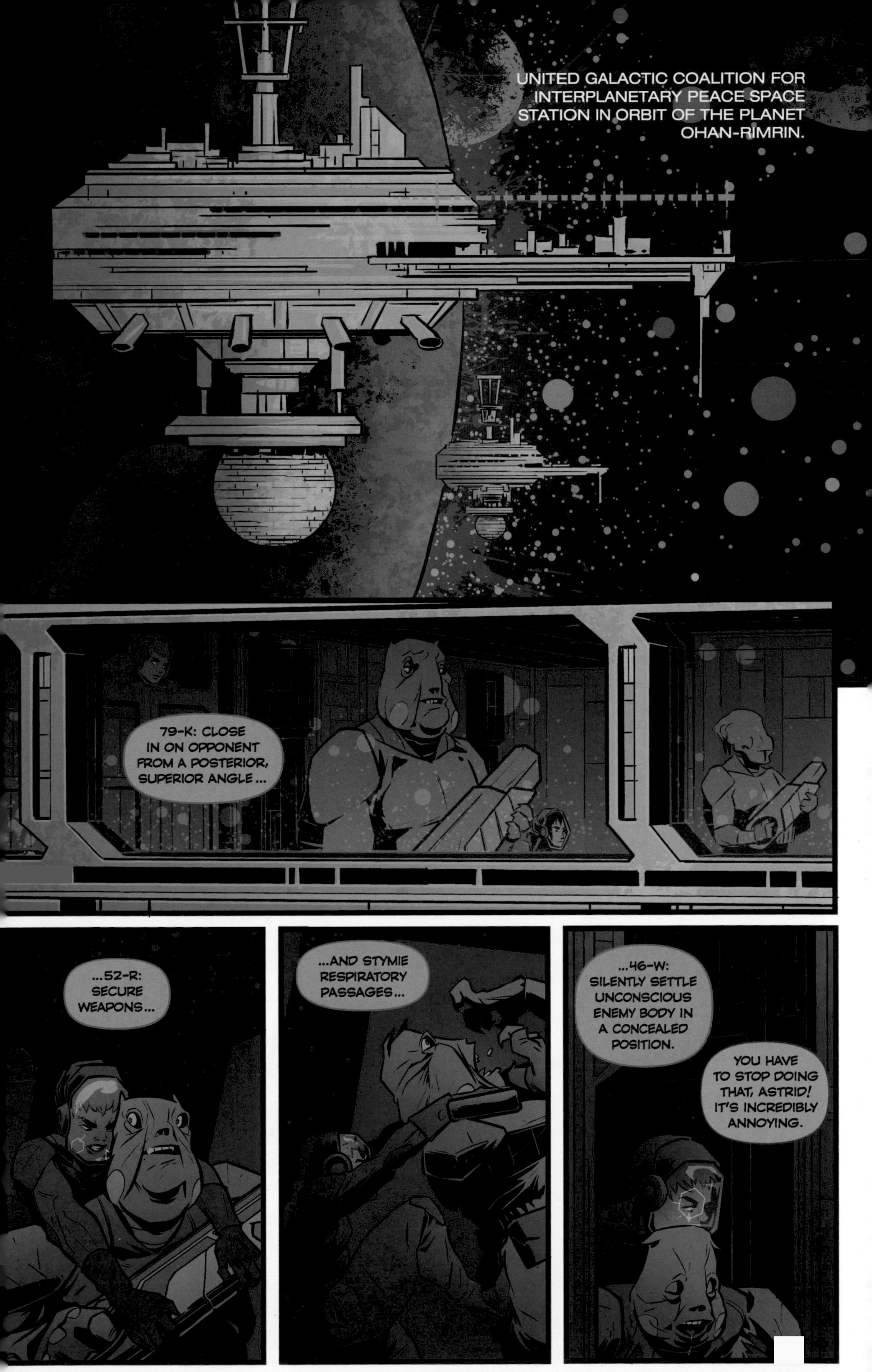
UNITED GALACTIC COALITION FOR INTERPLANETARY PEACE SPACE STATION IN ORBIT OF THE PLANET OHAN-RIMRIN.
79-K: CLOSE IN ON OPPONENT FROM A POSTERIOR, SUPERIOR ANGLE...
...52-R: SECURE WEAPONS...
...AND STYMIE RESPIRATORY PASSAGES...
...46-W: SILENTLY SETTLE UNCONSCIOUS ENEMY BODY IN A CONCEALED POSITION.
YOU HAVE TO STOP DOING THAT, ASTRID! IT'S INCREDIBLY ANNOYING.

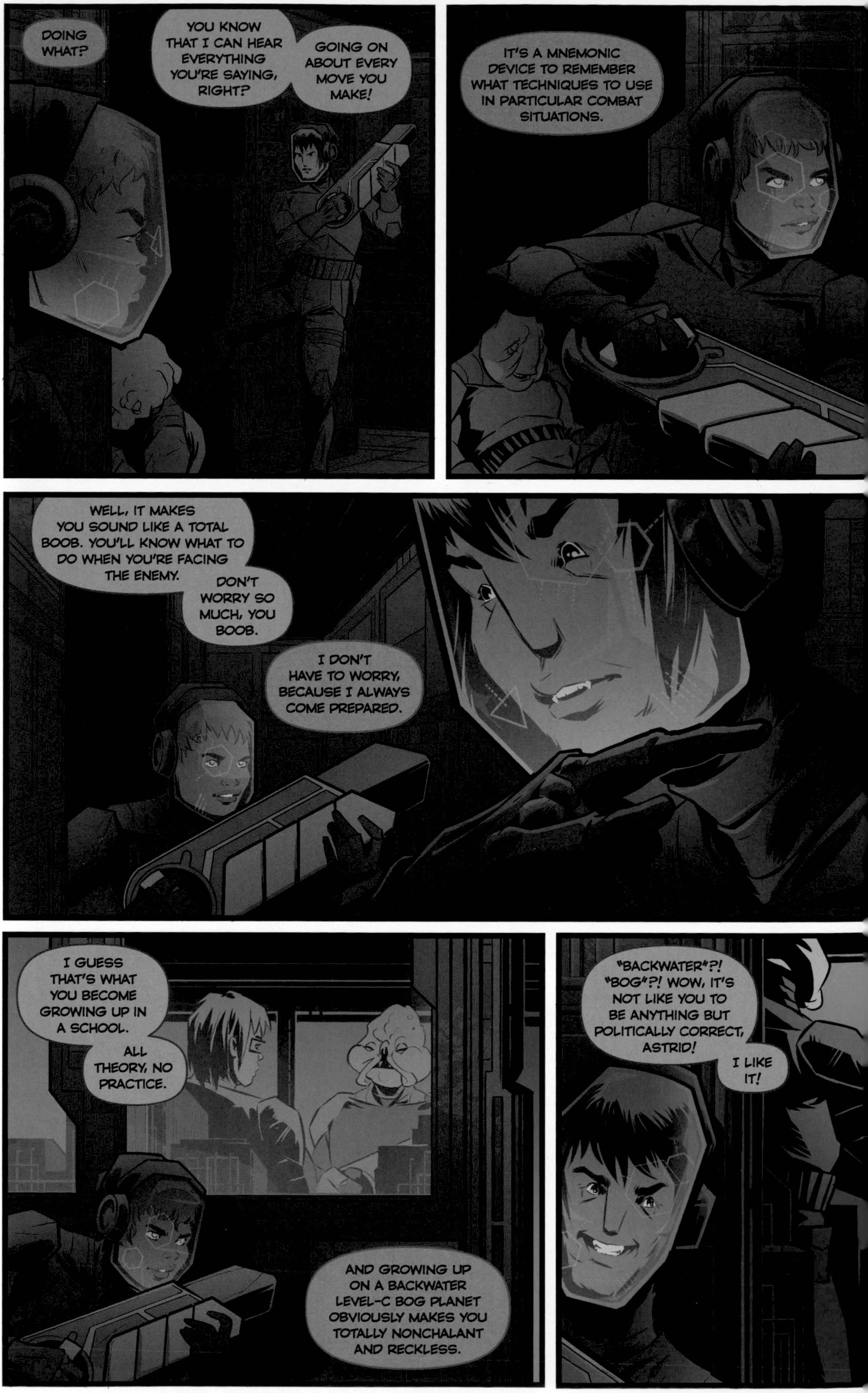
DOING WHAT?
YOU KNOW THAT I CAN HEAR EVERYTHING YOU'RE SAYING, RIGHT?
GOING ON ABOUT EVERY MOVE YOU MAKE!
IT'S A MNEMONIC DEVICE TO REMEMBER WHAT TECHNIQUES TO USE IN PARTICULAR COMBAT SITUATIONS.
WELL, IT MAKES YOU SOUND LIKE A TOTAL BOOB. YOU'LL KNOW WHAT TO DO WHEN YOU'RE FACING THE ENEMY.
DON'T WORRY SO MUCH, YOU BOOB.
I DON'T HAVE TO WORRY, BECAUSE I ALWAYS COME PREPARED.
I GUESS THAT'S WHAT YOU BECOME GROWING UP IN A SCHOOL.
ALL THEORY, NO PRACTICE.
AND GROWING UP ON A BACKWATER LEVEL-C BOG PLANET OBVIOUSLY MAKES YOU TOTALLY NONCHALANT AND RECKLESS.
"BACKWATER"?! "BOG"?! WOW, IT'S NOT LIKE YOU TO BE ANYTHING BUT POLITICALLY CORRECT, ASTRID!
I LIKE IT!

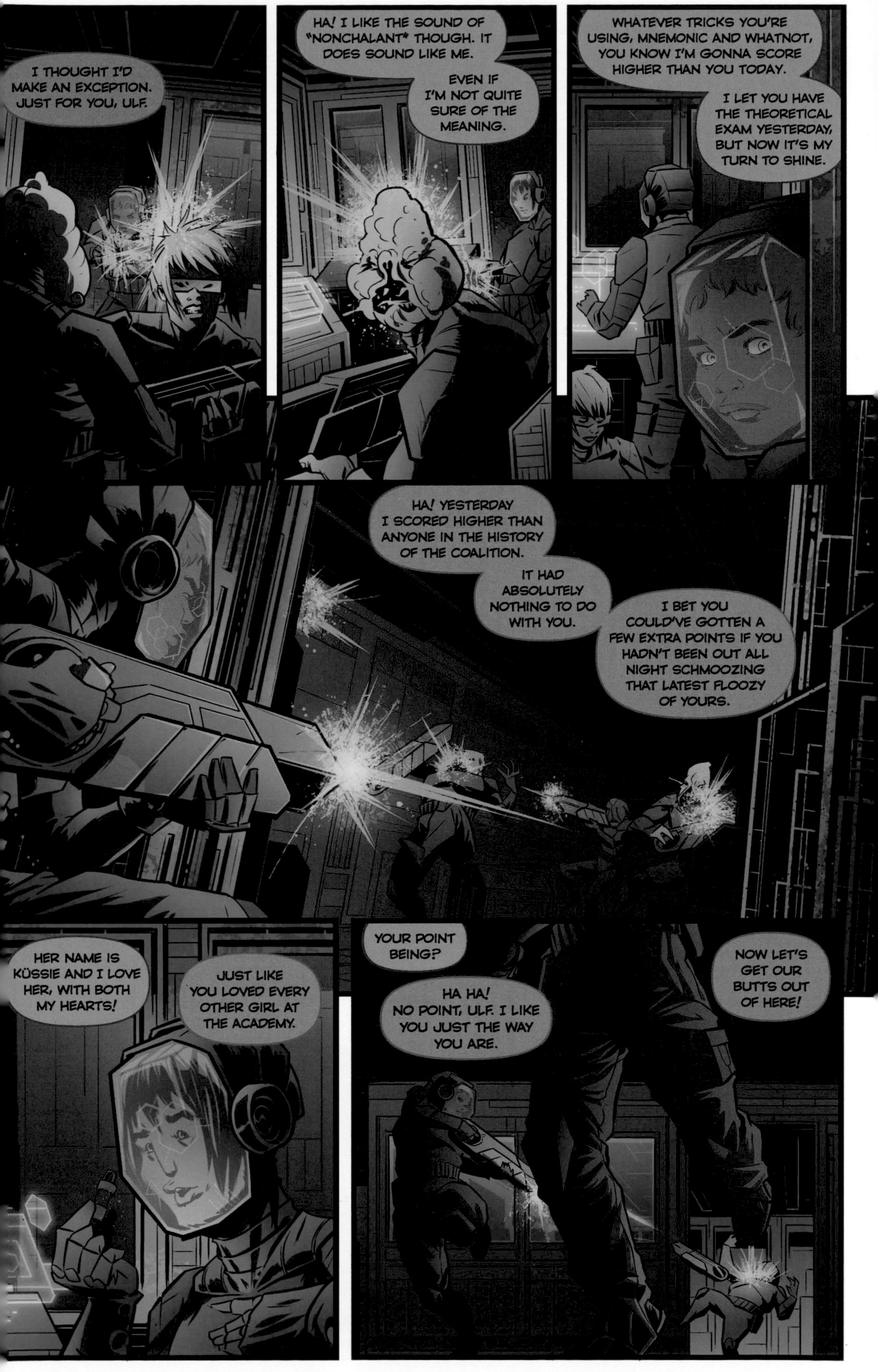
I THOUGHT I'D MAKE AN EXCEPTION. JUST FOR YOU, ULF.
HA! I LIKE THE SOUND OF "NONCHALANT" THOUGH. IT DOES SOUND LIKE ME.
EVEN IF I'M NOT QUITE SURE OF THE MEANING.
WHATEVER TRICKS YOU'RE USING, MNEMONIC AND WHATNOT, YOU KNOW I'M GONNA SCORE HIGHER THAN YOU TODAY.
I LET YOU HAVE THE THEORETICAL EXAM YESTERDAY, BUT NOW IT'S MY TURN TO SHINE.
HA! YESTERDAY I SCORED HIGHER THAN ANYONE IN THE HISTORY OF THE COALITION.
IT HAD ABSOLUTELY NOTHING TO DO WITH YOU.
I BET YOU COULD'VE GOTTEN A FEW EXTRA POINTS IF YOU HADN'T BEEN OUT ALL NIGHT SCHMOOZING THAT LATEST FLOOZY OF YOURS.
HER NAME IS KÜSSIE AND I LOVE HER, WITH BOTH MY HEARTS!
JUST LIKE YOU LOVED EVERY OTHER GIRL AT THE ACADEMY.
YOUR POINT BEING?
HA HA! NO POINT, ULF. I LIKE YOU JUST THE WAY YOU ARE.
NOW LET'S GET OUR BUTTS OUT OF HERE!

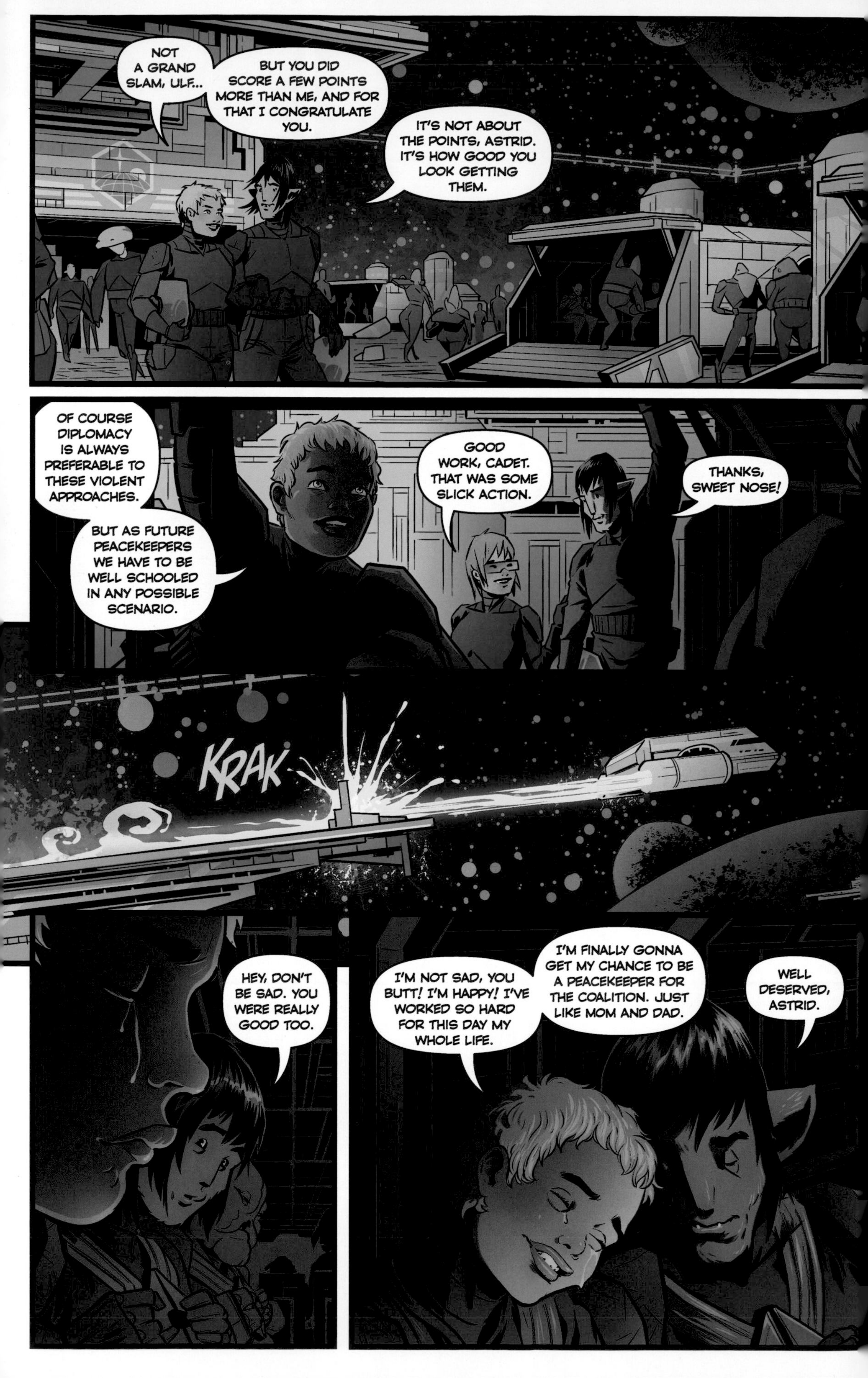
NOT A GRAND SLAM, ULF...
BUT YOU DID SCORE A FEW POINTS MORE THAN ME, AND FOR THAT I CONGRATULATE YOU.
IT'S NOT ABOUT THE POINTS, ASTRID. IT'S HOW GOOD YOU LOOK GETTING THEM.
OF COURSE DIPLOMACY IS ALWAYS PREFERABLE TO THESE VIOLENT APPROACHES.
BUT AS FUTURE PEACEKEEPERS WE HAVE TO BE WELL SCHOOLED IN ANY POSSIBLE SCENARIO.
GOOD WORK, CADET. THAT WAS SOME SLICK ACTION.
THANKS, SWEET NOSE!
KRAK
HEY, DON'T BE SAD. YOU WERE REALLY GOOD TOO.
I'M NOT SAD, YOU BUTT! I'M HAPPY! I'VE WORKED SO HARD FOR THIS DAY MY WHOLE LIFE.
I'M FINALLY GONNA GET MY CHANCE TO BE A PEACEKEEPER FOR THE COALITION. JUST LIKE MOM AND DAD.
WELL DESERVED, ASTRID.

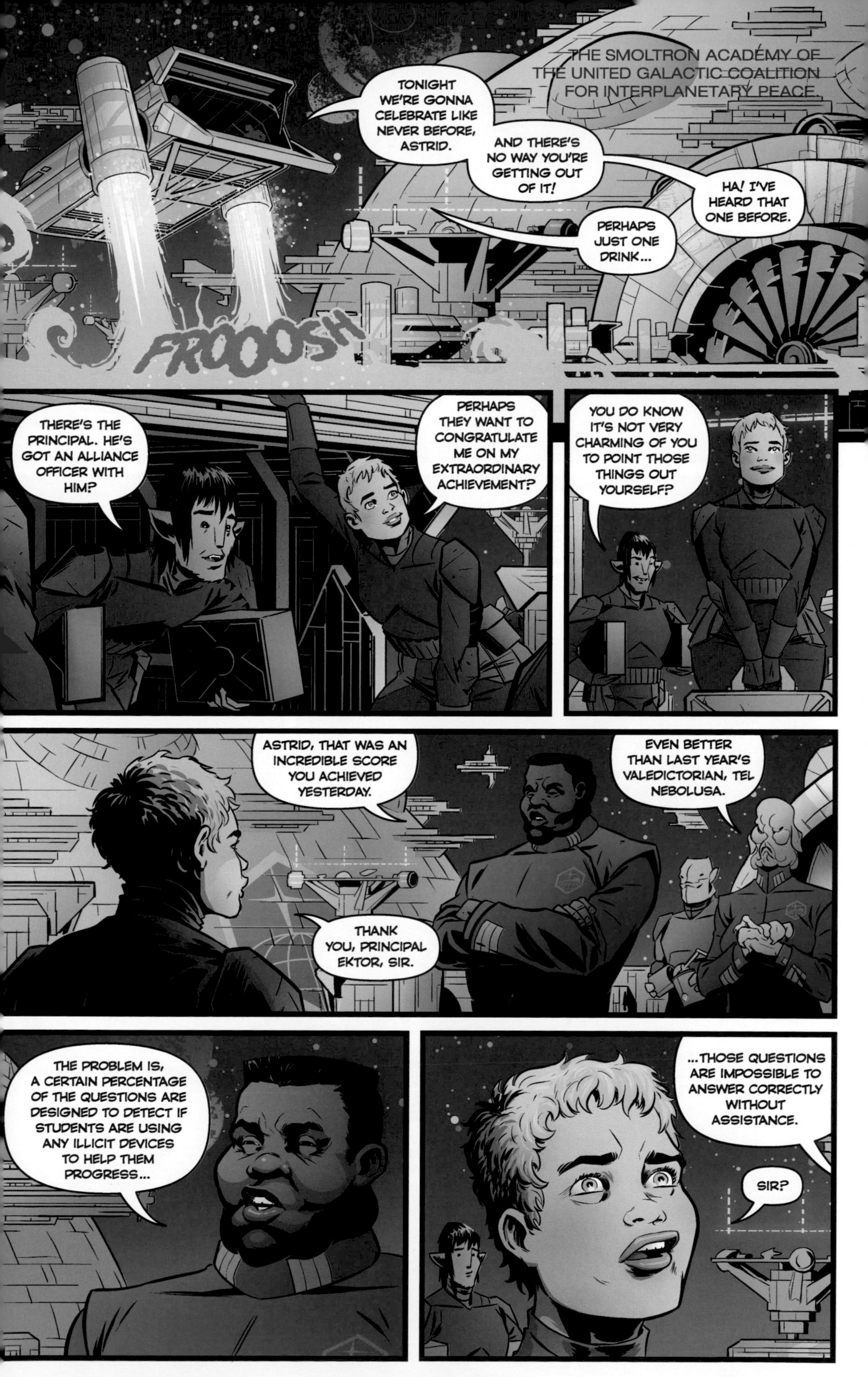
THE SMOLTRON ACADEMY OF THE UNITED GALACTIC COALITION FOR INTERPLANETARY PEACE.
TONIGHT WE'RE GONNA CELEBRATE LIKE NEVER BEFORE, ASTRID.
AND THERE'S NO WAY YOU'RE GETTING OUT OF IT!
HA! I'VE HEARD THAT ONE BEFORE.
PERHAPS JUST ONE DRINK...
FROOOSH
THERE'S THE PRINCIPAL. HE'S GOT AN ALLIANCE OFFICER WITH HIM?
PERHAPS THEY WANT TO CONGRATULATE ME ON MY EXTRAORDINARY ACHIEVEMENT?
YOU DO KNOW IT'S NOT VERY CHARMING OF YOU TO POINT THOSE THINGS OUT YOURSELF?
ASTRID, THAT WAS AN INCREDIBLE SCORE YOU ACHIEVED YESTERDAY.
EVEN BETTER THAN LAST YEAR'S VALEDICTORIAN, TEL NEBOLUSA.
THANK YOU, PRINCIPAL EKTOR, SIR.
THE PROBLEM IS, A CERTAIN PERCENTAGE OF THE QUESTIONS ARE DESIGNED TO DETECT IF STUDENTS ARE USING ANY ILLICIT DEVICES TO HELP THEM PROGRESS...
...THOSE QUESTIONS ARE IMPOSSIBLE TO ANSWER CORRECTLY WITHOUT ASSISTANCE.
SIR?

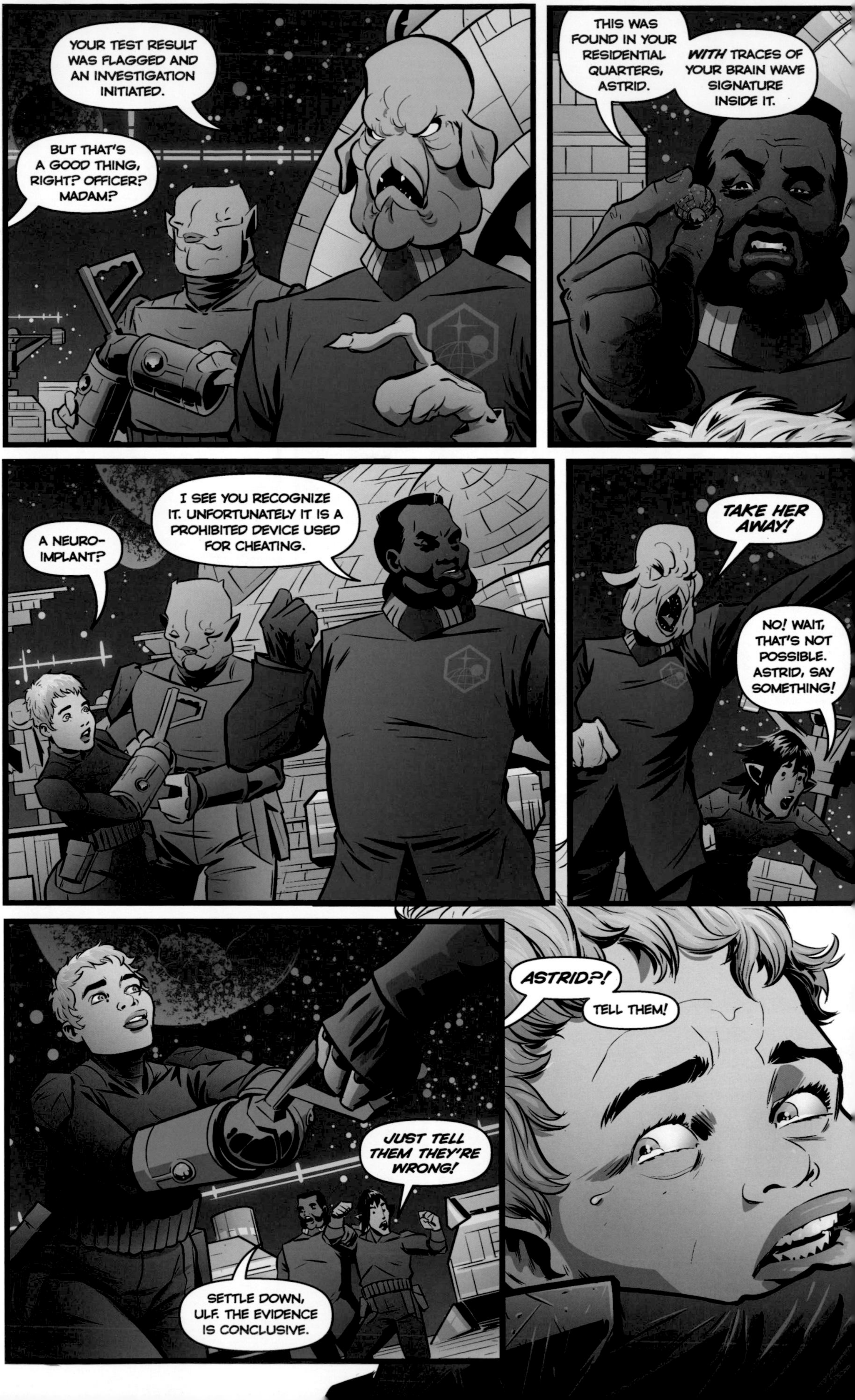
YOUR TEST RESULT WAS FLAGGED AND AN INVESTIGATION INITIATED.
BUT THAT'S A GOOD THING, RIGHT? OFFICER? MADAM?
THIS WAS FOUND IN YOUR RESIDENTIAL QUARTERS, ASTRID.
WITH TRACES OF YOUR BRAIN WAVE SIGNATURE INSIDE IT.
A NEURO-IMPLANT?
I SEE YOU RECOGNIZE IT. UNFORTUNATELY IT IS A PROHIBITED DEVICE USED FOR CHEATING.
TAKE HER AWAY!
NO! WAIT, THAT'S NOT POSSIBLE. ASTRID, SAY SOMETHING!
JUST TELL THEM THEY'RE WRONG!
SETTLE DOWN, ULF. THE EVIDENCE IS CONCLUSIVE.
ASTRID?!
TELL THEM!

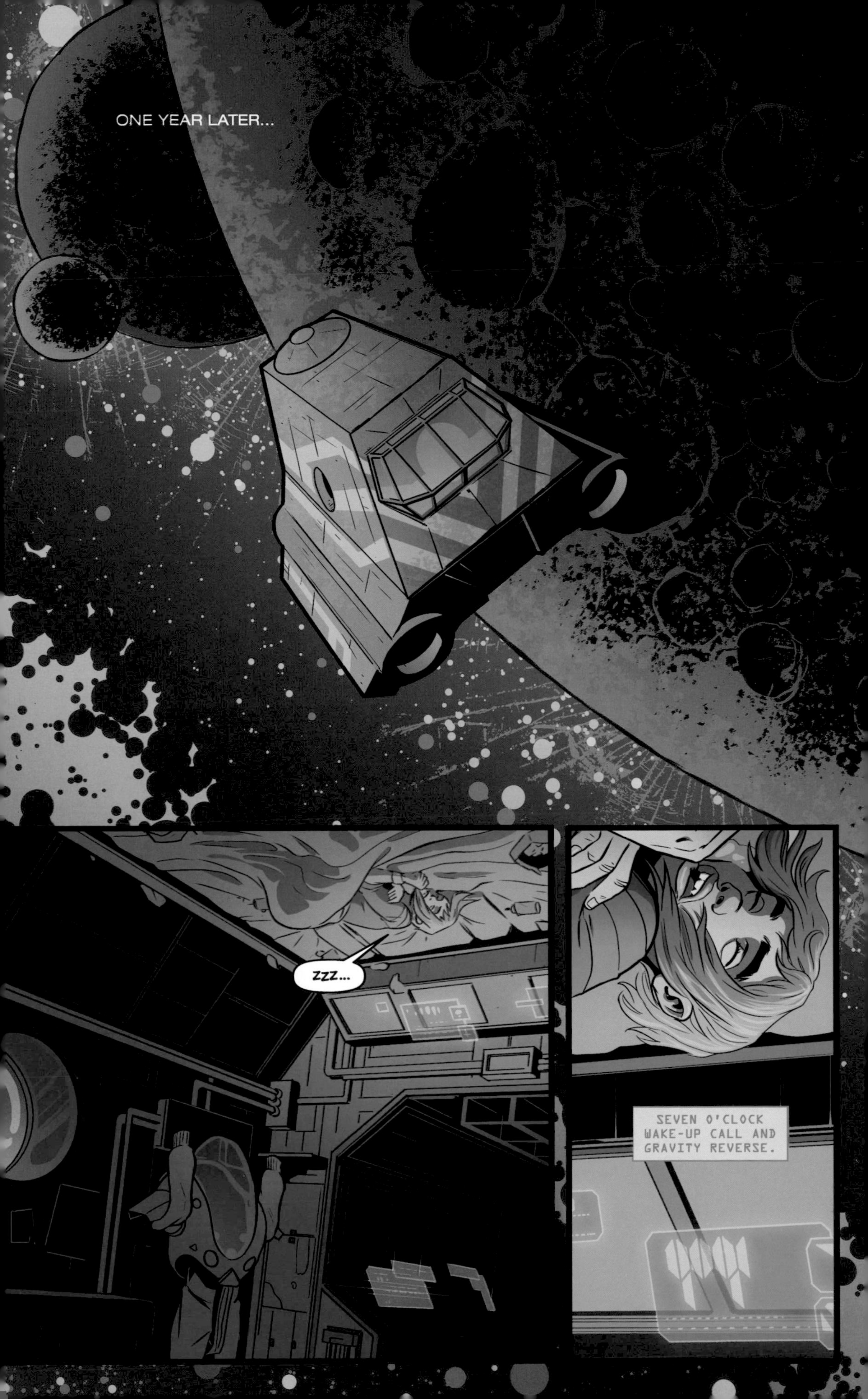
ONE YEAR LATER...
ZZZ...
SEVEN O'CLOCK WAKE-UP CALL AND GRAVITY REVERSE.

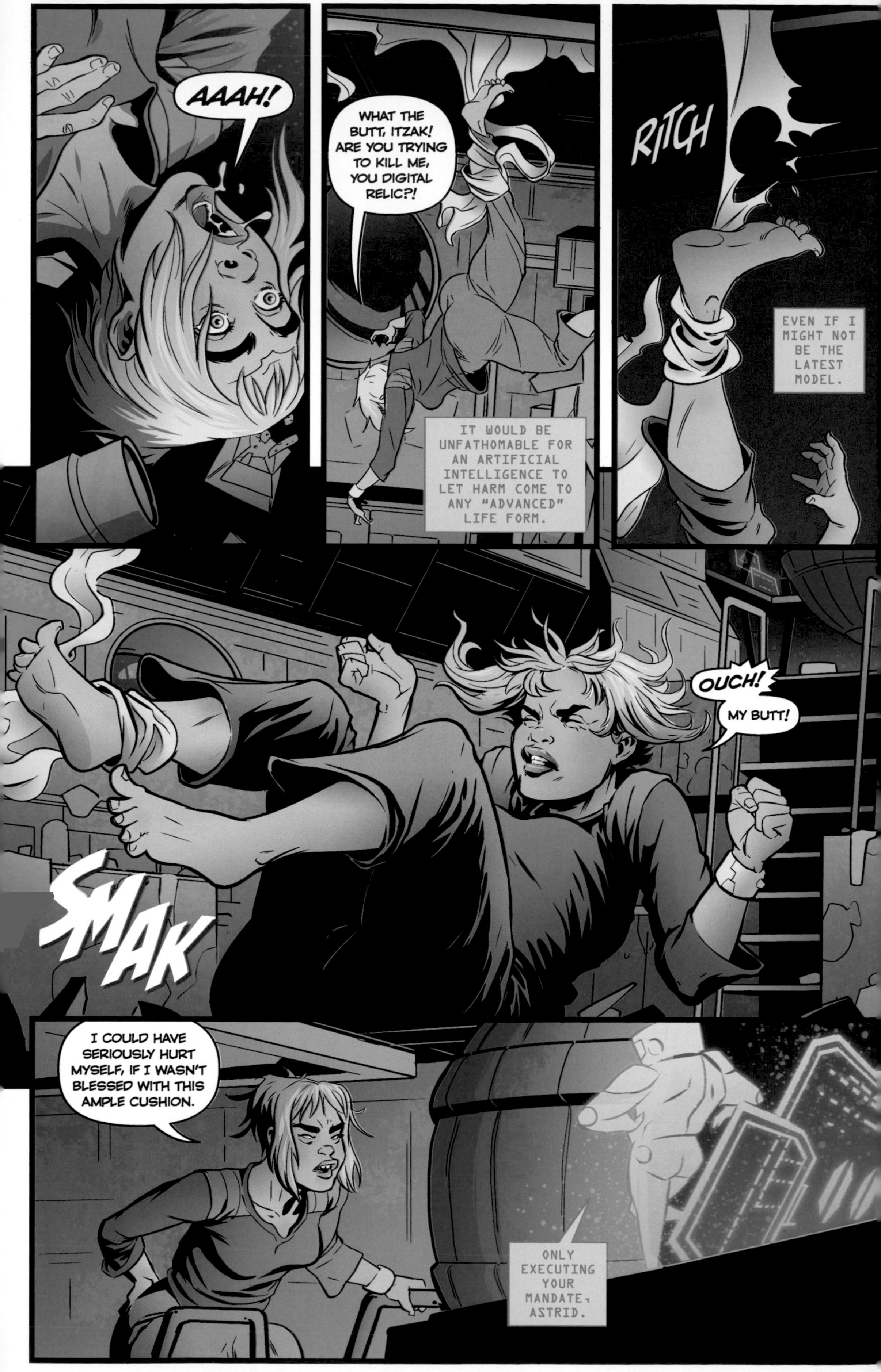
AAAH!
WHAT THE BUTT, ITZAK! ARE YOU TRYING TO KILL ME, YOU DIGITAL RELIC?!
IT WOULD BE UNFATHOMABLE FOR AN ARTIFICIAL INTELLIGENCE TO LET HARM COME TO ANY "ADVANCED" LIFE FORM.
RITCH
EVEN IF I MIGHT NOT BE THE LATEST MODEL.
SMAK
OUCH!
MY BUTT!
I COULD HAVE SERIOUSLY HURT MYSELF, IF I WASN'T BLESSED WITH THIS AMPLE CUSHION.
ONLY EXECUTING YOUR MANDATE, ASTRID.

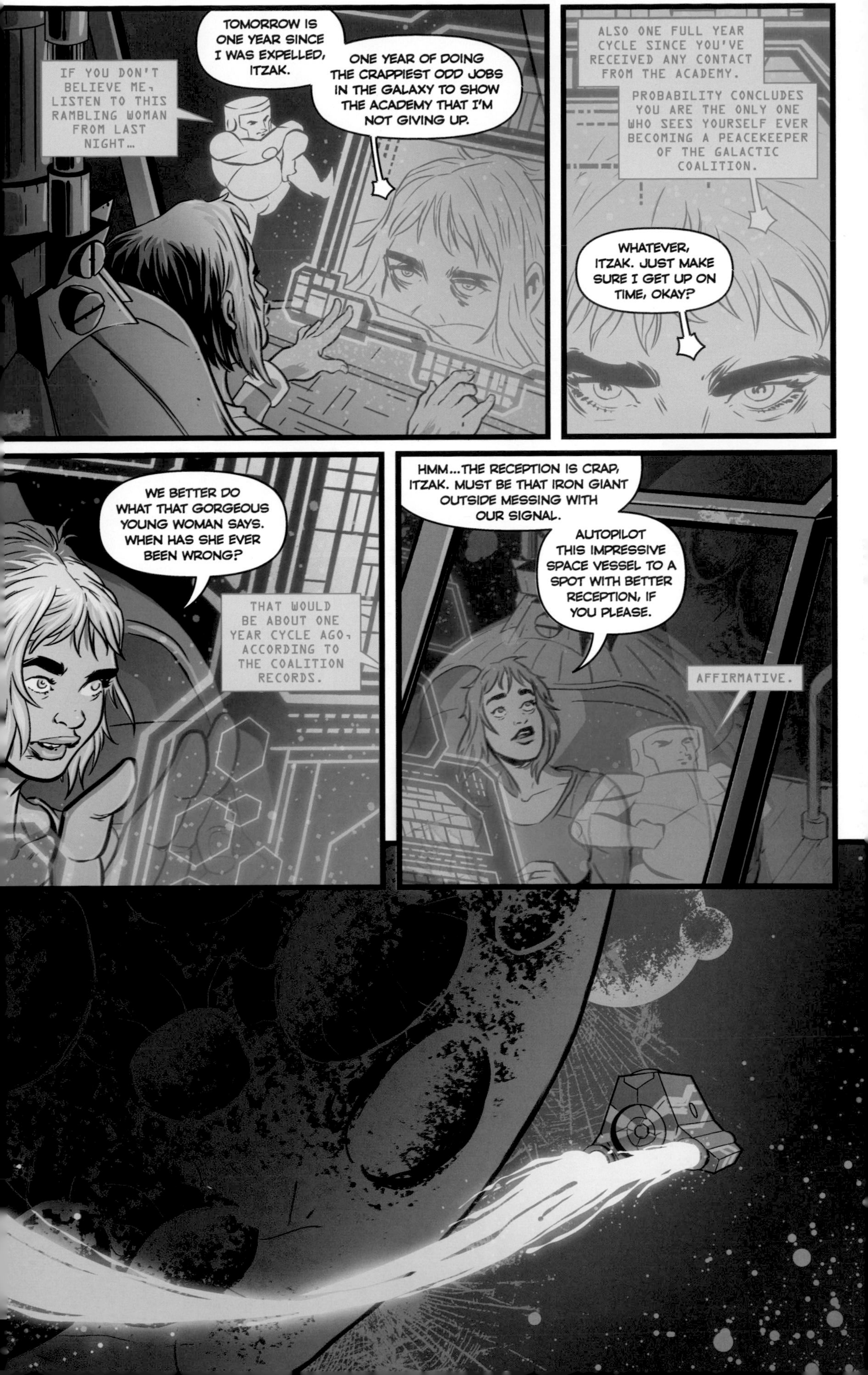
IF YOU DON'T BELIEVE ME, LISTEN TO THIS RAMBLING WOMAN FROM LAST NIGHT...
TOMORROW IS ONE YEAR SINCE I WAS EXPELLED, ITZAK.
ONE YEAR OF DOING THE CRAPPIEST ODD JOBS IN THE GALAXY TO SHOW THE ACADEMY THAT I'M NOT GIVING UP.
ALSO ONE FULL YEAR CYCLE SINCE YOU'VE RECEIVED ANY CONTACT FROM THE ACADEMY.
PROBABILITY CONCLUDES YOU ARE THE ONLY ONE WHO SEES YOURSELF EVER BECOMING A PEACEKEEPER OF THE GALACTIC COALITION.
WHATEVER, ITZAK. JUST MAKE SURE I GET UP ON TIME, OKAY?
WE BETTER DO WHAT THAT GORGEOUS YOUNG WOMAN SAYS. WHEN HAS SHE EVER BEEN WRONG?
THAT WOULD BE ABOUT ONE YEAR CYCLE AGO, ACCORDING TO THE COALITION RECORDS.
HMM...THE RECEPTION IS CRAP, ITZAK. MUST BE THAT IRON GIANT OUTSIDE MESSING WITH OUR SIGNAL.
AUTOPILOT THIS IMPRESSIVE SPACE VESSEL TO A SPOT WITH BETTER RECEPTION, IF YOU PLEASE.
AFFIRMATIVE.

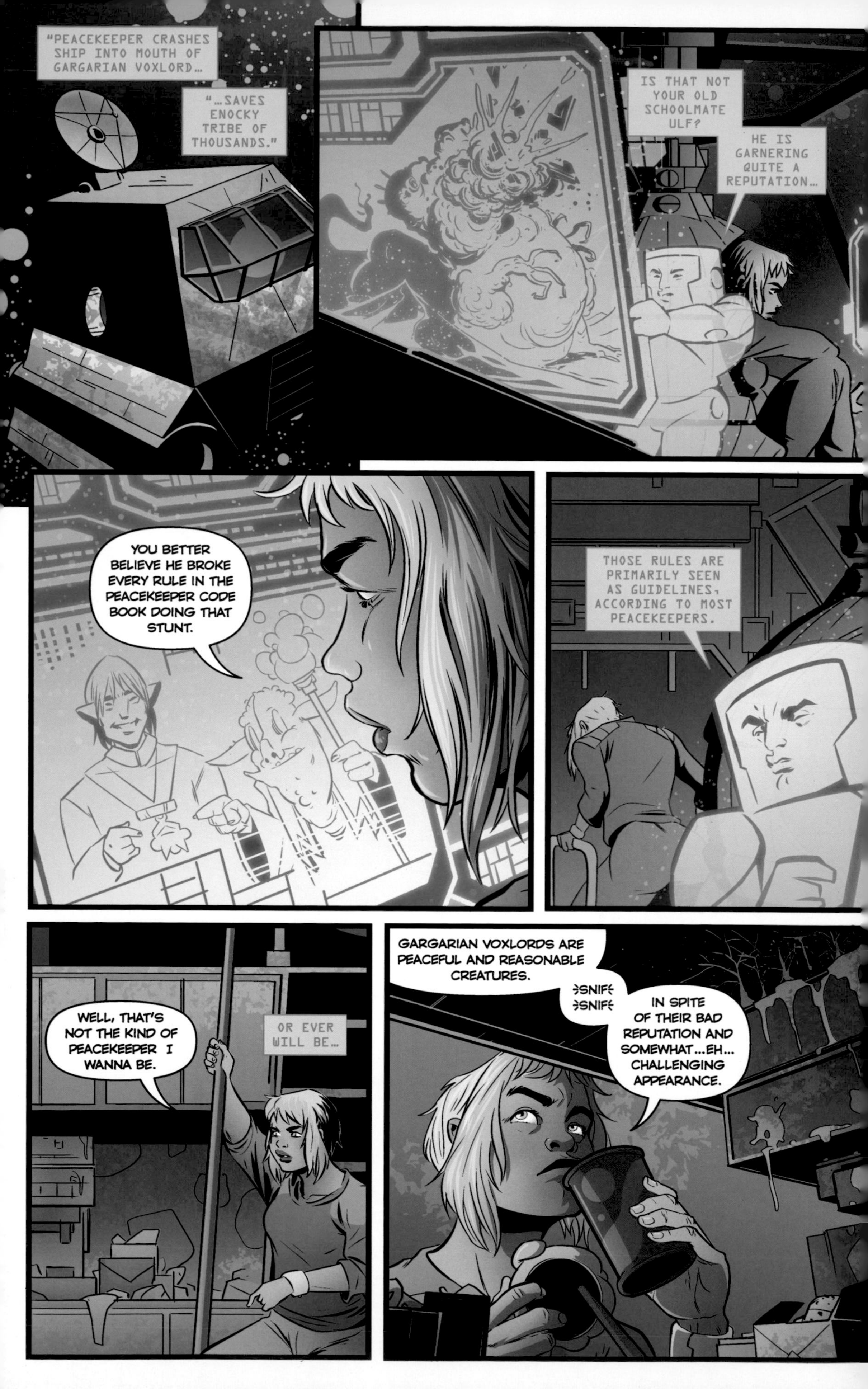
"PEACEKEEPER CRASHES SHIP INTO MOUTH OF GARGARIAN VOXLORD...
"...SAVES ENOCKY TRIBE OF THOUSANDS."
IS THAT NOT YOUR OLD SCHOOLMATE ULF?
HE IS GARNERING QUITE A REPUTATION...
YOU BETTER BELIEVE HE BROKE EVERY RULE IN THE PEACEKEEPER CODE BOOK DOING THAT STUNT.
THOSE RULES ARE PRIMARILY SEEN AS GUIDELINES, ACCORDING TO MOST PEACEKEEPERS.
WELL, THAT'S NOT THE KIND OF PEACEKEEPER I WANNA BE.
OR EVER WILL BE...
GARGARIAN VOXLORDS ARE PEACEFUL AND REASONABLE CREATURES.
SNIF
SNIF
IN SPITE OF THEIR BAD REPUTATION AND SOMEWHAT...EH... CHALLENGING APPEARANCE.

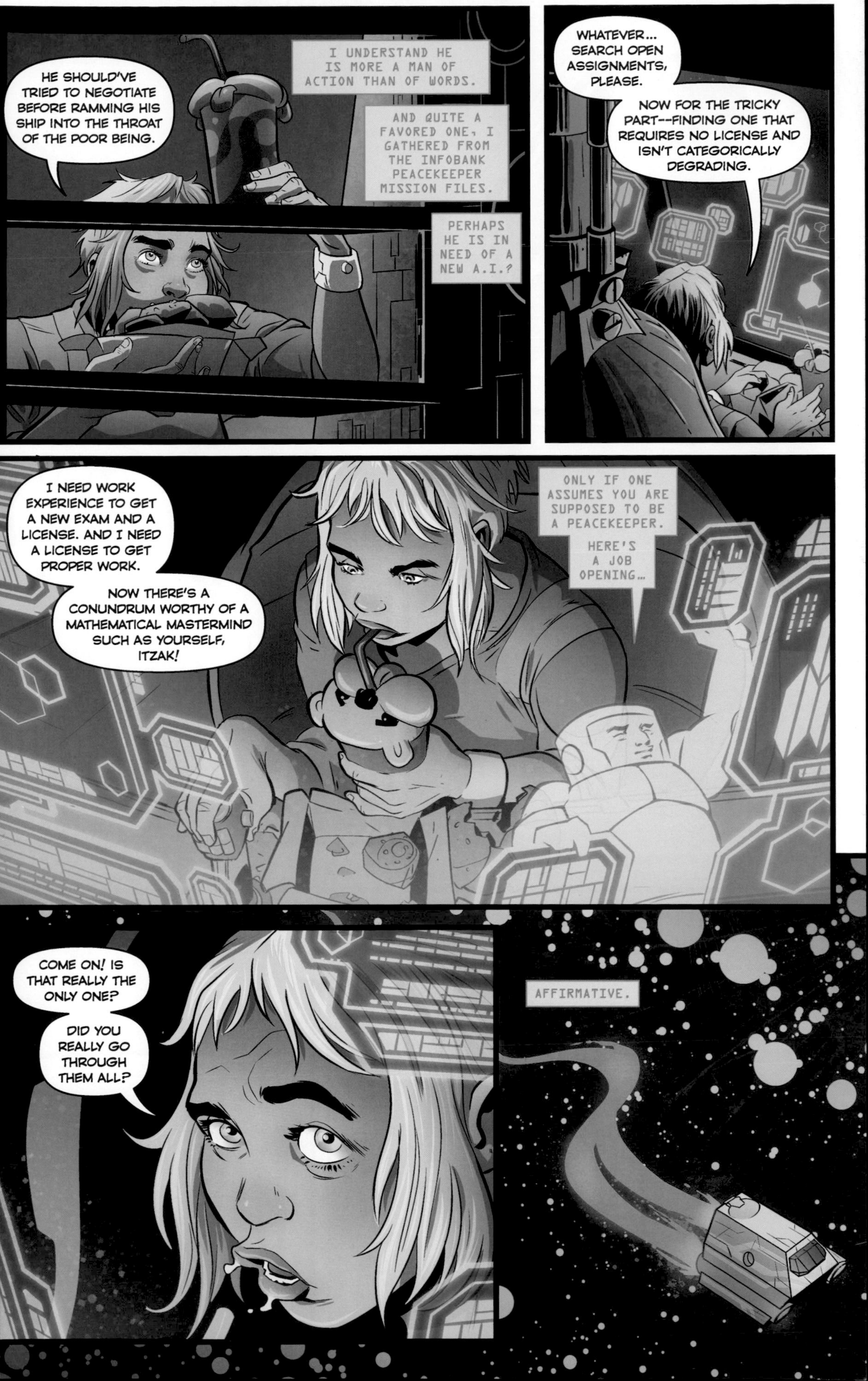
HE SHOULD'VE TRIED TO NEGOTIATE BEFORE RAMMING HIS SHIP INTO THE THROAT OF THE POOR BEING.
I UNDERSTAND HE IS MORE A MAN OF ACTION THAN OF WORDS.
AND QUITE A FAVORED ONE, I GATHERED FROM THE INFOBANK PEACEKEEPER MISSION FILES.
PERHAPS HE IS IN NEED OF A NEW A.I.?
WHATEVER... SEARCH OPEN ASSIGNMENTS, PLEASE.
NOW FOR THE TRICKY PART--FINDING ONE THAT REQUIRES NO LICENSE AND ISN'T CATEGORICALLY DEGRADING.
I NEED WORK EXPERIENCE TO GET A NEW EXAM AND A LICENSE. AND I NEED A LICENSE TO GET PROPER WORK.
NOW THERE'S A CONUNDRUM WORTHY OF A MATHEMATICAL MASTERMIND SUCH AS YOURSELF, ITZAK!
ONLY IF ONE ASSUMES YOU ARE SUPPOSED TO BE A PEACEKEEPER.
HERE'S A JOB OPENING...
COME ON! IS THAT REALLY THE ONLY ONE?
DID YOU REALLY GO THROUGH THEM ALL?
AFFIRMATIVE.

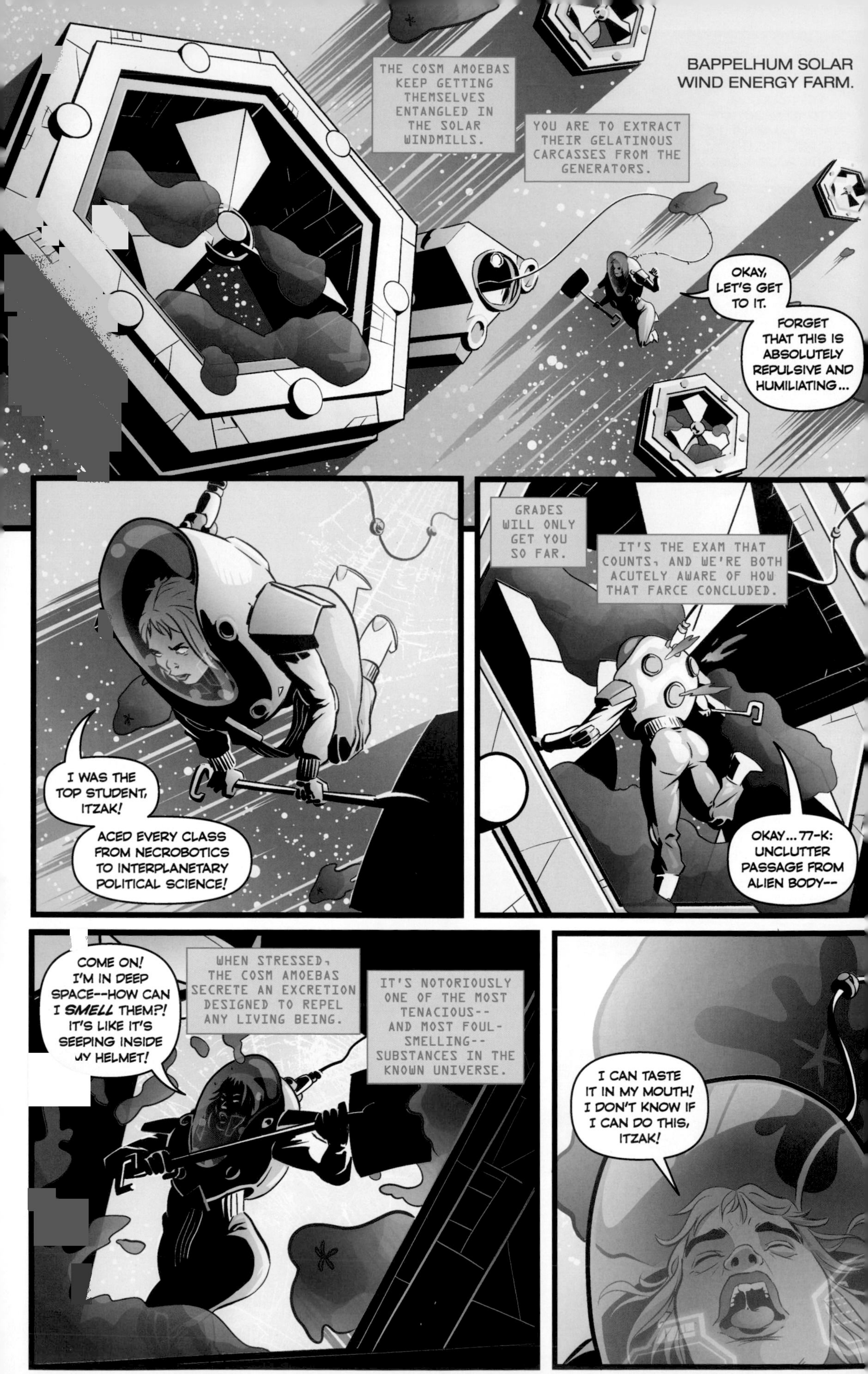
BAPPELHUM SOLAR WIND ENERGY FARM.
THE COSM AMOEBAS KEEP GETTING THEMSELVES ENTANGLED IN THE SOLAR WINDMILLS.
YOU ARE TO EXTRACT THEIR GELATINOUS CARCASSES FROM THE GENERATORS.
OKAY, LET'S GET TO IT.
FORGET THAT THIS IS ABSOLUTELY REPULSIVE AND HUMILIATING...
I WAS THE TOP STUDENT, ITZAK!
ACED EVERY CLASS FROM NECROBOTICS TO INTERPLANETARY POLITICAL SCIENCE!
GRADES WILL ONLY GET YOU SO FAR.
IT'S THE EXAM THAT COUNTS, AND WE'RE BOTH ACUTELY AWARE OF HOW THAT FARCE CONCLUDED.
OKAY... 77-K: UNCLUTTER PASSAGE FROM ALIEN BODY--
COME ON! I'M IN DEEP SPACE--HOW CAN I SMELL THEM?! IT'S LIKE IT'S SEEPING INSIDE MY HELMET!
WHEN STRESSED, THE COSM AMOEBAS SECRETE AN EXCRETION DESIGNED TO REPEL ANY LIVING BEING.
IT'S NOTORIOUSLY ONE OF THE MOST TENACIOUS-- AND MOST FOUL-SMELLING-- SUBSTANCES IN THE KNOWN UNIVERSE.
I CAN TASTE IT IN MY MOUTH! I DON'T KNOW IF I CAN DO THIS, ITZAK!

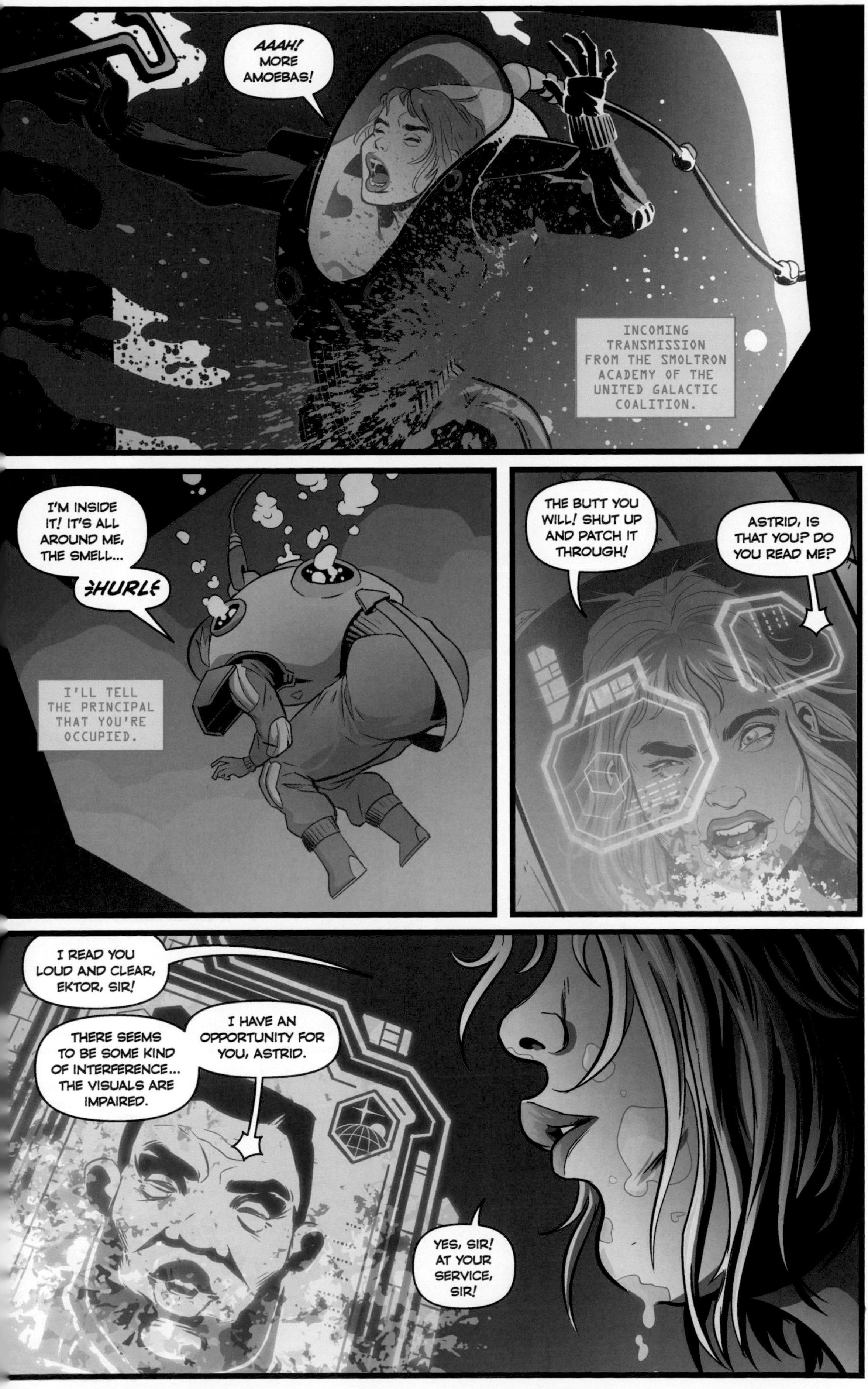
AAAH! MORE AMOEBAS!
INCOMING TRANSMISSION FROM THE SMOLTRON ACADEMY OF THE UNITED GALACTIC COALITION.
I'M INSIDE IT! IT'S ALL AROUND ME, THE SMELL...
HURL
I'LL TELL THE PRINCIPAL THAT YOU'RE OCCUPIED.
THE BUTT YOU WILL! SHUT UP AND PATCH IT THROUGH!
ASTRID, IS THAT YOU? DO YOU READ ME?
I READ YOU LOUD AND CLEAR, EKTOR, SIR!
THERE SEEMS TO BE SOME KIND OF INTERFERENCE... THE VISUALS ARE IMPAIRED.
I HAVE AN OPPORTUNITY FOR YOU, ASTRID.
YES, SIR! AT YOUR SERVICE, SIR!

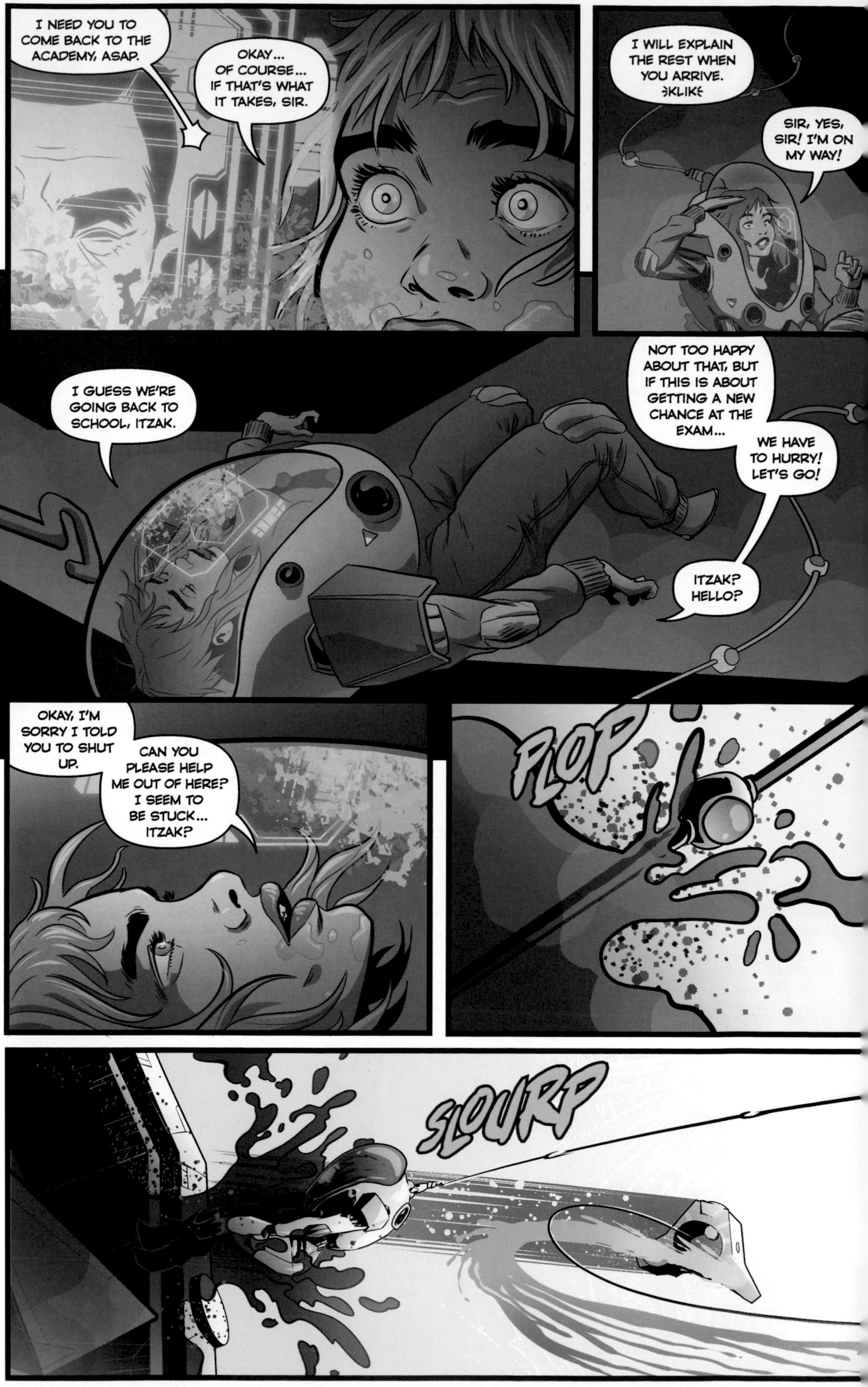
I NEED YOU TO COME BACK TO THE ACADEMY, ASAP.
OKAY... OF COURSE... IF THAT'S WHAT IT TAKES, SIR.
I WILL EXPLAIN THE REST WHEN YOU ARRIVE. ⩥KLIK⩤
SIR, YES, SIR! I'M ON MY WAY!
I GUESS WE'RE GOING BACK TO SCHOOL, ITZAK.
NOT TOO HAPPY ABOUT THAT, BUT IF THIS IS ABOUT GETTING A NEW CHANCE AT THE EXAM...
WE HAVE TO HURRY! LET'S GO!
ITZAK? HELLO?
OKAY, I'M SORRY I TOLD YOU TO SHUT UP.
CAN YOU PLEASE HELP ME OUT OF HERE? I SEEM TO BE STUCK... ITZAK?
PLOP
SLOURP

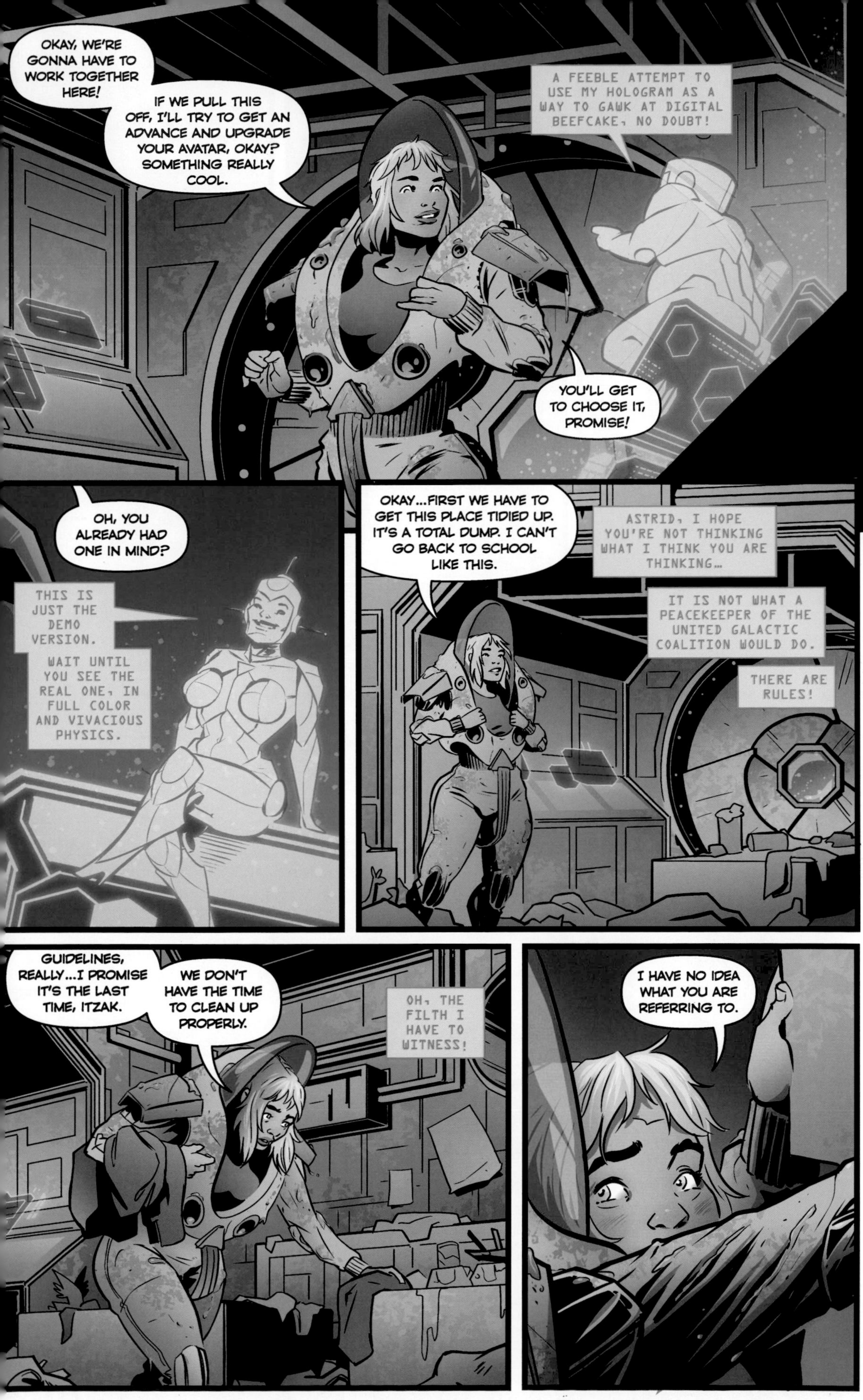
OKAY, WE'RE GONNA HAVE TO WORK TOGETHER HERE!
IF WE PULL THIS OFF, I'LL TRY TO GET AN ADVANCE AND UPGRADE YOUR AVATAR, OKAY? SOMETHING REALLY COOL.
A FEEBLE ATTEMPT TO USE MY HOLOGRAM AS A WAY TO GAWK AT DIGITAL BEEFCAKE, NO DOUBT!
YOU'LL GET TO CHOOSE IT, PROMISE!
OH, YOU ALREADY HAD ONE IN MIND?
THIS IS JUST THE DEMO VERSION.
WAIT UNTIL YOU SEE THE REAL ONE, IN FULL COLOR AND VIVACIOUS PHYSICS.
OKAY...FIRST WE HAVE TO GET THIS PLACE TIDIED UP. IT'S A TOTAL DUMP. I CAN'T GO BACK TO SCHOOL LIKE THIS.
ASTRID, I HOPE YOU'RE NOT THINKING WHAT I THINK YOU ARE THINKING...
IT IS NOT WHAT A PEACEKEEPER OF THE UNITED GALACTIC COALITION WOULD DO.
THERE ARE RULES!
GUIDELINES, REALLY...I PROMISE IT'S THE LAST TIME, ITZAK.
WE DON'T HAVE THE TIME TO CLEAN UP PROPERLY.
OH, THE FILTH I HAVE TO WITNESS!
I HAVE NO IDEA WHAT YOU ARE REFERRING TO.

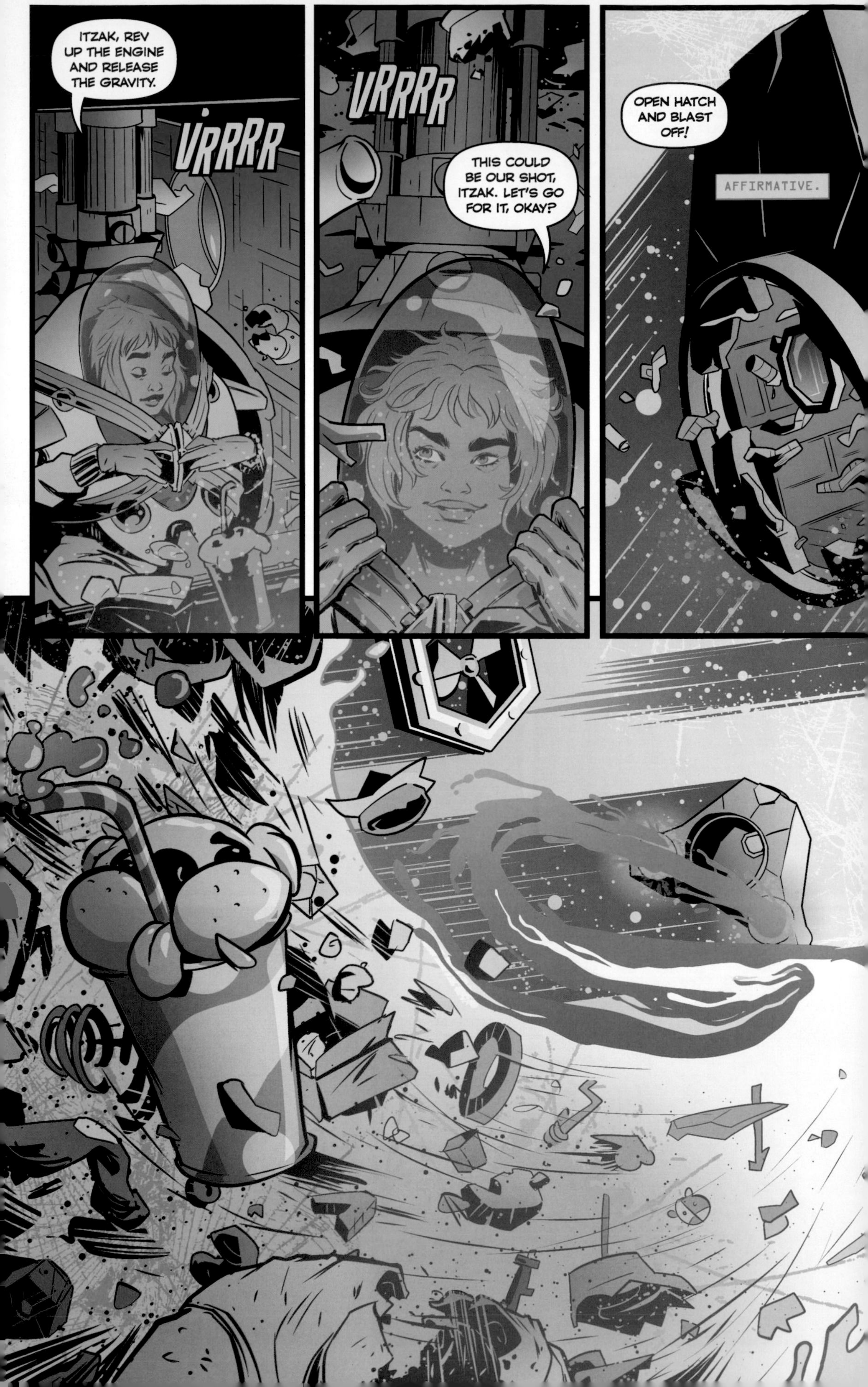
ITZAK, REV UP THE ENGINE AND RELEASE THE GRAVITY.
VRRRR
VRRRR
THIS COULD BE OUR SHOT, ITZAK. LET'S GO FOR IT, OKAY?
OPEN HATCH AND BLAST OFF!
AFFIRMATIVE.

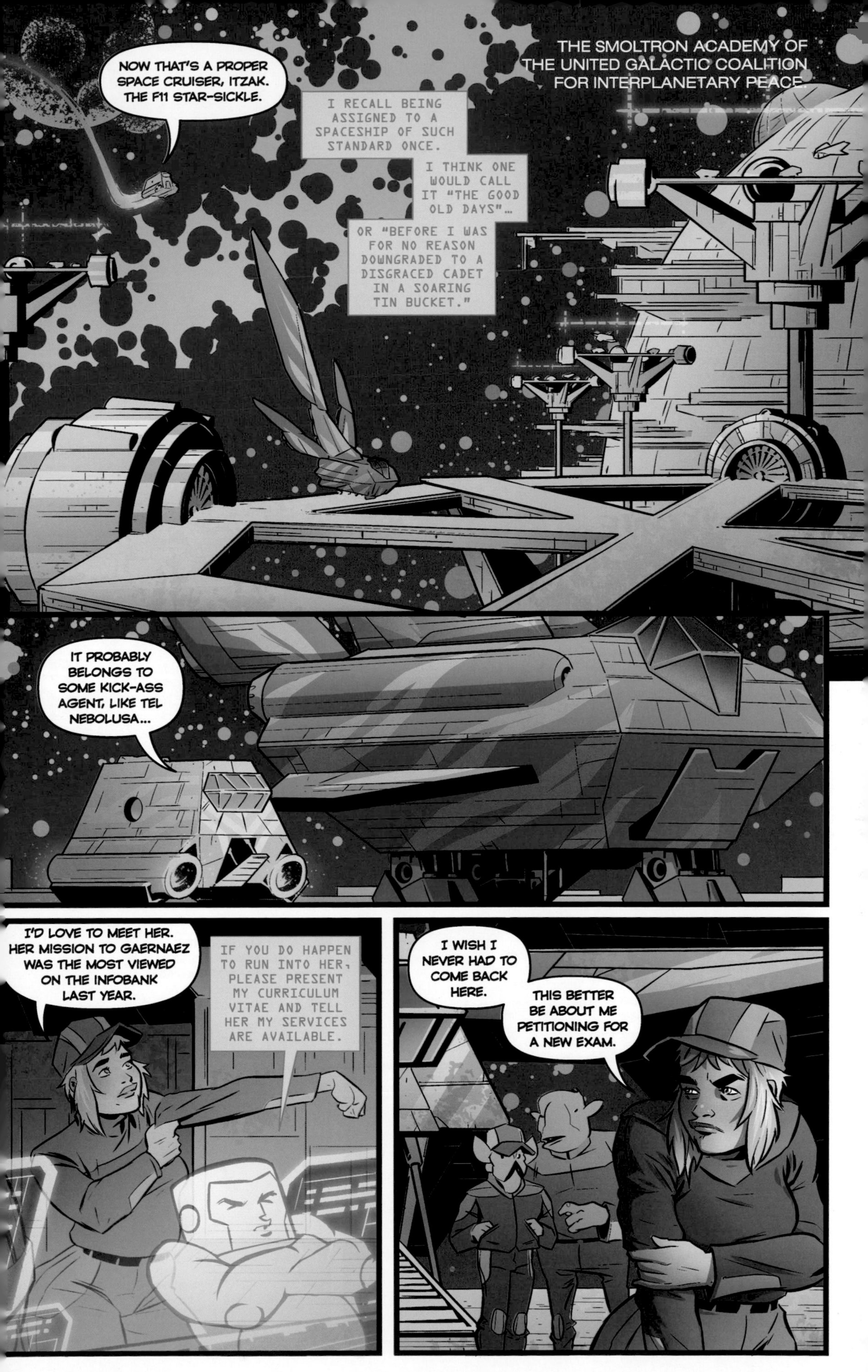
THE SMOLTRON ACADEMY OF THE UNITED GALACTIC COALITION FOR INTERPLANETARY PEACE.
NOW THAT'S A PROPER SPACE CRUISER, ITZAK. THE F11 STAR-SICKLE.
I RECALL BEING ASSIGNED TO A SPACESHIP OF SUCH STANDARD ONCE.
I THINK ONE WOULD CALL IT "THE GOOD OLD DAYS"...
OR "BEFORE I WAS FOR NO REASON DOWNGRADED TO A DISGRACED CADET IN A SOARING TIN BUCKET."
IT PROBABLY BELONGS TO SOME KICK-ASS AGENT, LIKE TEL NEBOLUSA...
I'D LOVE TO MEET HER. HER MISSION TO GAERNAEZ WAS THE MOST VIEWED ON THE INFOBANK LAST YEAR.
IF YOU DO HAPPEN TO RUN INTO HER, PLEASE PRESENT MY CURRICULUM VITAE AND TELL HER MY SERVICES ARE AVAILABLE.
I WISH I NEVER HAD TO COME BACK HERE.
THIS BETTER BE ABOUT ME PETITIONING FOR A NEW EXAM.

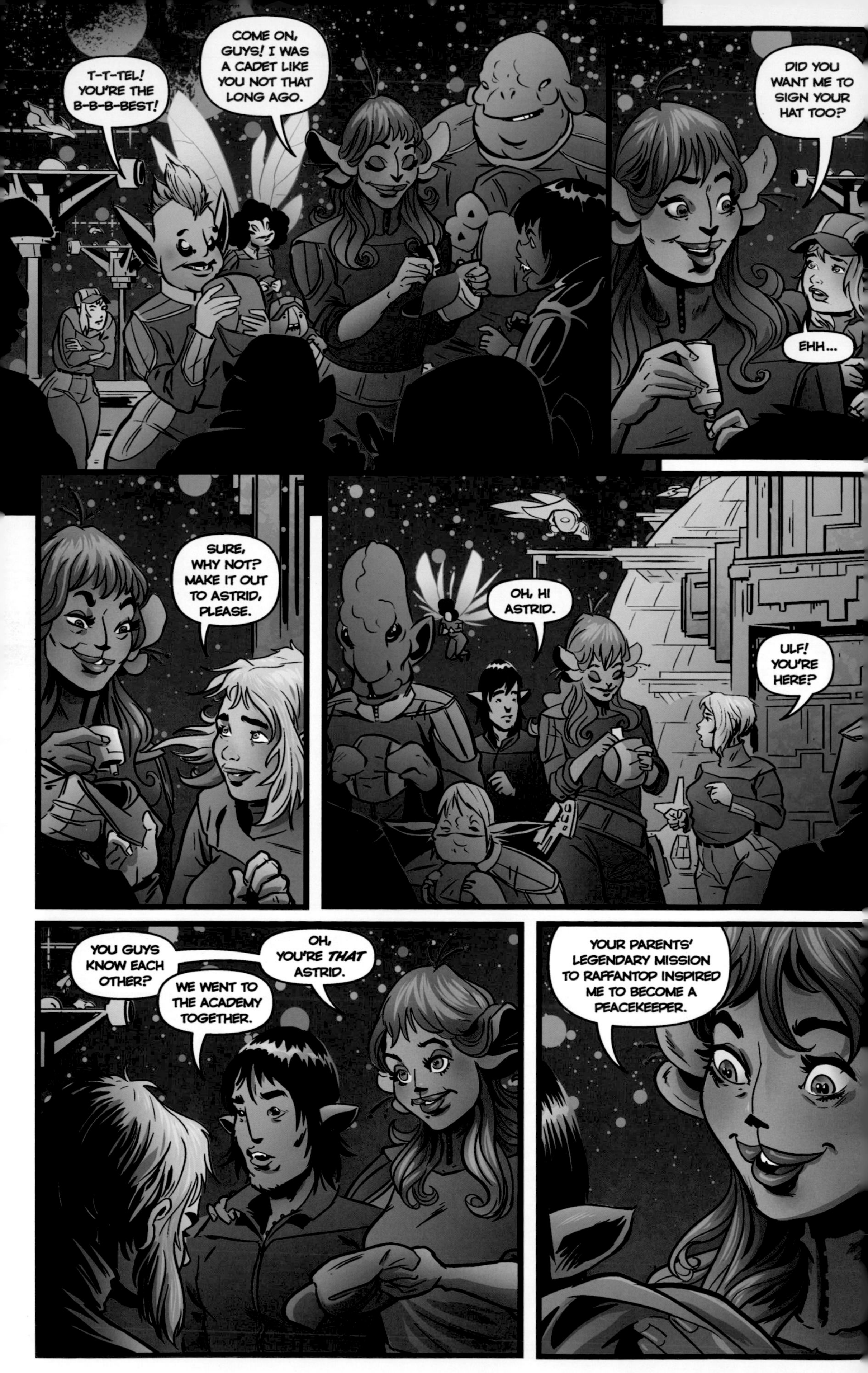
T-T-TEL! YOU'RE THE B-B-B-BEST!
COME ON, GUYS! I WAS A CADET LIKE YOU NOT THAT LONG AGO.
DID YOU WANT ME TO SIGN YOUR HAT TOO?
EHH...
SURE, WHY NOT? MAKE IT OUT TO ASTRID, PLEASE.
OH, HI ASTRID.
ULF! YOU'RE HERE?
YOU GUYS KNOW EACH OTHER?
WE WENT TO THE ACADEMY TOGETHER.
OH, YOU'RE *THAT* ASTRID.
YOUR PARENTS' LEGENDARY MISSION TO RAFFANTOP INSPIRED ME TO BECOME A PEACEKEEPER.

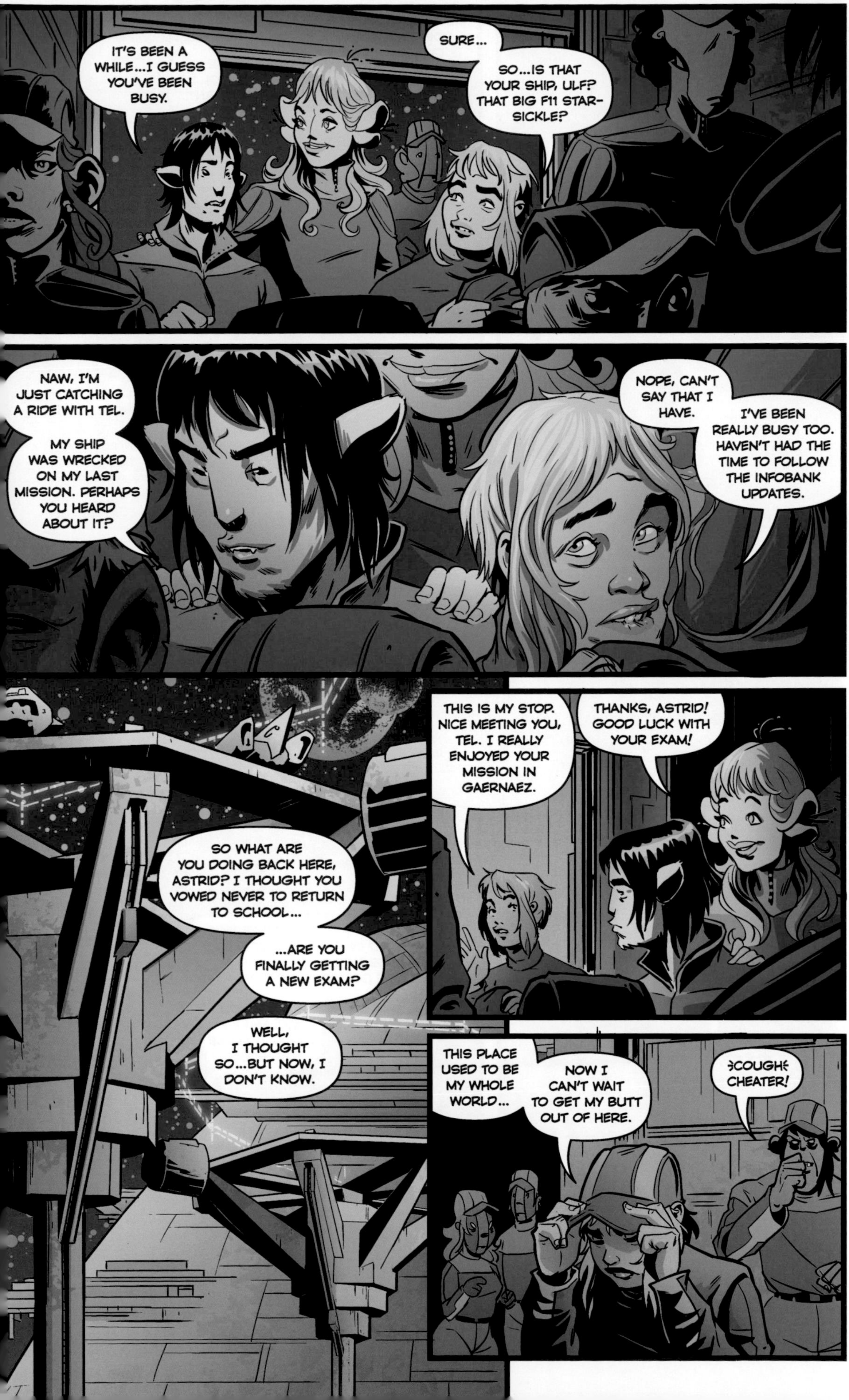
IT'S BEEN A WHILE...I GUESS YOU'VE BEEN BUSY.
SURE...
SO...IS THAT YOUR SHIP, ULF? THAT BIG F11 STAR-SICKLE?
NAW, I'M JUST CATCHING A RIDE WITH TEL.
MY SHIP WAS WRECKED ON MY LAST MISSION. PERHAPS YOU HEARD ABOUT IT?
NOPE, CAN'T SAY THAT I HAVE.
I'VE BEEN REALLY BUSY TOO. HAVEN'T HAD THE TIME TO FOLLOW THE INFOBANK UPDATES.
SO WHAT ARE YOU DOING BACK HERE, ASTRID? I THOUGHT YOU VOWED NEVER TO RETURN TO SCHOOL...
...ARE YOU FINALLY GETTING A NEW EXAM?
WELL, I THOUGHT SO...BUT NOW, I DON'T KNOW.
THIS IS MY STOP. NICE MEETING YOU, TEL. I REALLY ENJOYED YOUR MISSION IN GAERNAEZ.
THANKS, ASTRID! GOOD LUCK WITH YOUR EXAM!
THIS PLACE USED TO BE MY WHOLE WORLD...
NOW I CAN'T WAIT TO GET MY BUTT OUT OF HERE.
*COUGH* CHEATER!

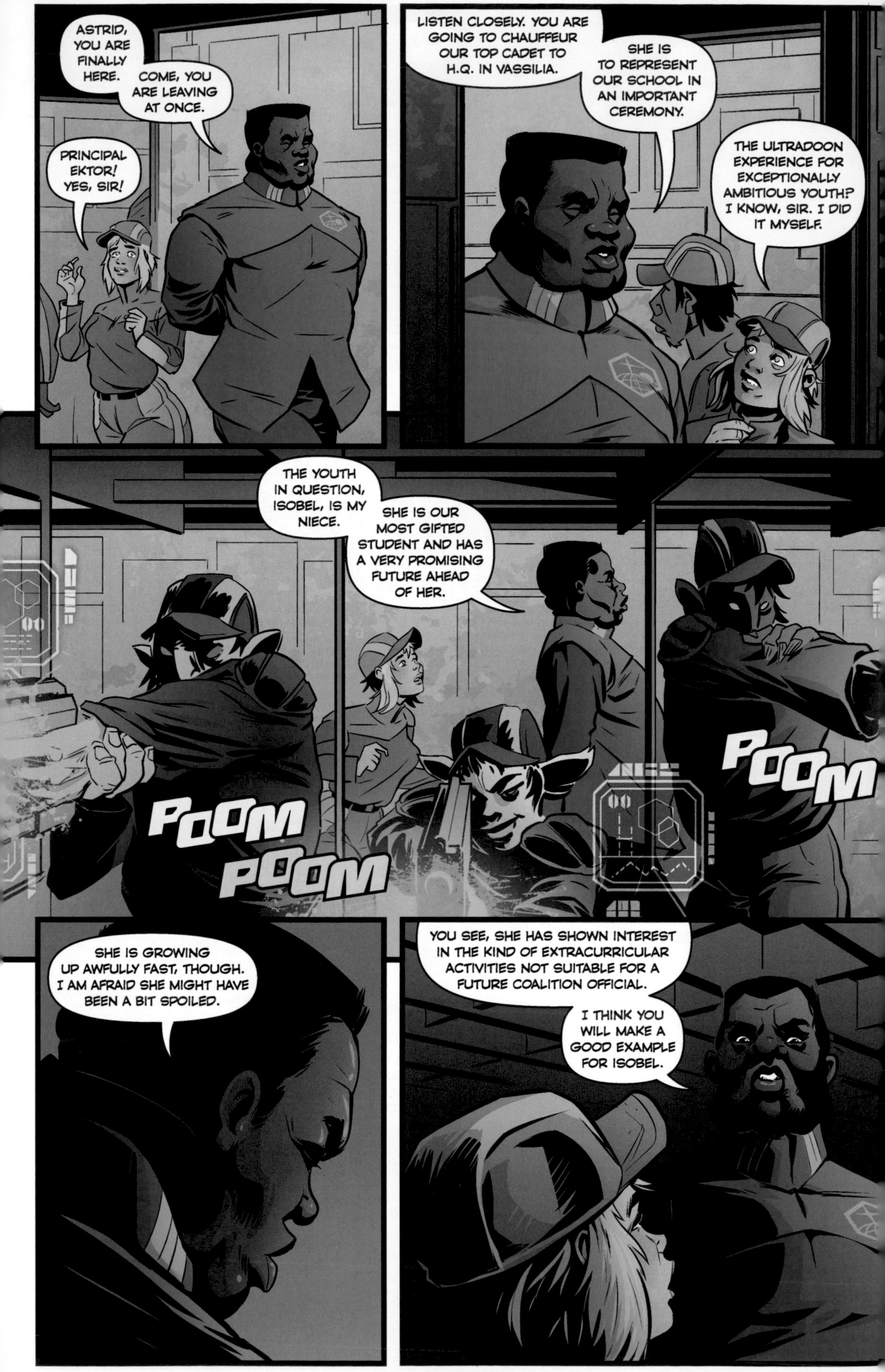
ASTRID, YOU ARE FINALLY HERE.
COME, YOU ARE LEAVING AT ONCE.
PRINCIPAL EKTOR! YES, SIR!
LISTEN CLOSELY. YOU ARE GOING TO CHAUFFEUR OUR TOP CADET TO H.Q. IN VASSILIA.
SHE IS TO REPRESENT OUR SCHOOL IN AN IMPORTANT CEREMONY.
THE ULTRADOON EXPERIENCE FOR EXCEPTIONALLY AMBITIOUS YOUTH? I KNOW, SIR. I DID IT MYSELF.
THE YOUTH IN QUESTION, ISOBEL, IS MY NIECE.
SHE IS OUR MOST GIFTED STUDENT AND HAS A VERY PROMISING FUTURE AHEAD OF HER.
POOM
POOM
POOM
SHE IS GROWING UP AWFULLY FAST, THOUGH. I AM AFRAID SHE MIGHT HAVE BEEN A BIT SPOILED.
YOU SEE, SHE HAS SHOWN INTEREST IN THE KIND OF EXTRACURRICULAR ACTIVITIES NOT SUITABLE FOR A FUTURE COALITION OFFICIAL.
I THINK YOU WILL MAKE A GOOD EXAMPLE FOR ISOBEL.

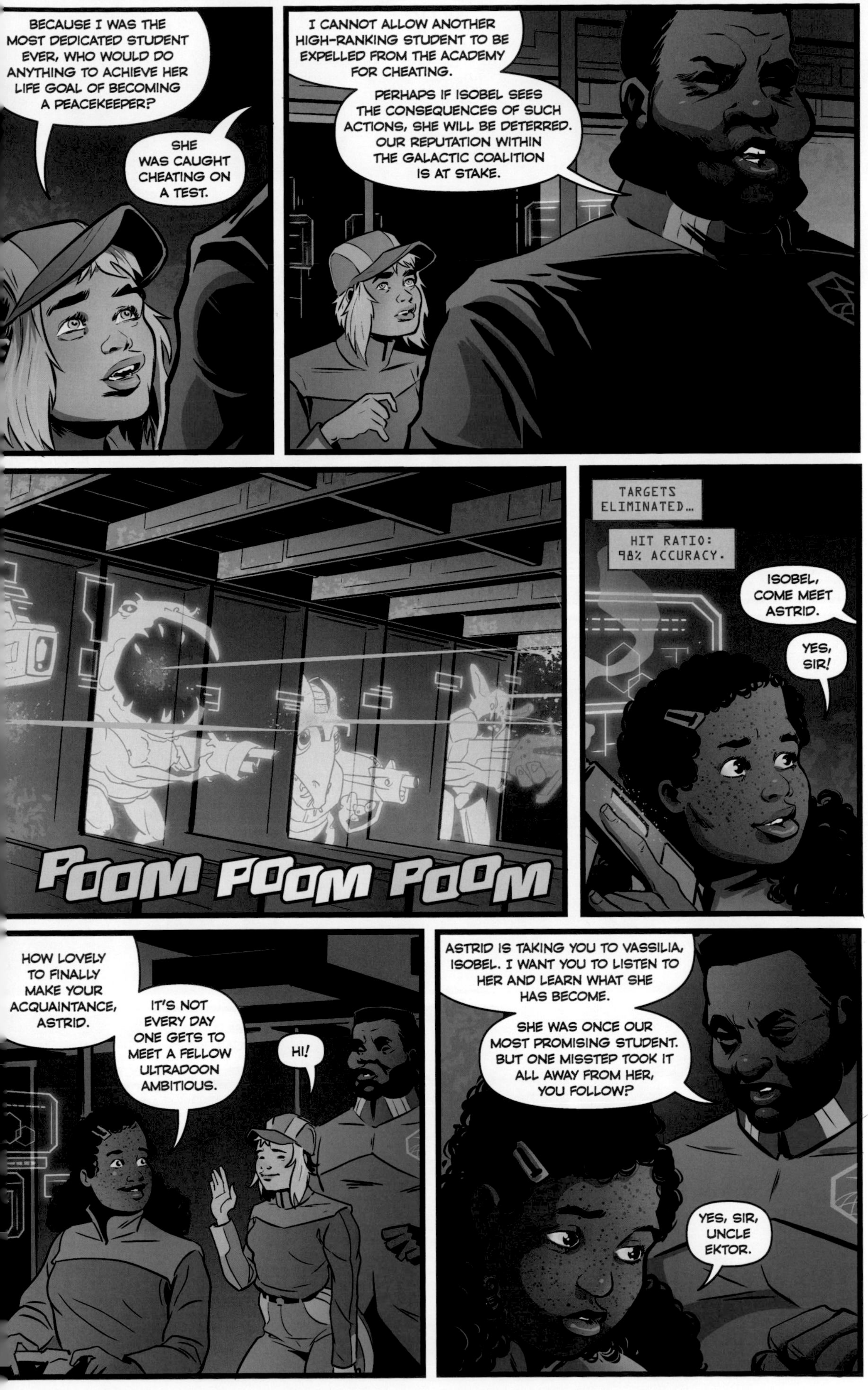
BECAUSE I WAS THE MOST DEDICATED STUDENT EVER, WHO WOULD DO ANYTHING TO ACHIEVE HER LIFE GOAL OF BECOMING A PEACEKEEPER?
SHE WAS CAUGHT CHEATING ON A TEST.
I CANNOT ALLOW ANOTHER HIGH-RANKING STUDENT TO BE EXPELLED FROM THE ACADEMY FOR CHEATING.
PERHAPS IF ISOBEL SEES THE CONSEQUENCES OF SUCH ACTIONS, SHE WILL BE DETERRED. OUR REPUTATION WITHIN THE GALACTIC COALITION IS AT STAKE.
POOM POOM POOM
TARGETS ELIMINATED...
HIT RATIO: 98% ACCURACY.
ISOBEL, COME MEET ASTRID.
YES, SIR!
HOW LOVELY TO FINALLY MAKE YOUR ACQUAINTANCE, ASTRID.
IT'S NOT EVERY DAY ONE GETS TO MEET A FELLOW ULTRADOON AMBITIOUS.
HI!
ASTRID IS TAKING YOU TO VASSILIA, ISOBEL. I WANT YOU TO LISTEN TO HER AND LEARN WHAT SHE HAS BECOME.
SHE WAS ONCE OUR MOST PROMISING STUDENT. BUT ONE MISSTEP TOOK IT ALL AWAY FROM HER, YOU FOLLOW?
YES, SIR, UNCLE EKTOR.

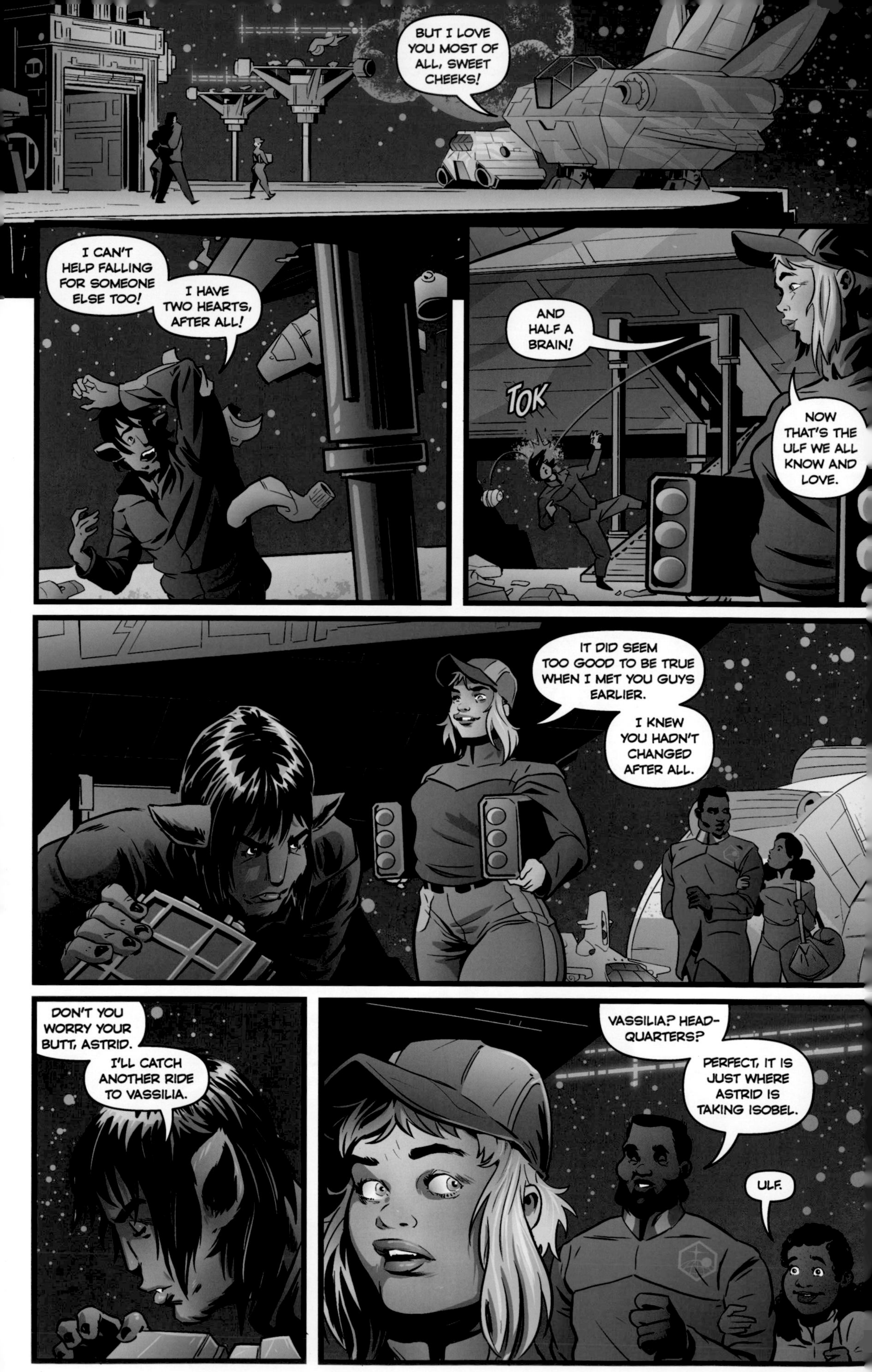
BUT I LOVE YOU MOST OF ALL, SWEET CHEEKS!
I CAN'T HELP FALLING FOR SOMEONE ELSE TOO!
I HAVE TWO HEARTS, AFTER ALL!
AND HALF A BRAIN!
TOK
NOW THAT'S THE ULF WE ALL KNOW AND LOVE.
IT DID SEEM TOO GOOD TO BE TRUE WHEN I MET YOU GUYS EARLIER.
I KNEW YOU HADN'T CHANGED AFTER ALL.
DON'T YOU WORRY YOUR BUTT, ASTRID.
I'LL CATCH ANOTHER RIDE TO VASSILIA.
VASSILIA? HEAD-QUARTERS?
PERFECT, IT IS JUST WHERE ASTRID IS TAKING ISOBEL.
ULF.

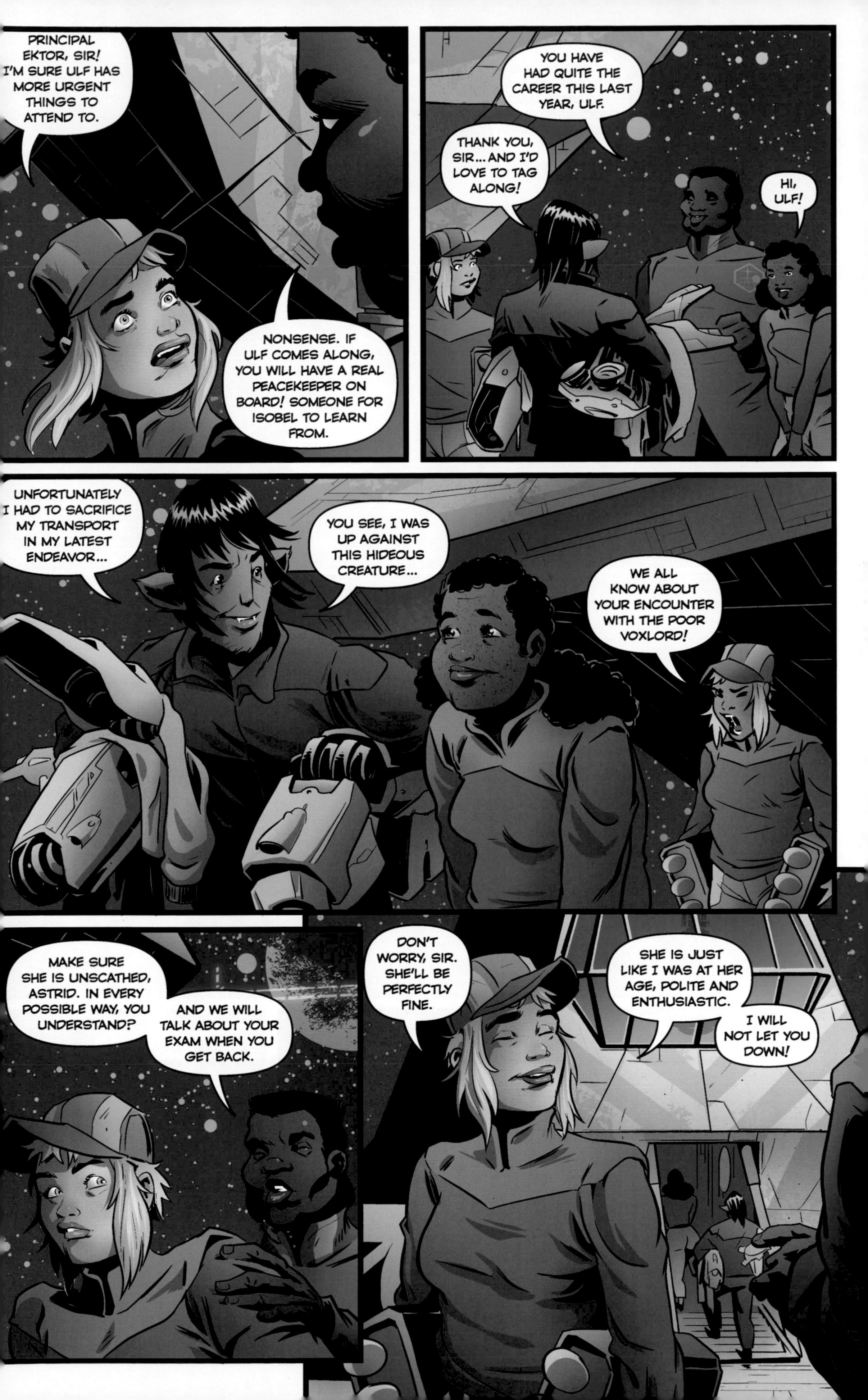
PRINCIPAL EKTOR, SIR! I'M SURE ULF HAS MORE URGENT THINGS TO ATTEND TO.
NONSENSE. IF ULF COMES ALONG, YOU WILL HAVE A REAL PEACEKEEPER ON BOARD! SOMEONE FOR ISOBEL TO LEARN FROM.
YOU HAVE HAD QUITE THE CAREER THIS LAST YEAR, ULF.
THANK YOU, SIR... AND I'D LOVE TO TAG ALONG!
HI, ULF!
UNFORTUNATELY I HAD TO SACRIFICE MY TRANSPORT IN MY LATEST ENDEAVOR...
YOU SEE, I WAS UP AGAINST THIS HIDEOUS CREATURE...
WE ALL KNOW ABOUT YOUR ENCOUNTER WITH THE POOR VOXLORD!
MAKE SURE SHE IS UNSCATHED, ASTRID. IN EVERY POSSIBLE WAY, YOU UNDERSTAND?
AND WE WILL TALK ABOUT YOUR EXAM WHEN YOU GET BACK.
DON'T WORRY, SIR. SHE'LL BE PERFECTLY FINE.
SHE IS JUST LIKE I WAS AT HER AGE, POLITE AND ENTHUSIASTIC.
I WILL NOT LET YOU DOWN!

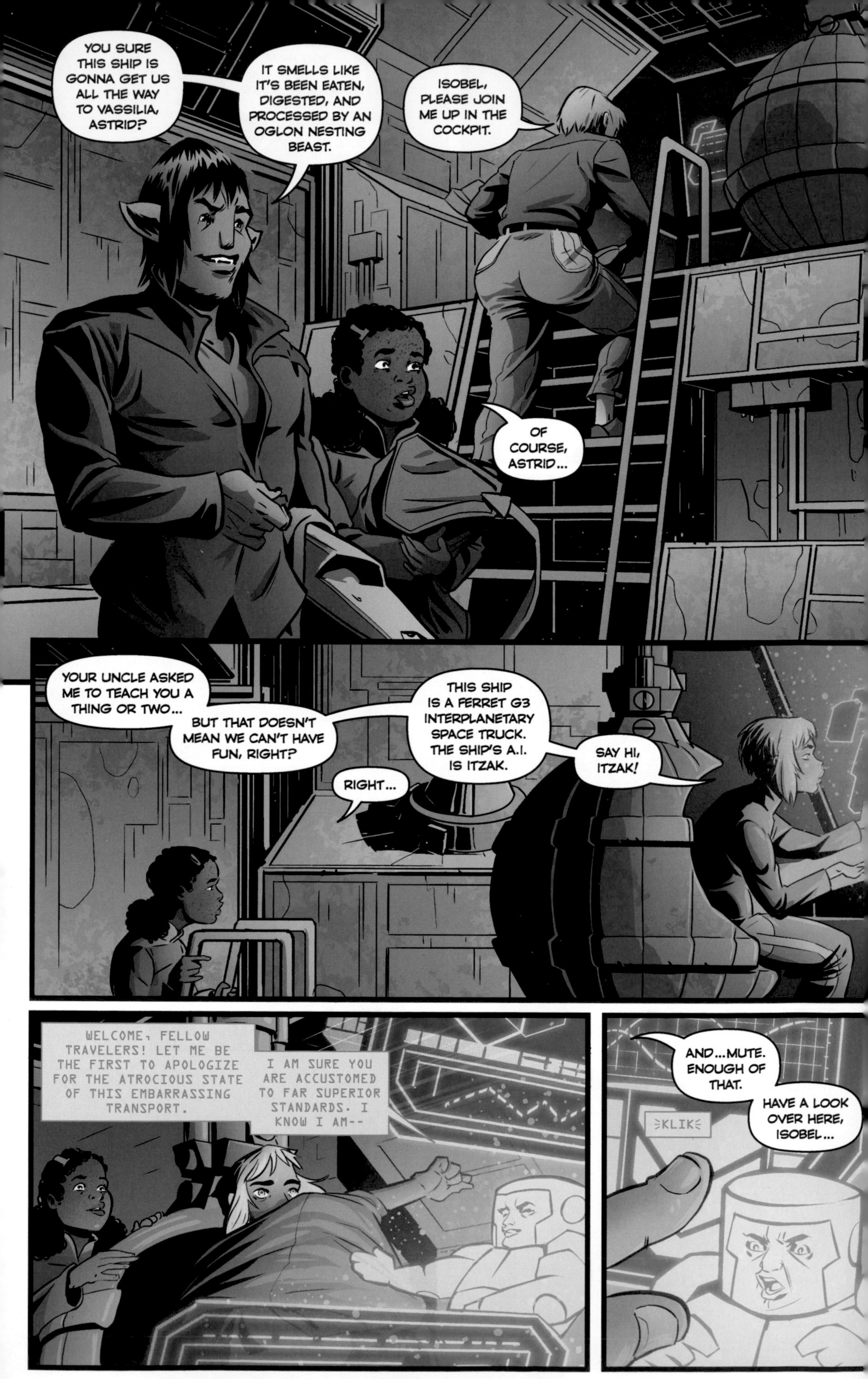
YOU SURE THIS SHIP IS GONNA GET US ALL THE WAY TO VASSILIA, ASTRID?
IT SMELLS LIKE IT'S BEEN EATEN, DIGESTED, AND PROCESSED BY AN OGLON NESTING BEAST.
ISOBEL, PLEASE JOIN ME UP IN THE COCKPIT.
OF COURSE, ASTRID...
YOUR UNCLE ASKED ME TO TEACH YOU A THING OR TWO...
BUT THAT DOESN'T MEAN WE CAN'T HAVE FUN, RIGHT?
RIGHT...
THIS SHIP IS A FERRET G3 INTERPLANETARY SPACE TRUCK. THE SHIP'S A.I. IS ITZAK.
SAY HI, ITZAK!
WELCOME, FELLOW TRAVELERS! LET ME BE THE FIRST TO APOLOGIZE FOR THE ATROCIOUS STATE OF THIS EMBARRASSING TRANSPORT.
I AM SURE YOU ARE ACCUSTOMED TO FAR SUPERIOR STANDARDS. I KNOW I AM--
AND...MUTE. ENOUGH OF THAT.
KLIK
HAVE A LOOK OVER HERE, ISOBEL...

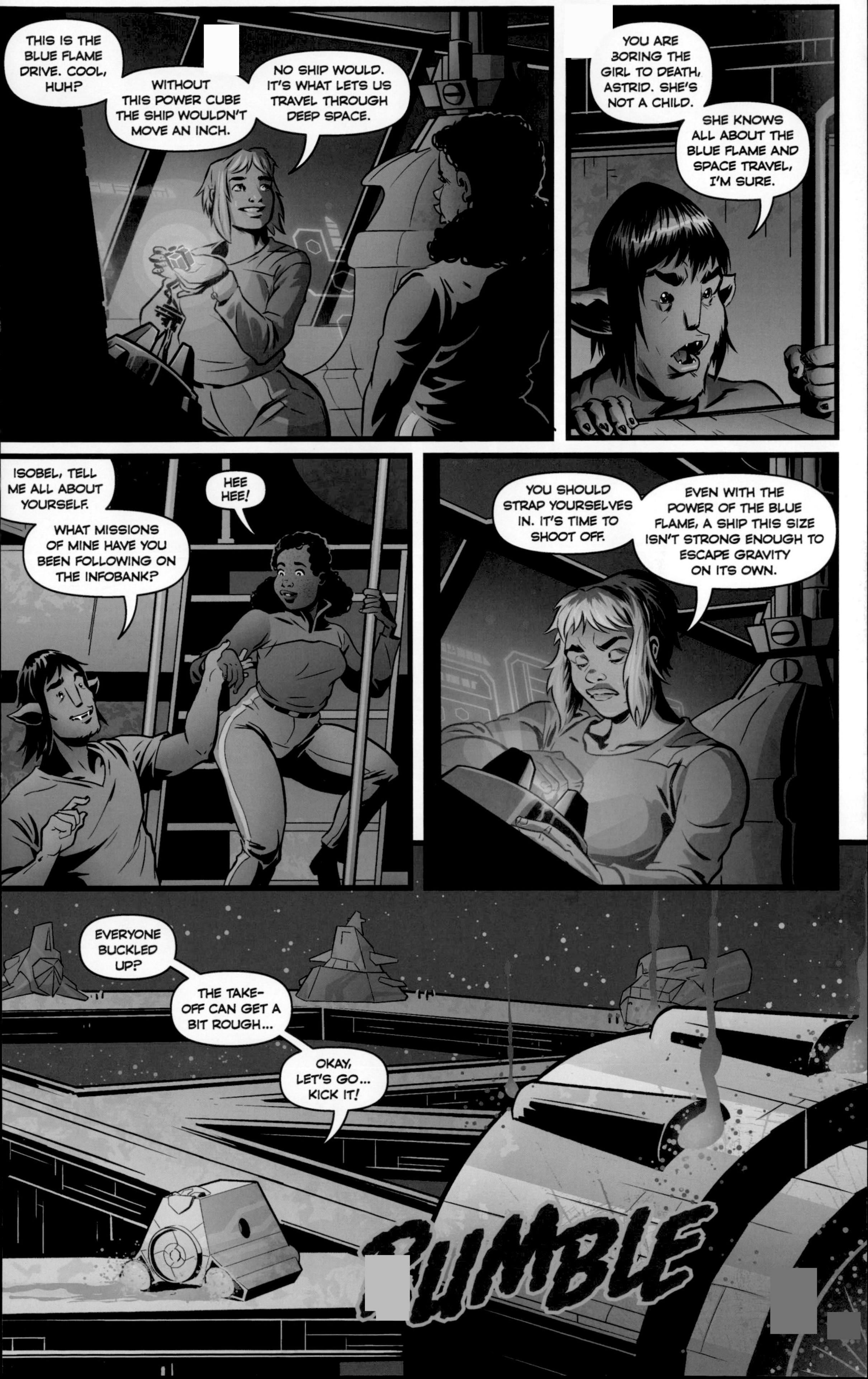
THIS IS THE BLUE FLAME DRIVE. COOL, HUH?
WITHOUT THIS POWER CUBE THE SHIP WOULDN'T MOVE AN INCH.
NO SHIP WOULD. IT'S WHAT LETS US TRAVEL THROUGH DEEP SPACE.
YOU ARE BORING THE GIRL TO DEATH, ASTRID. SHE'S NOT A CHILD.
SHE KNOWS ALL ABOUT THE BLUE FLAME AND SPACE TRAVEL, I'M SURE.
ISOBEL, TELL ME ALL ABOUT YOURSELF.
WHAT MISSIONS OF MINE HAVE YOU BEEN FOLLOWING ON THE INFOBANK?
HEE HEE!
YOU SHOULD STRAP YOURSELVES IN. IT'S TIME TO SHOOT OFF.
EVEN WITH THE POWER OF THE BLUE FLAME, A SHIP THIS SIZE ISN'T STRONG ENOUGH TO ESCAPE GRAVITY ON ITS OWN.
EVERYONE BUCKLED UP?
THE TAKE-OFF CAN GET A BIT ROUGH...
OKAY, LET'S GO... KICK IT!
RUMBLE

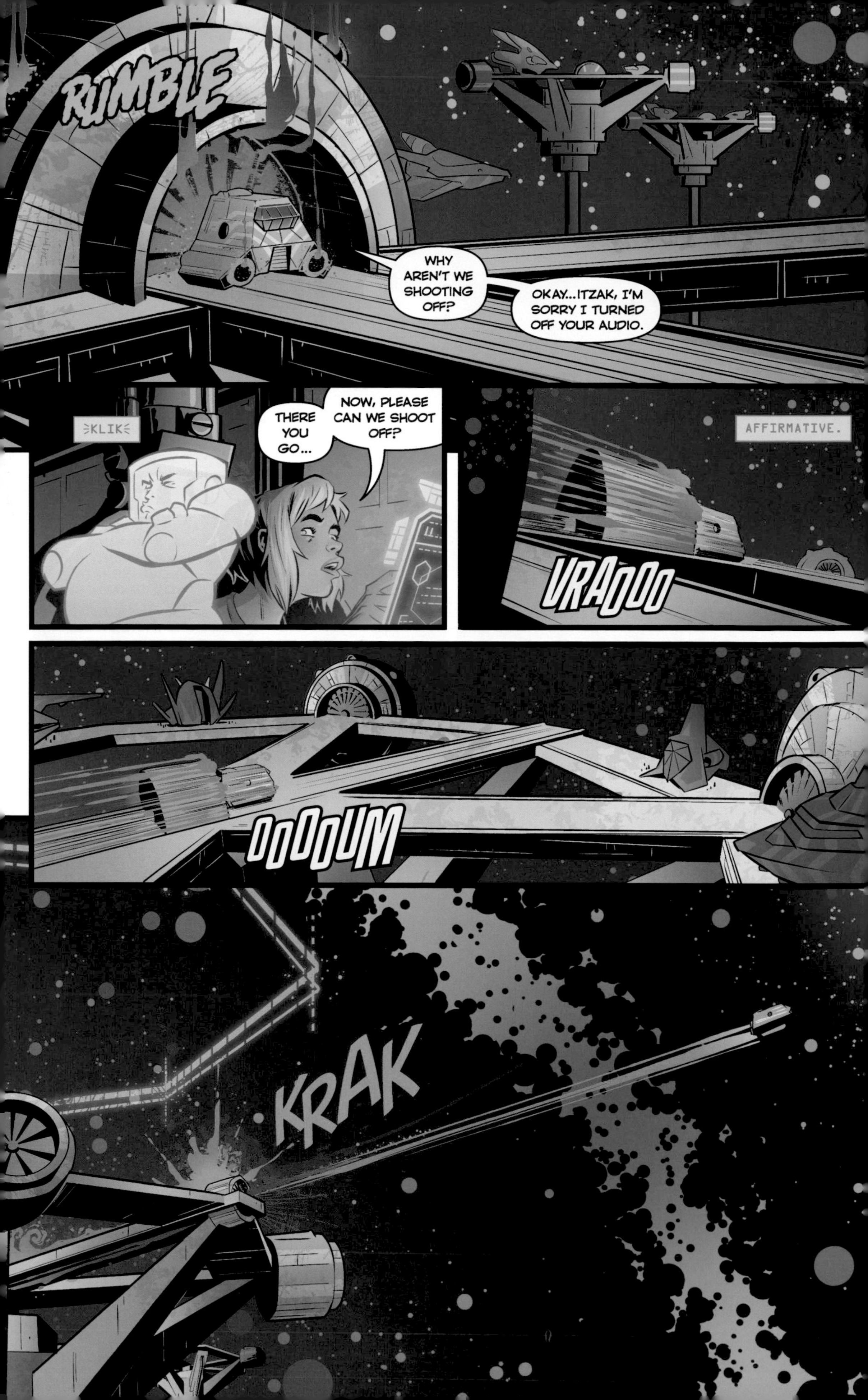
RUMBLE
WHY AREN'T WE SHOOTING OFF?
OKAY...ITZAK, I'M SORRY I TURNED OFF YOUR AUDIO.
KLIK
THERE YOU GO...
NOW, PLEASE CAN WE SHOOT OFF?
AFFIRMATIVE.
VRAOOO
OOOOUM
KRAK

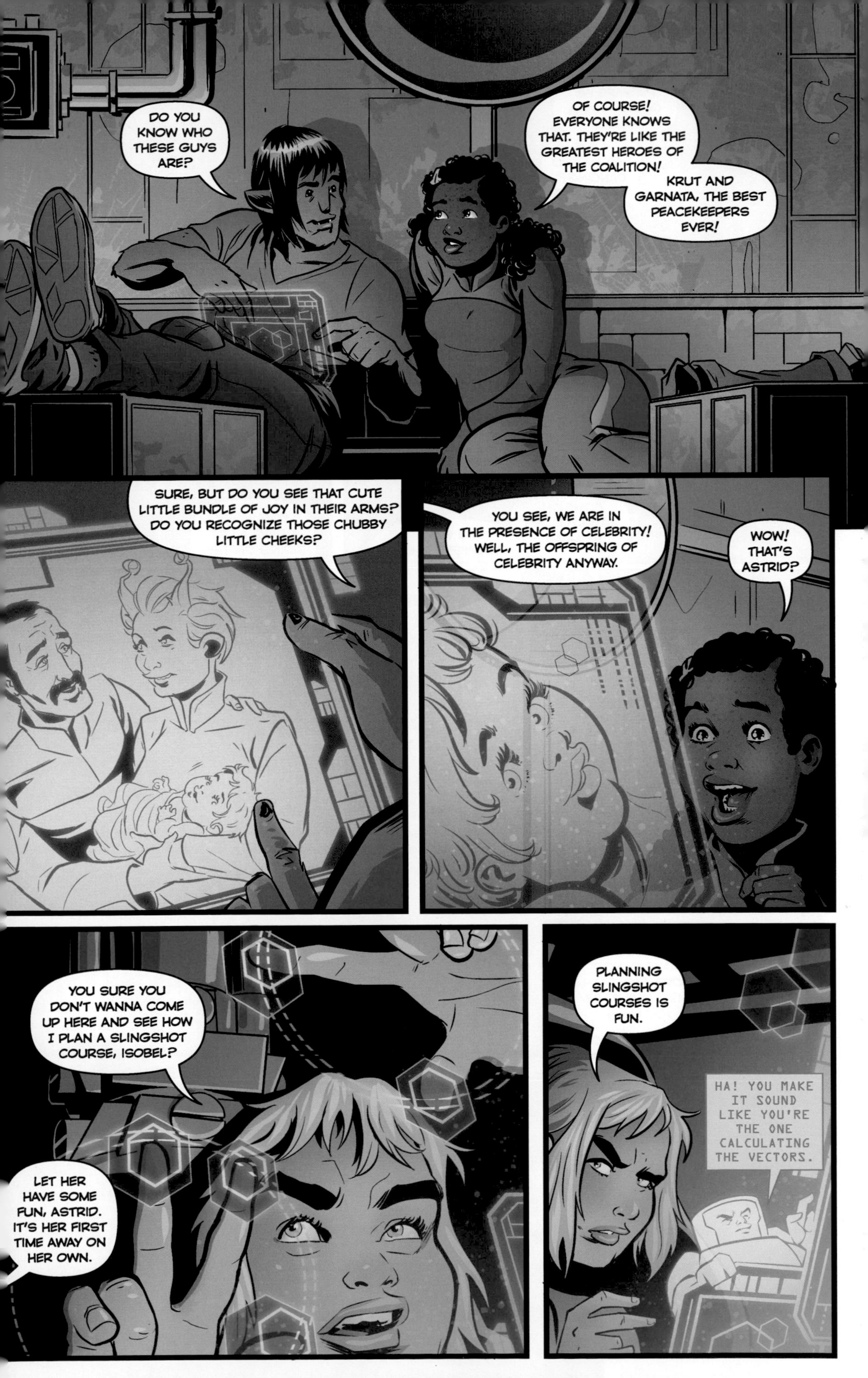
DO YOU KNOW WHO THESE GUYS ARE?
OF COURSE! EVERYONE KNOWS THAT. THEY'RE LIKE THE GREATEST HEROES OF THE COALITION!
KRUT AND GARNATA, THE BEST PEACEKEEPERS EVER!
SURE, BUT DO YOU SEE THAT CUTE LITTLE BUNDLE OF JOY IN THEIR ARMS? DO YOU RECOGNIZE THOSE CHUBBY LITTLE CHEEKS?
YOU SEE, WE ARE IN THE PRESENCE OF CELEBRITY! WELL, THE OFFSPRING OF CELEBRITY ANYWAY.
WOW! THAT'S ASTRID?
YOU SURE YOU DON'T WANNA COME UP HERE AND SEE HOW I PLAN A SLINGSHOT COURSE, ISOBEL?
LET HER HAVE SOME FUN, ASTRID. IT'S HER FIRST TIME AWAY ON HER OWN.
PLANNING SLINGSHOT COURSES IS FUN.
HA! YOU MAKE IT SOUND LIKE YOU'RE THE ONE CALCULATING THE VECTORS.

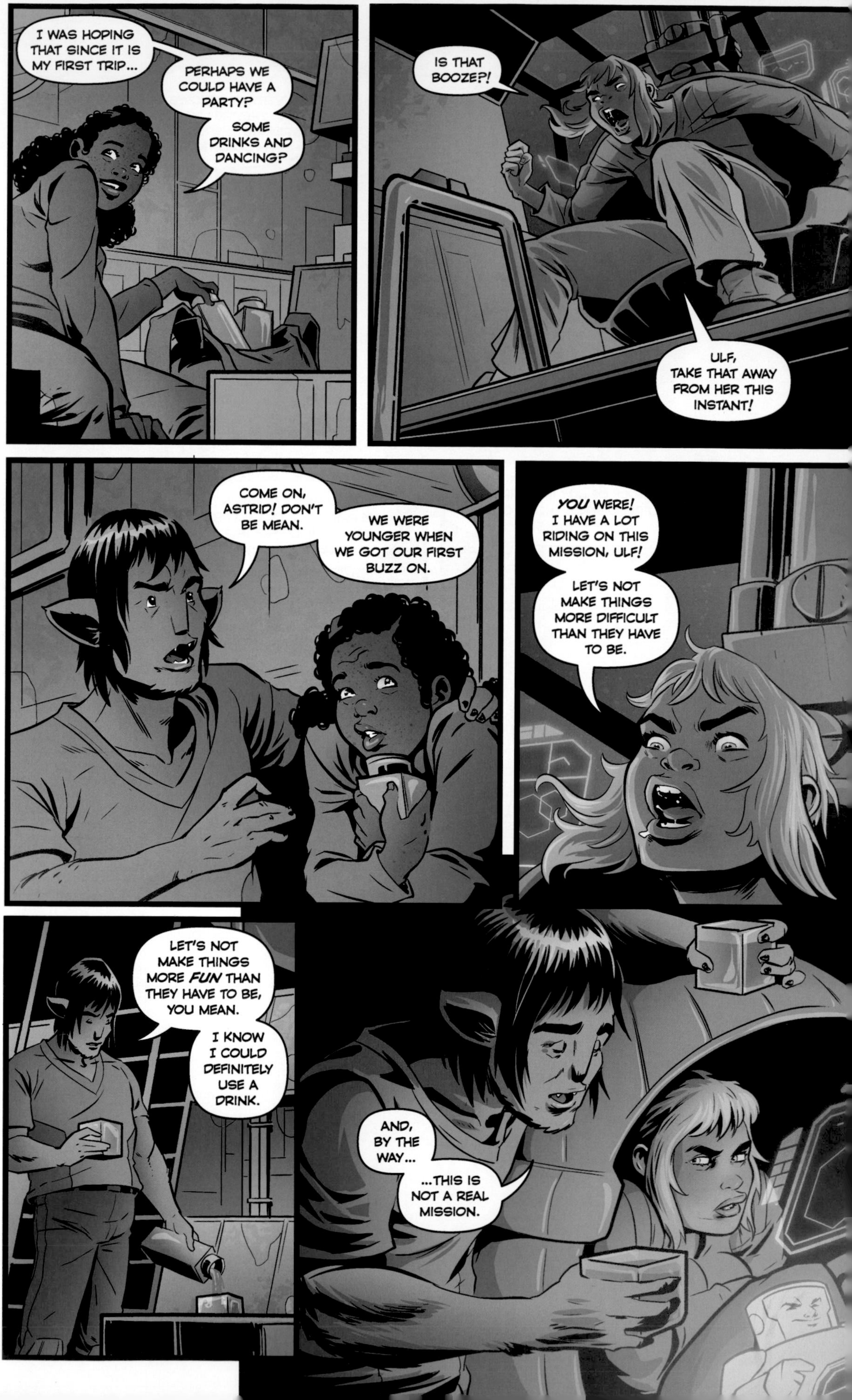
I WAS HOPING THAT SINCE IT IS MY FIRST TRIP...
PERHAPS WE COULD HAVE A PARTY?
SOME DRINKS AND DANCING?
IS THAT BOOZE?!
ULF, TAKE THAT AWAY FROM HER THIS INSTANT!
COME ON, ASTRID! DON'T BE MEAN.
WE WERE YOUNGER WHEN WE GOT OUR FIRST BUZZ ON.
*YOU* WERE! I HAVE A LOT RIDING ON THIS MISSION, ULF!
LET'S NOT MAKE THINGS MORE DIFFICULT THAN THEY HAVE TO BE.
LET'S NOT MAKE THINGS MORE *FUN* THAN THEY HAVE TO BE, YOU MEAN.
I KNOW I COULD DEFINITELY USE A DRINK.
AND, BY THE WAY...
...THIS IS NOT A REAL MISSION.

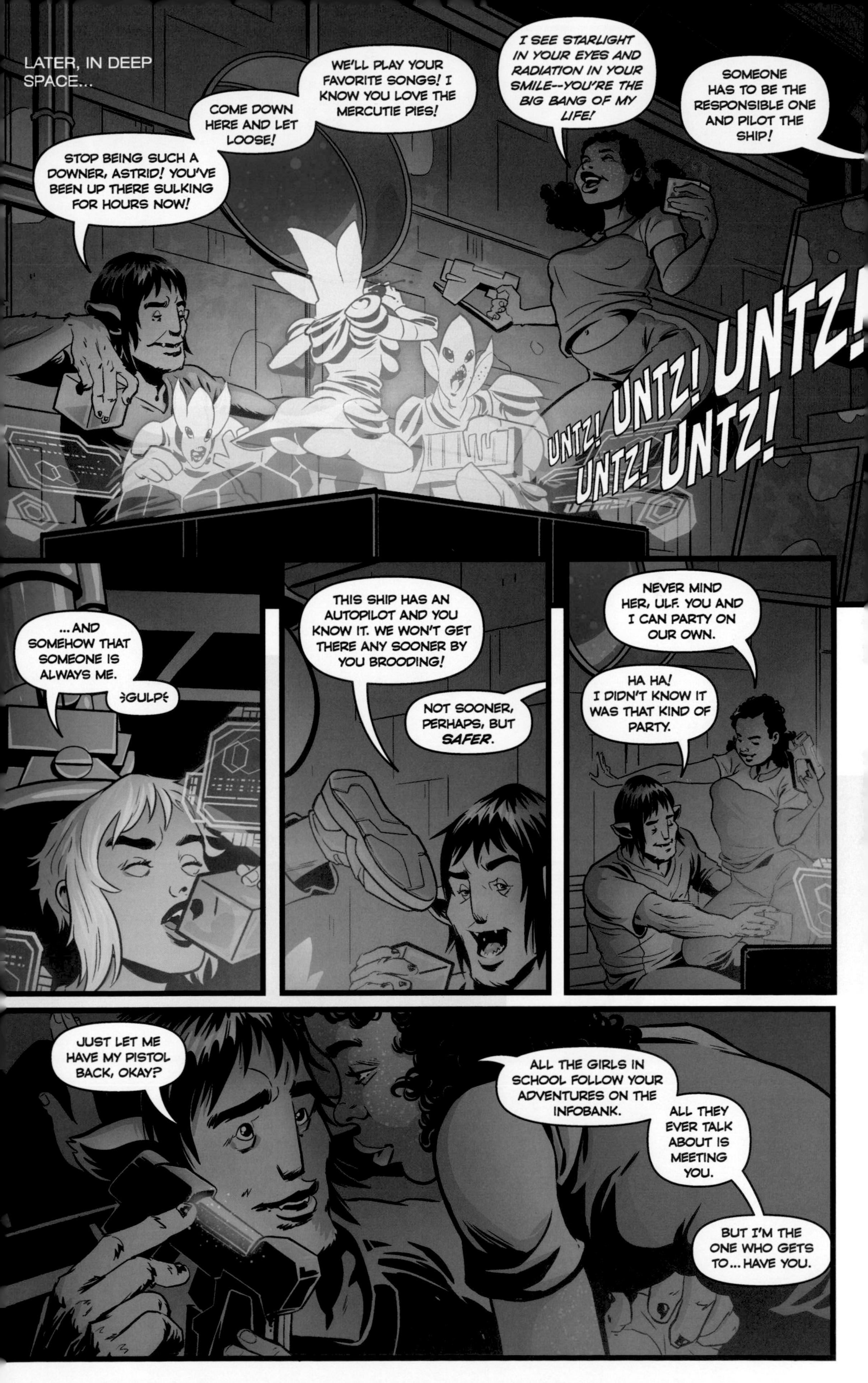
LATER, IN DEEP SPACE...
STOP BEING SUCH A DOWNER, ASTRID! YOU'VE BEEN UP THERE SULKING FOR HOURS NOW!
COME DOWN HERE AND LET LOOSE!
WE'LL PLAY YOUR FAVORITE SONGS! I KNOW YOU LOVE THE MERCUTIE PIES!
I SEE STARLIGHT IN YOUR EYES AND RADIATION IN YOUR SMILE--YOU'RE THE BIG BANG OF MY LIFE!
SOMEONE HAS TO BE THE RESPONSIBLE ONE AND PILOT THE SHIP!
UNTZ! UNTZ! UNTZ! UNTZ! UNTZ!
...AND SOMEHOW THAT SOMEONE IS ALWAYS ME.
GULP
THIS SHIP HAS AN AUTOPILOT AND YOU KNOW IT. WE WON'T GET THERE ANY SOONER BY YOU BROODING!
NOT SOONER, PERHAPS, BUT SAFER.
NEVER MIND HER, ULF. YOU AND I CAN PARTY ON OUR OWN.
HA HA! I DIDN'T KNOW IT WAS THAT KIND OF PARTY.
JUST LET ME HAVE MY PISTOL BACK, OKAY?
ALL THE GIRLS IN SCHOOL FOLLOW YOUR ADVENTURES ON THE INFOBANK.
ALL THEY EVER TALK ABOUT IS MEETING YOU.
BUT I'M THE ONE WHO GETS TO... HAVE YOU.

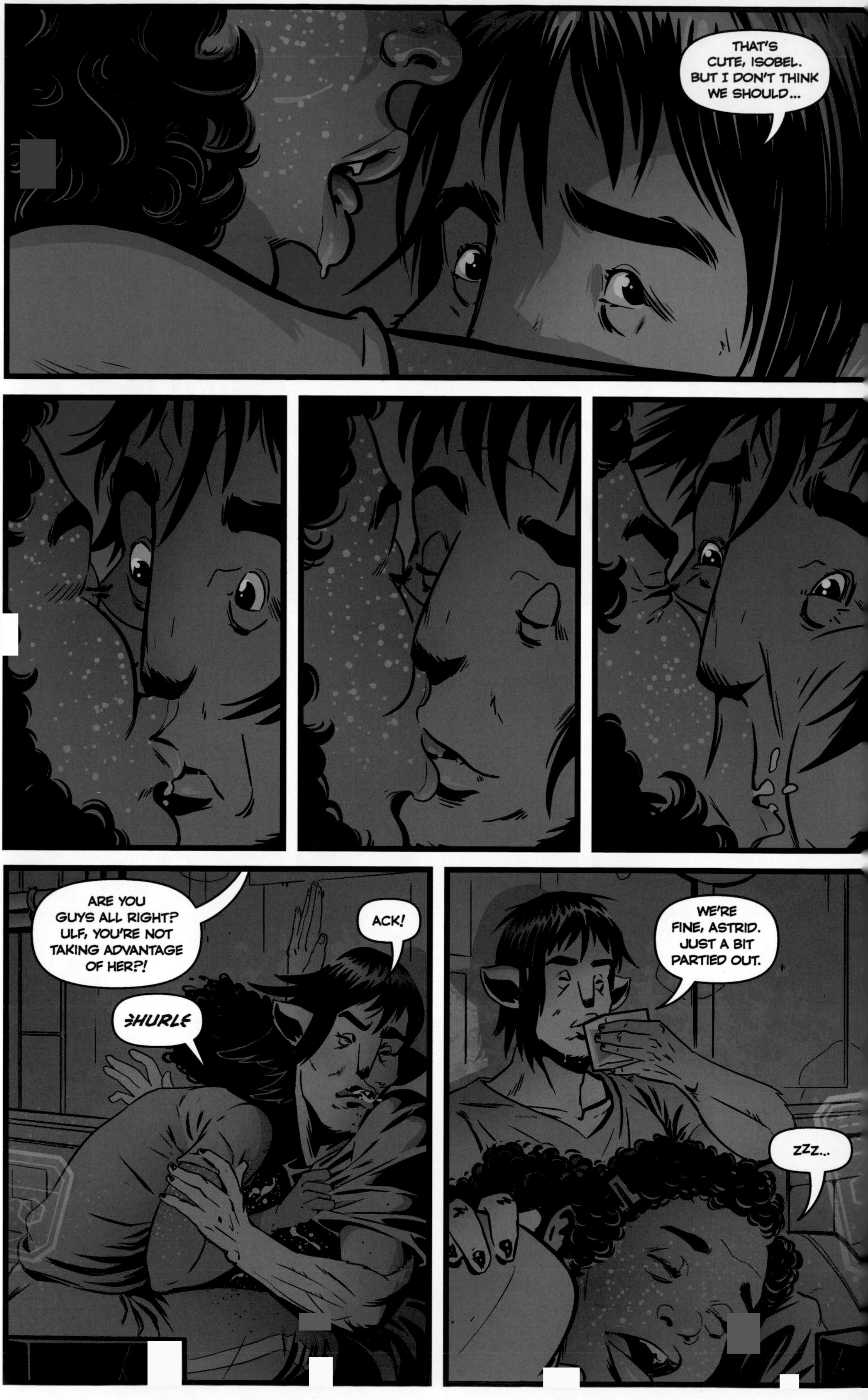
THAT'S CUTE, ISOBEL. BUT I DON'T THINK WE SHOULD...
ARE YOU GUYS ALL RIGHT? ULF, YOU'RE NOT TAKING ADVANTAGE OF HER?!
ACK!
HURL
WE'RE FINE, ASTRID. JUST A BIT PARTIED OUT.
ZZZ...

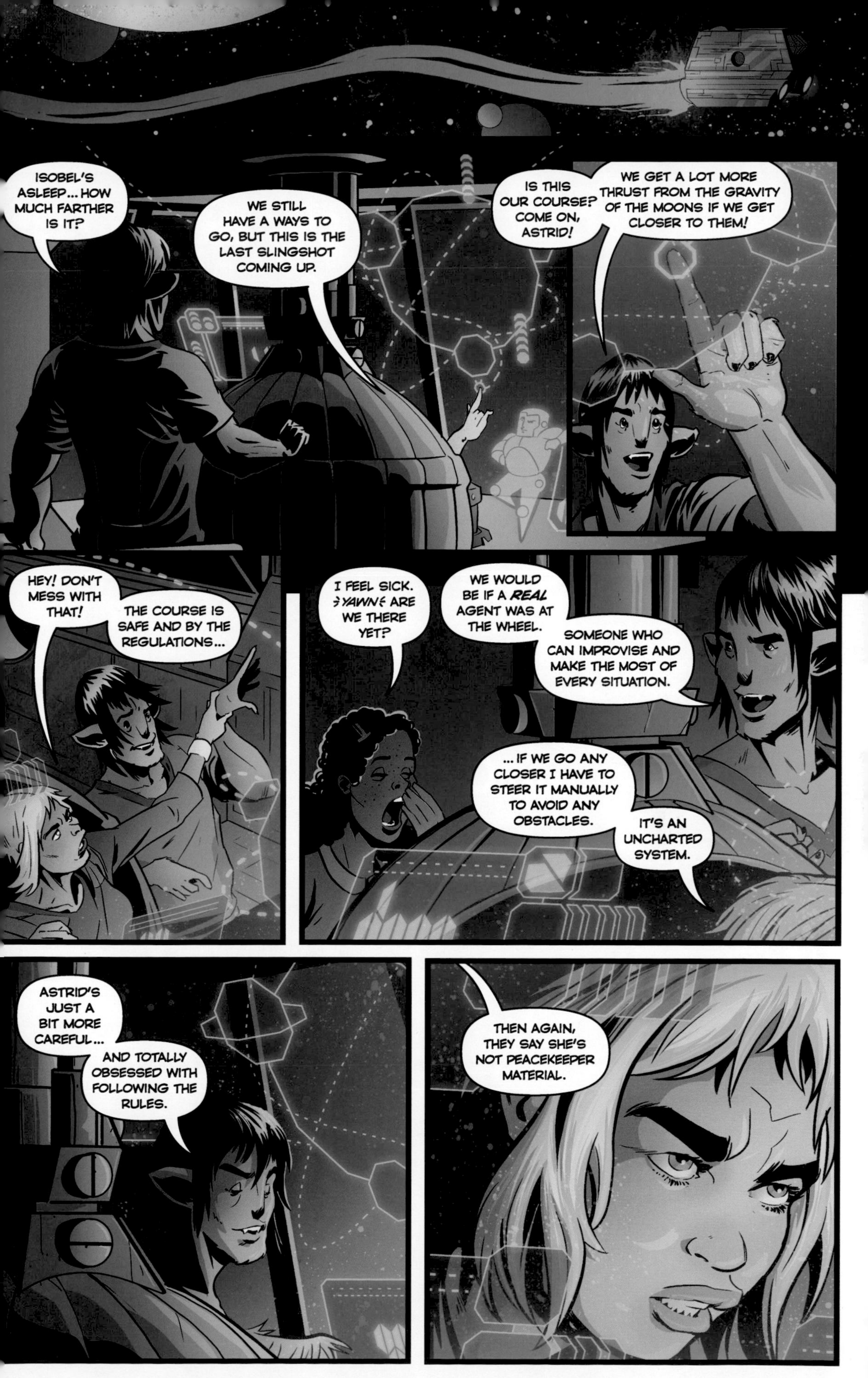
ISOBEL'S ASLEEP... HOW MUCH FARTHER IS IT?
WE STILL HAVE A WAYS TO GO, BUT THIS IS THE LAST SLINGSHOT COMING UP.
IS THIS OUR COURSE? COME ON, ASTRID!
WE GET A LOT MORE THRUST FROM THE GRAVITY OF THE MOONS IF WE GET CLOSER TO THEM!
HEY! DON'T MESS WITH THAT!
THE COURSE IS SAFE AND BY THE REGULATIONS...
I FEEL SICK. *YAWN* ARE WE THERE YET?
WE WOULD BE IF A REAL AGENT WAS AT THE WHEEL.
SOMEONE WHO CAN IMPROVISE AND MAKE THE MOST OF EVERY SITUATION.
...IF WE GO ANY CLOSER I HAVE TO STEER IT MANUALLY TO AVOID ANY OBSTACLES.
IT'S AN UNCHARTED SYSTEM.
ASTRID'S JUST A BIT MORE CAREFUL...
AND TOTALLY OBSESSED WITH FOLLOWING THE RULES.
THEN AGAIN, THEY SAY SHE'S NOT PEACEKEEPER MATERIAL.

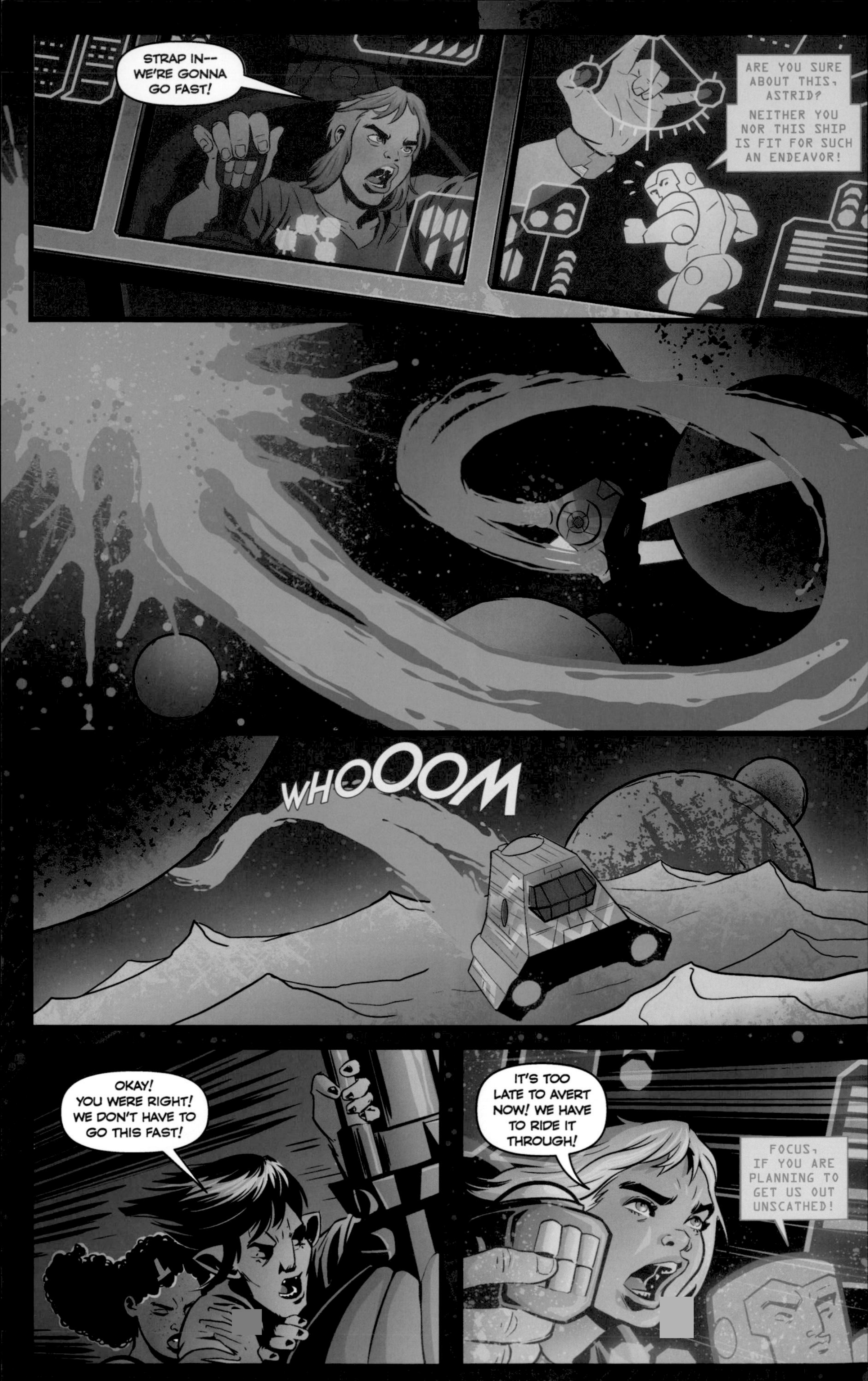
STRAP IN--
WE'RE GONNA
GO FAST!
ARE YOU SURE ABOUT THIS, ASTRID?
NEITHER YOU NOR THIS SHIP IS FIT FOR SUCH AN ENDEAVOR!
WHOOOOM
OKAY!
YOU WERE RIGHT!
WE DON'T HAVE TO
GO THIS FAST!
IT'S TOO LATE TO AVERT NOW! WE HAVE TO RIDE IT THROUGH!
FOCUS, IF YOU ARE PLANNING TO GET US OUT UNSCATHED!

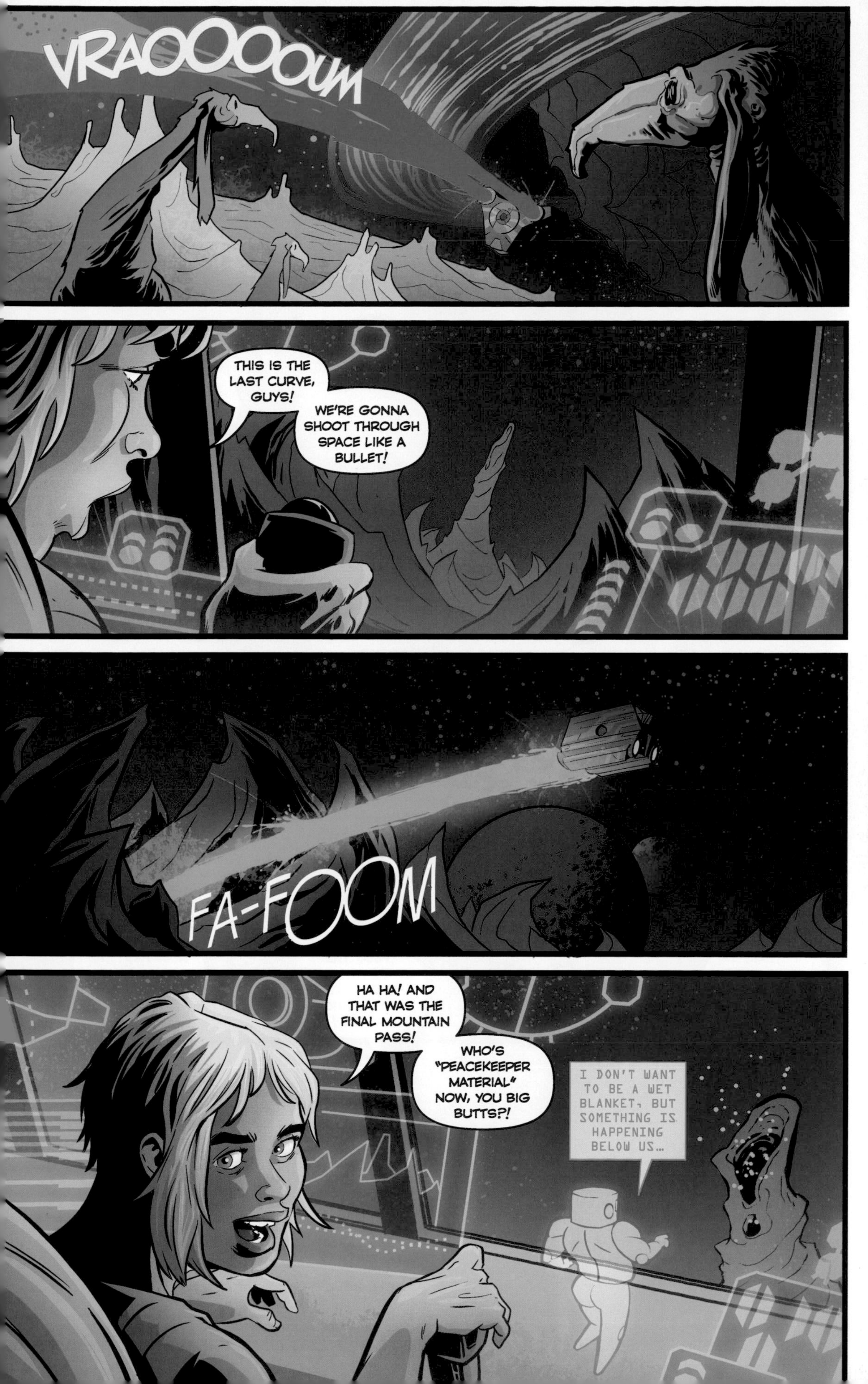
VRAOOOOUM
THIS IS THE LAST CURVE, GUYS!
WE'RE GONNA SHOOT THROUGH SPACE LIKE A BULLET!
FA-FOOM
HA HA! AND THAT WAS THE FINAL MOUNTAIN PASS!
WHO'S "PEACEKEEPER MATERIAL" NOW, YOU BIG BUTTS?!
I DON'T WANT TO BE A WET BLANKET, BUT SOMETHING IS HAPPENING BELOW US...

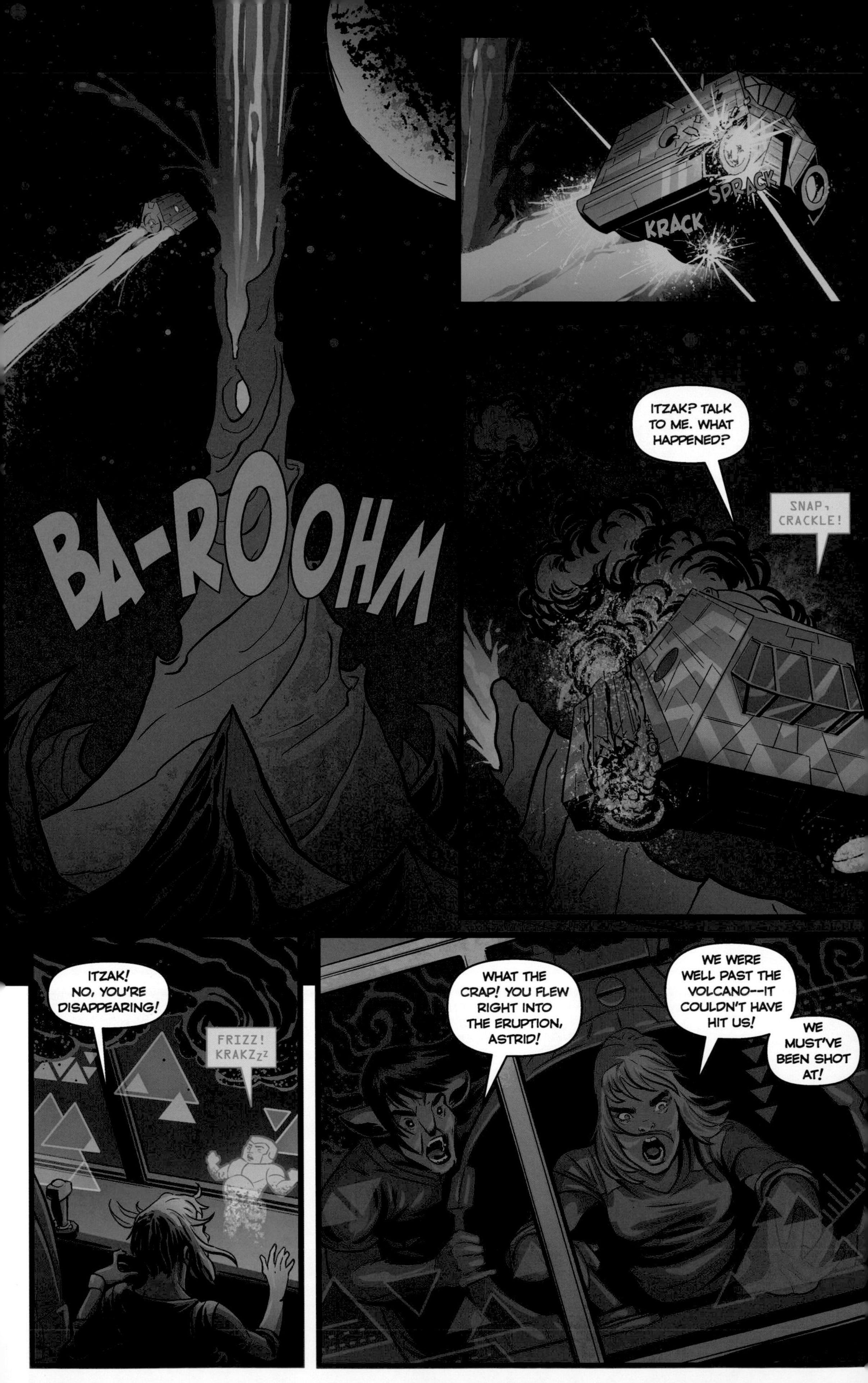
SPRACK
KRACK
BA-ROOHM
ITZAK? TALK TO ME. WHAT HAPPENED?
SNAP, CRACKLE!
ITZAK! NO, YOU'RE DISAPPEARING!
FRIZZ! KRAKZzz
WHAT THE CRAP! YOU FLEW RIGHT INTO THE ERUPTION, ASTRID!
WE WERE WELL PAST THE VOLCANO--IT COULDN'T HAVE HIT US!
WE MUST'VE BEEN SHOT AT!

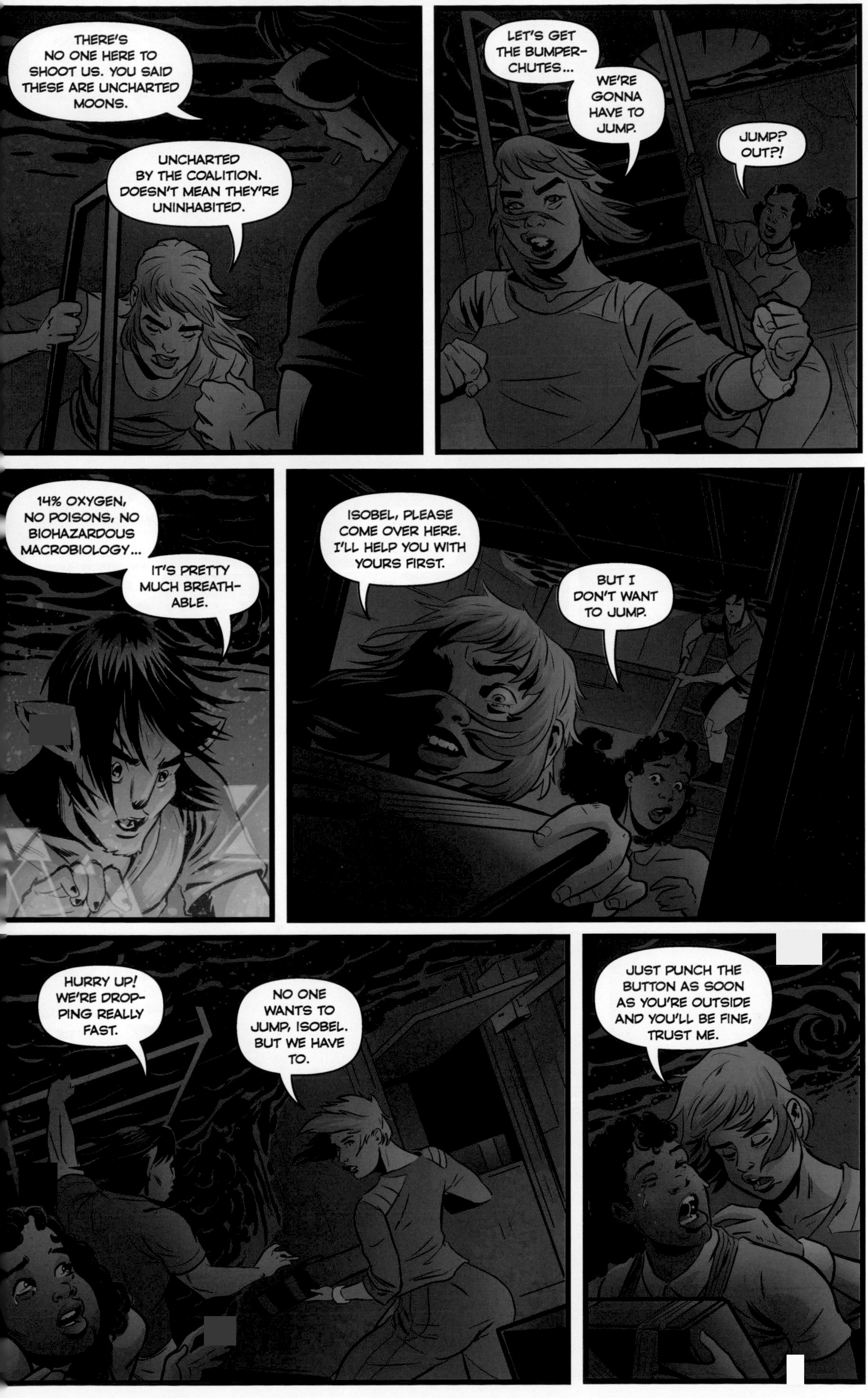
THERE'S NO ONE HERE TO SHOOT US. YOU SAID THESE ARE UNCHARTED MOONS.
UNCHARTED BY THE COALITION. DOESN'T MEAN THEY'RE UNINHABITED.
LET'S GET THE BUMPER-CHUTES...
WE'RE GONNA HAVE TO JUMP.
JUMP? OUT?!
14% OXYGEN, NO POISONS, NO BIOHAZARDOUS MACROBIOLOGY...
IT'S PRETTY MUCH BREATH-ABLE.
ISOBEL, PLEASE COME OVER HERE. I'LL HELP YOU WITH YOURS FIRST.
BUT I DON'T WANT TO JUMP.
HURRY UP! WE'RE DROP-PING REALLY FAST.
NO ONE WANTS TO JUMP, ISOBEL. BUT WE HAVE TO.
JUST PUNCH THE BUTTON AS SOON AS YOU'RE OUTSIDE AND YOU'LL BE FINE, TRUST ME.

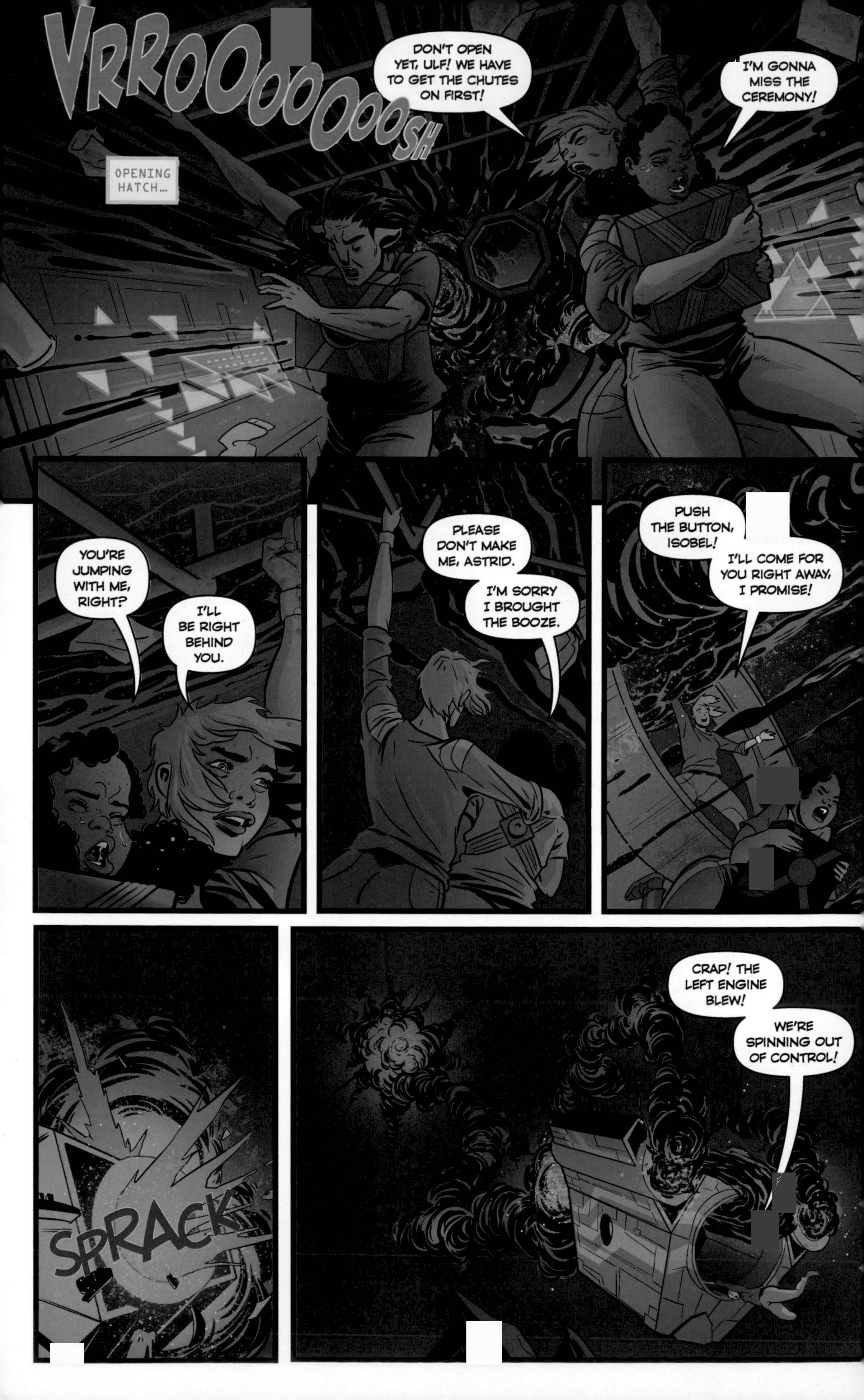
VRROOOOOOOOSH
OPENING HATCH...
DON'T OPEN YET, ULF! WE HAVE TO GET THE CHUTES ON FIRST!
I'M GONNA MISS THE CEREMONY!
YOU'RE JUMPING WITH ME, RIGHT?
I'LL BE RIGHT BEHIND YOU.
PLEASE DON'T MAKE ME, ASTRID.
I'M SORRY I BROUGHT THE BOOZE.
PUSH THE BUTTON, ISOBEL!
I'LL COME FOR YOU RIGHT AWAY, I PROMISE!
SPRACK
CRAP! THE LEFT ENGINE BLEW!
WE'RE SPINNING OUT OF CONTROL!

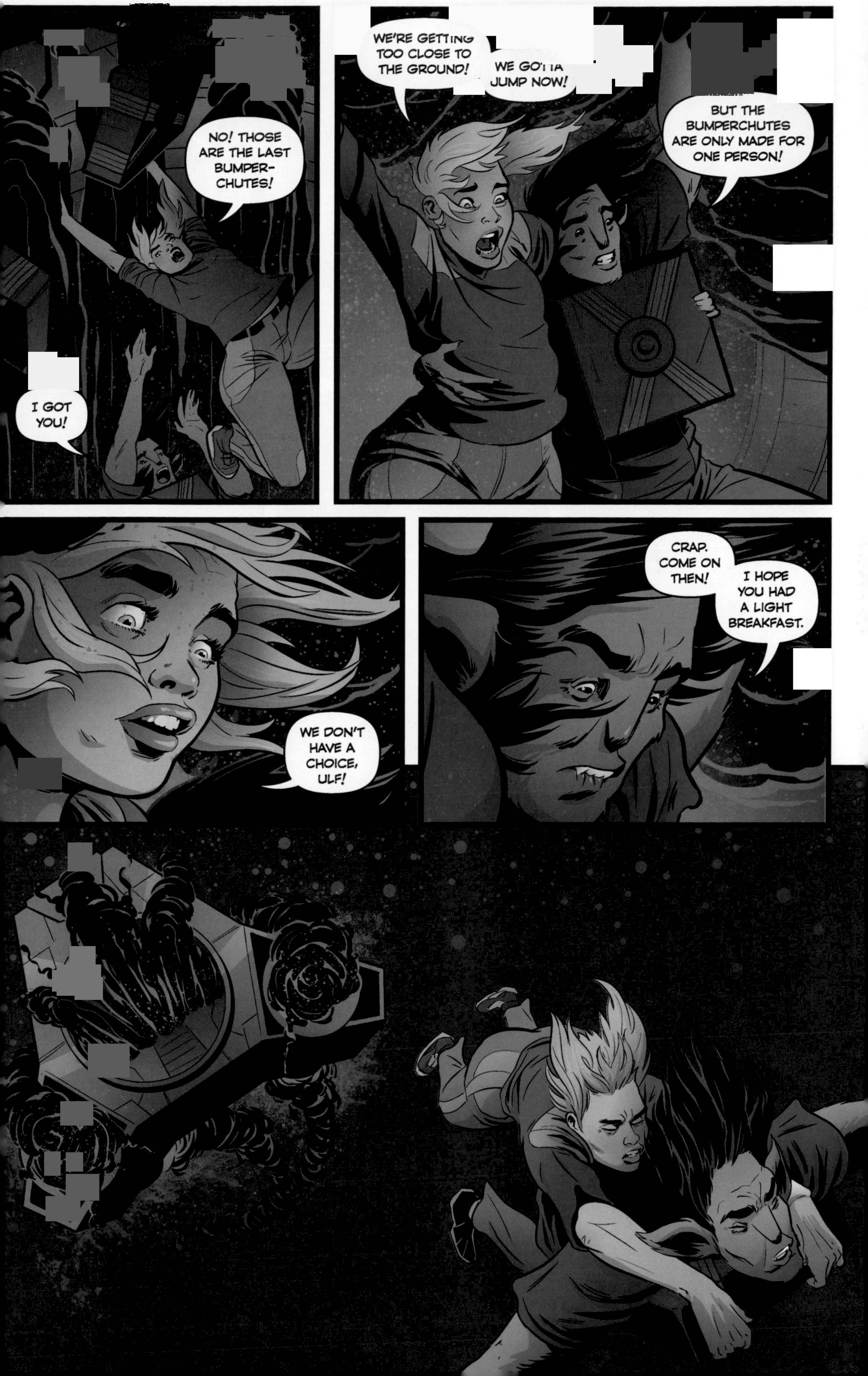
NO! THOSE ARE THE LAST BUMPER-CHUTES!
I GOT YOU!
WE'RE GETTING TOO CLOSE TO THE GROUND!
WE GOTTA JUMP NOW!
BUT THE BUMPERCHUTES ARE ONLY MADE FOR ONE PERSON!
WE DON'T HAVE A CHOICE, ULF!
CRAP. COME ON THEN!
I HOPE YOU HAD A LIGHT BREAKFAST.

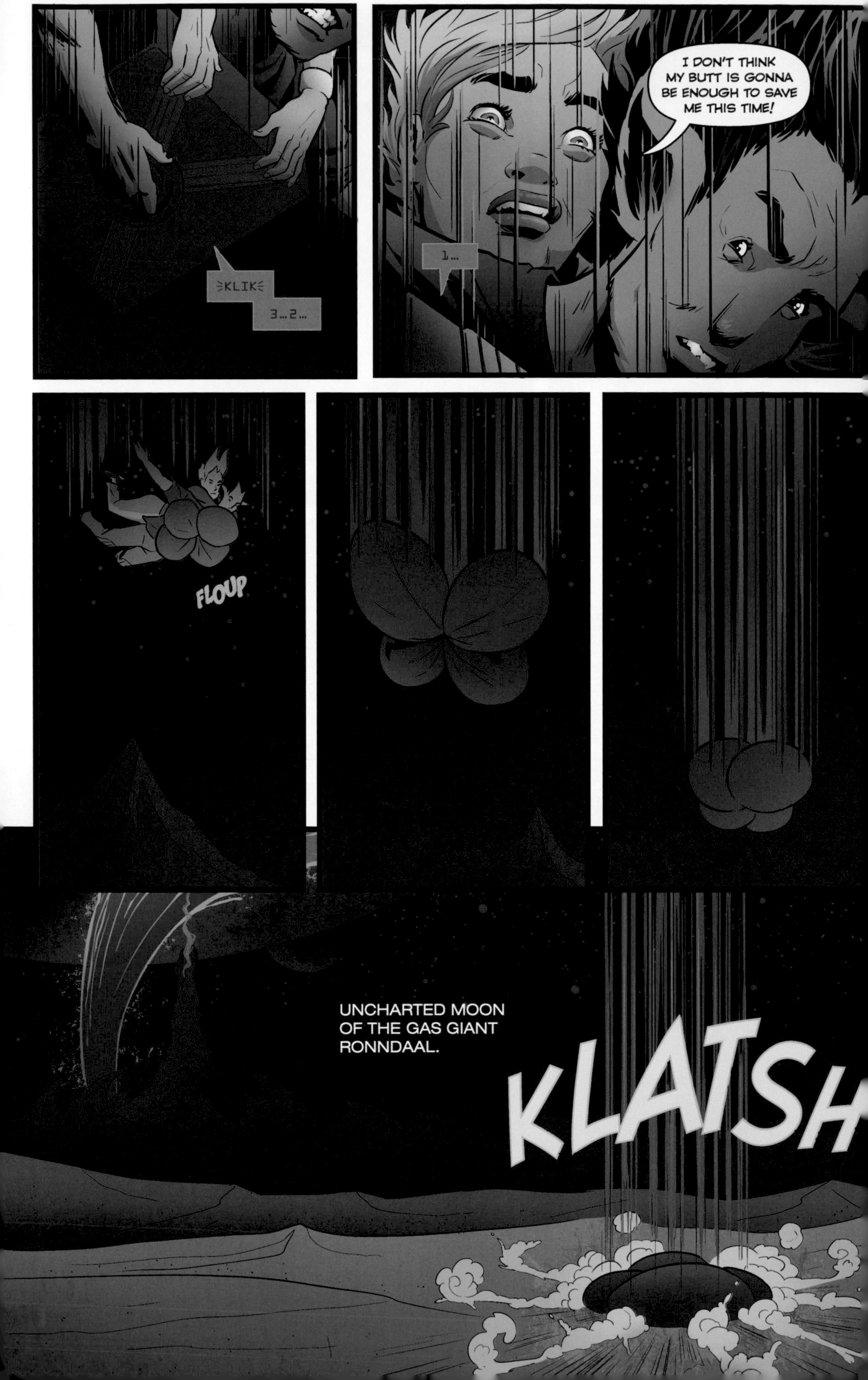

KLIK
3...2...
1...
I DON'T THINK MY BUTT IS GONNA BE ENOUGH TO SAVE ME THIS TIME!
FLOUP
UNCHARTED MOON OF THE GAS GIANT RONNDAAL.
KLATSH

*¿HUFF!¿*

**PSSH**

**PSSSH**

**PSSH**

COME ON, ULF! WE HAVE TO GET YOU OUT BEFORE THE CHUTE DEFLATES.

ARGH! MY BEAUTIFUL PAW IS BROKEN! I'LL NEVER WALK AGAIN!

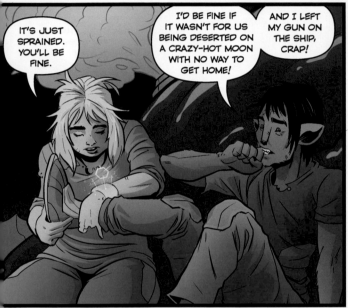

IT'S JUST SPRAINED. YOU'LL BE FINE.

I'D BE FINE IF IT WASN'T FOR US BEING DESERTED ON A CRAZY-HOT MOON WITH NO WAY TO GET HOME!

AND I LEFT MY GUN ON THE SHIP, CRAP!

FIRST OF ALL WE HAVE TO FIND ISOBEL--

NO, WE'RE GOING TO THE SHIP TO SEND FOR THE COALITION.

WE DIDN'T GET A CHANCE TO SEND A DISTRESS SIGNAL BEFORE WE WENT DOWN.

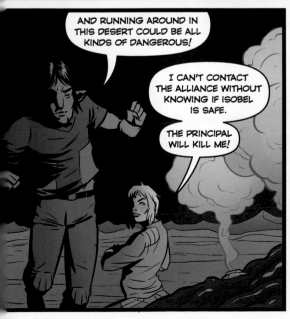

AND RUNNING AROUND IN THIS DESERT COULD BE ALL KINDS OF DANGEROUS!

I CAN'T CONTACT THE ALLIANCE WITHOUT KNOWING IF ISOBEL IS SAFE.

THE PRINCIPAL WILL KILL ME!

SO THAT'S WHAT THIS IS ABOUT? YOU WANNA IMPRESS THE PRINCIPAL TO GET A NEW CHANCE AT THE EXAM?!

WELL, PERHAPS... BUT I PROMISED ISOBEL TOO.

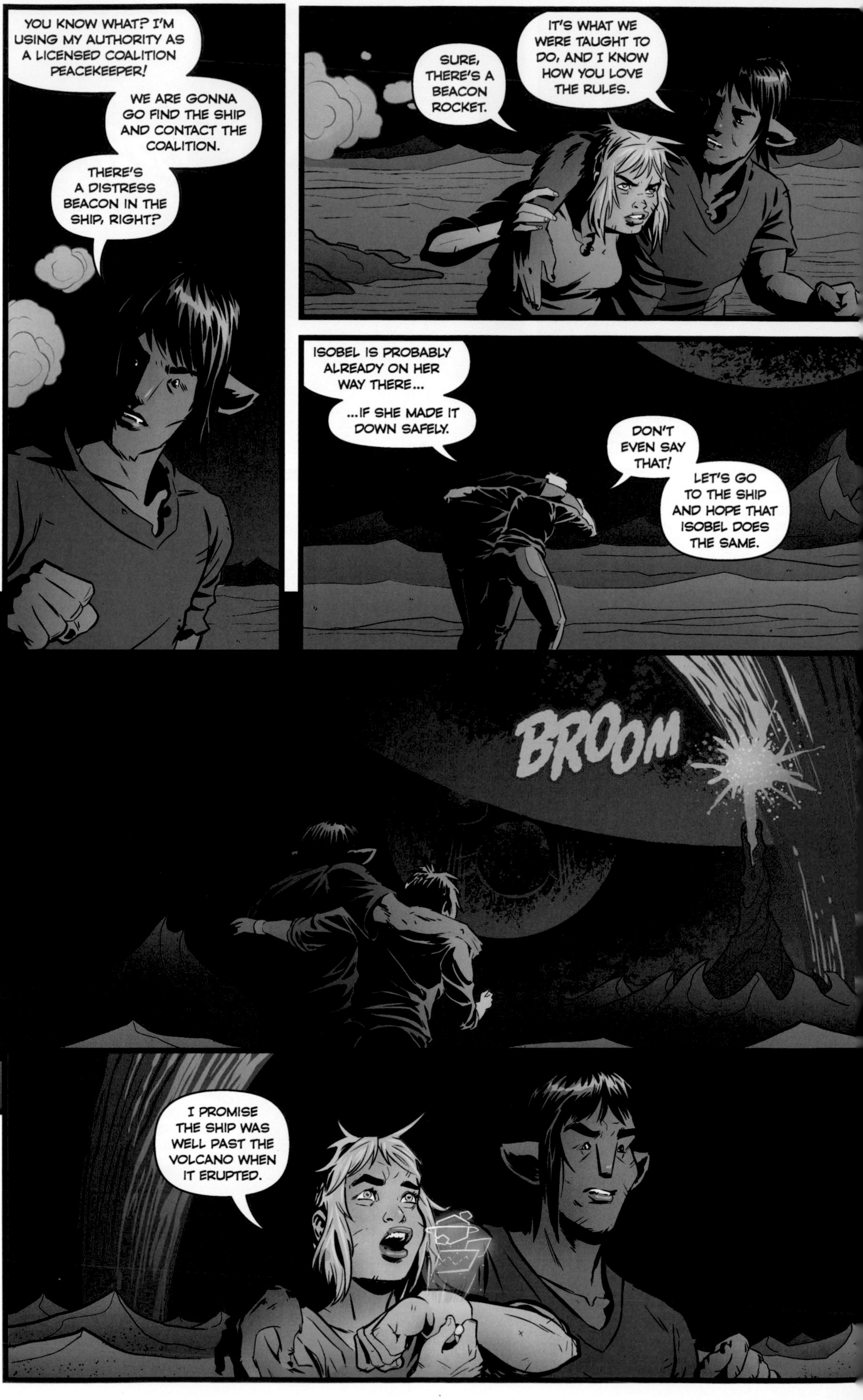
YOU KNOW WHAT? I'M USING MY AUTHORITY AS A LICENSED COALITION PEACEKEEPER!
WE ARE GONNA GO FIND THE SHIP AND CONTACT THE COALITION.
THERE'S A DISTRESS BEACON IN THE SHIP, RIGHT?
SURE, THERE'S A BEACON ROCKET.
IT'S WHAT WE WERE TAUGHT TO DO, AND I KNOW HOW YOU LOVE THE RULES.
ISOBEL IS PROBABLY ALREADY ON HER WAY THERE...
...IF SHE MADE IT DOWN SAFELY.
DON'T EVEN SAY THAT!
LET'S GO TO THE SHIP AND HOPE THAT ISOBEL DOES THE SAME.
BROOM
I PROMISE THE SHIP WAS WELL PAST THE VOLCANO WHEN IT ERUPTED.

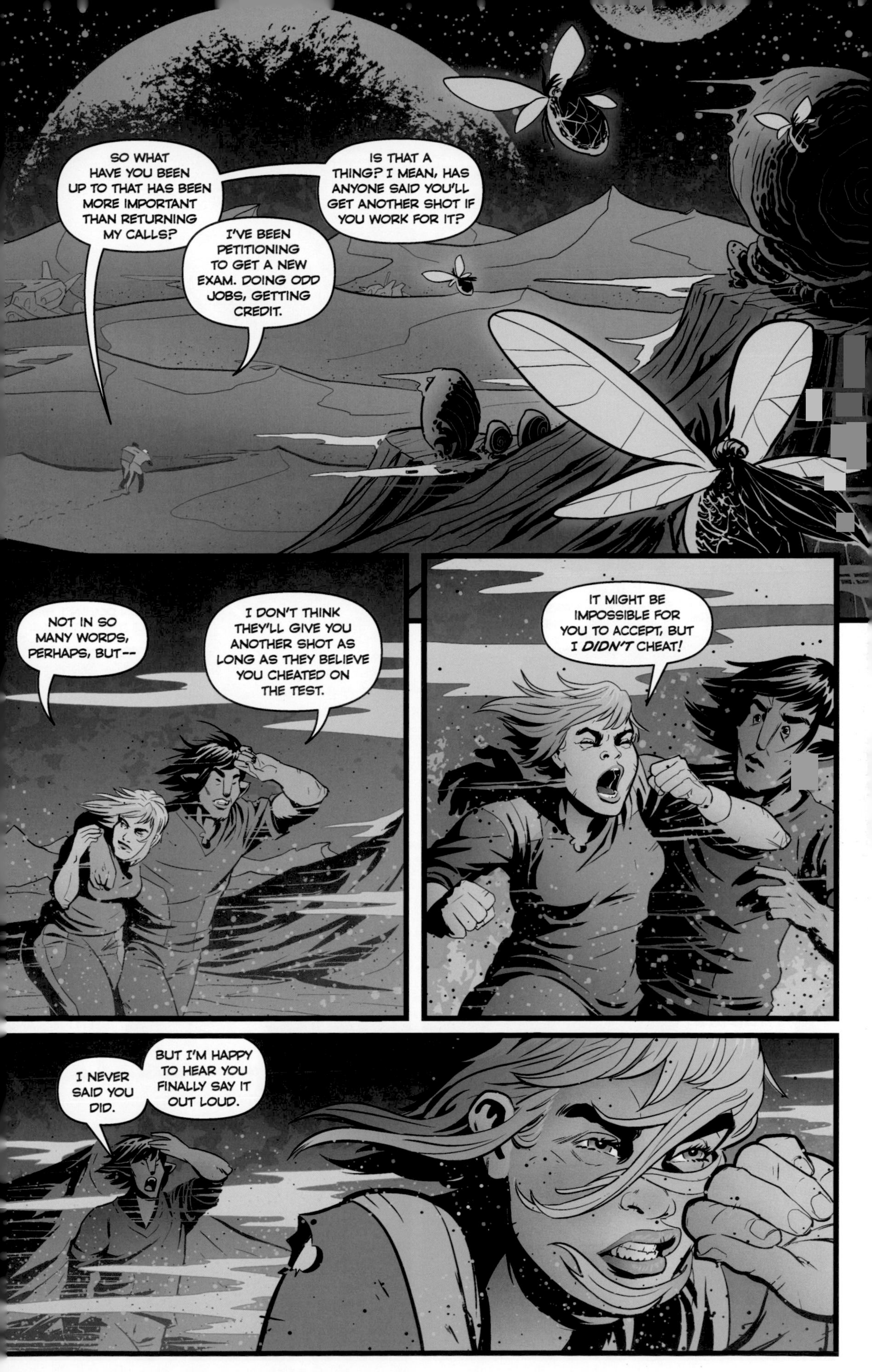
SO WHAT HAVE YOU BEEN UP TO THAT HAS BEEN MORE IMPORTANT THAN RETURNING MY CALLS?
I'VE BEEN PETITIONING TO GET A NEW EXAM. DOING ODD JOBS, GETTING CREDIT.
IS THAT A THING? I MEAN, HAS ANYONE SAID YOU'LL GET ANOTHER SHOT IF YOU WORK FOR IT?
NOT IN SO MANY WORDS, PERHAPS, BUT--
I DON'T THINK THEY'LL GIVE YOU ANOTHER SHOT AS LONG AS THEY BELIEVE YOU CHEATED ON THE TEST.
IT MIGHT BE IMPOSSIBLE FOR YOU TO ACCEPT, BUT I *DIDN'T* CHEAT!
I NEVER SAID YOU DID.
BUT I'M HAPPY TO HEAR YOU FINALLY SAY IT OUT LOUD.

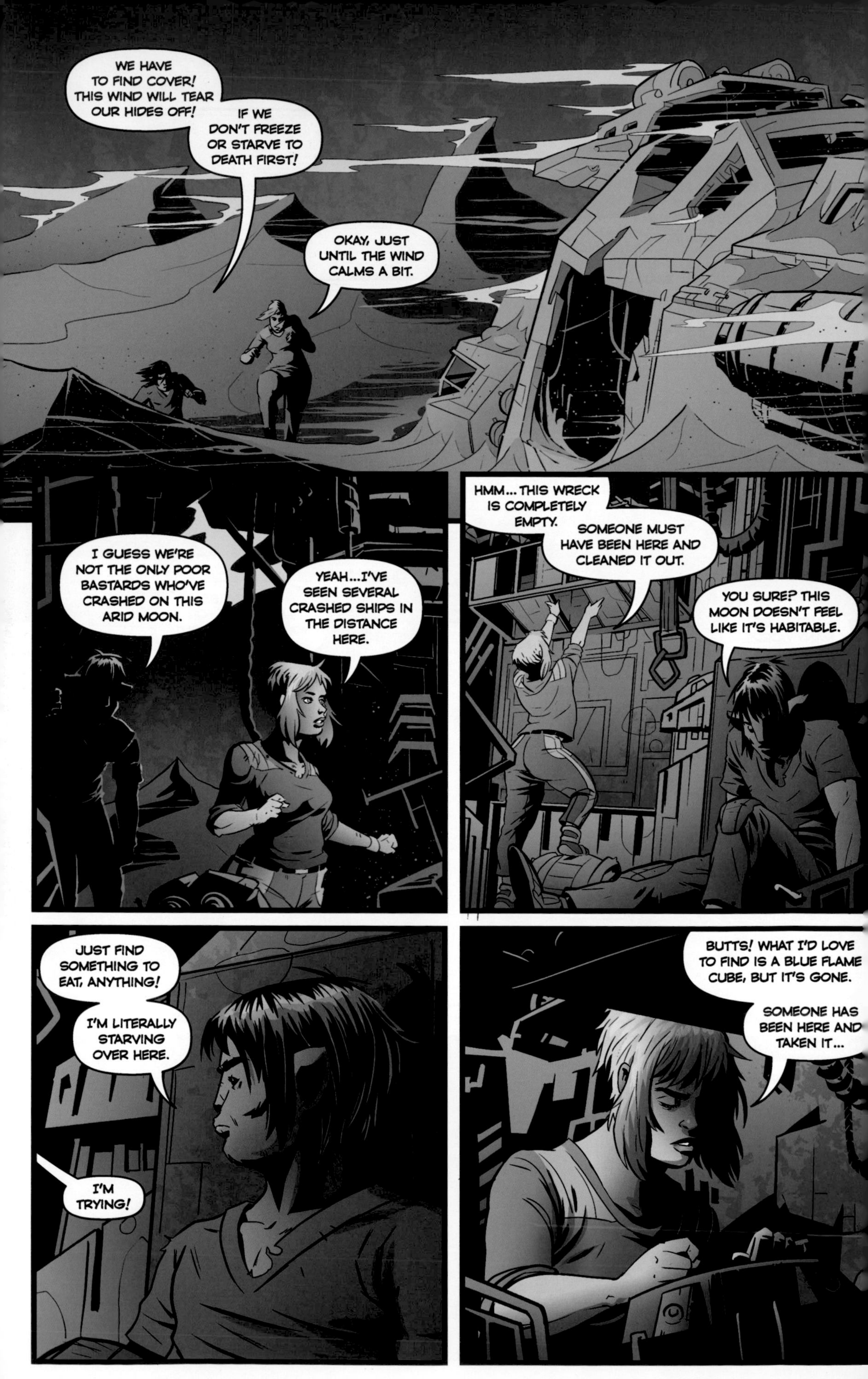
WE HAVE TO FIND COVER! THIS WIND WILL TEAR OUR HIDES OFF!
IF WE DON'T FREEZE OR STARVE TO DEATH FIRST!
OKAY, JUST UNTIL THE WIND CALMS A BIT.
I GUESS WE'RE NOT THE ONLY POOR BASTARDS WHO'VE CRASHED ON THIS ARID MOON.
YEAH...I'VE SEEN SEVERAL CRASHED SHIPS IN THE DISTANCE HERE.
HMM... THIS WRECK IS COMPLETELY EMPTY.
SOMEONE MUST HAVE BEEN HERE AND CLEANED IT OUT.
YOU SURE? THIS MOON DOESN'T FEEL LIKE IT'S HABITABLE.
JUST FIND SOMETHING TO EAT, ANYTHING!
I'M LITERALLY STARVING OVER HERE.
I'M TRYING!
BUTTS! WHAT I'D LOVE TO FIND IS A BLUE FLAME CUBE, BUT IT'S GONE.
SOMEONE HAS BEEN HERE AND TAKEN IT...

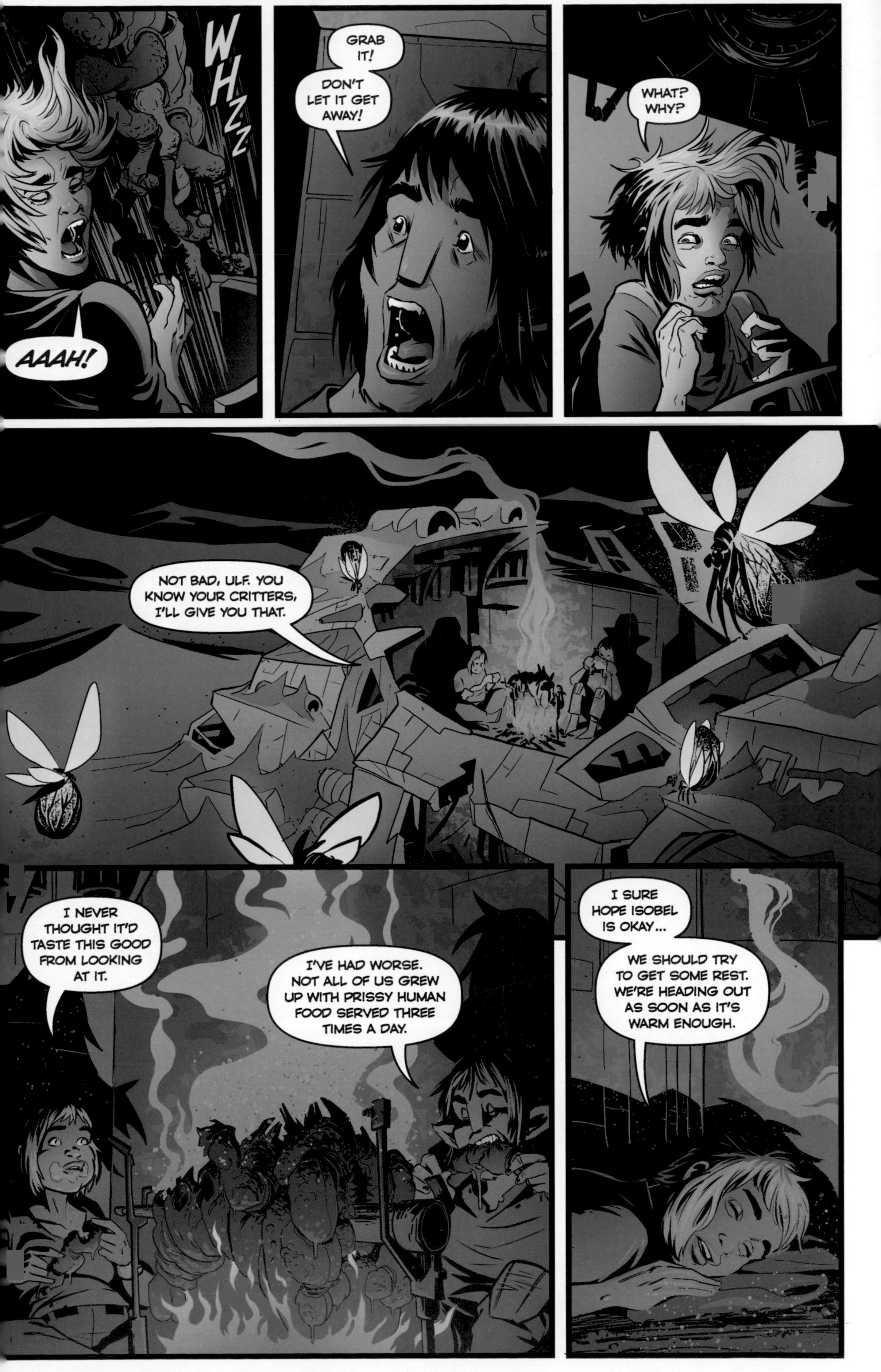
WHZZZ
AAAH!
GRAB IT!
DON'T LET IT GET AWAY!
WHAT? WHY?
NOT BAD, ULF. YOU KNOW YOUR CRITTERS, I'LL GIVE YOU THAT.
I NEVER THOUGHT IT'D TASTE THIS GOOD FROM LOOKING AT IT.
I'VE HAD WORSE. NOT ALL OF US GREW UP WITH PRISSY HUMAN FOOD SERVED THREE TIMES A DAY.
I SURE HOPE ISOBEL IS OKAY...
WE SHOULD TRY TO GET SOME REST. WE'RE HEADING OUT AS SOON AS IT'S WARM ENOUGH.

WAKE UP!

HUH?

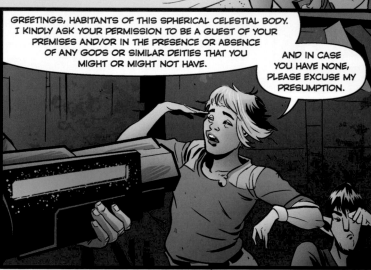

GREETINGS, HABITANTS OF THIS SPHERICAL CELESTIAL BODY. I KINDLY ASK YOUR PERMISSION TO BE A GUEST OF YOUR PREMISES AND/OR IN THE PRESENCE OR ABSENCE OF ANY GODS OR SIMILAR DEITIES THAT YOU MIGHT OR MIGHT NOT HAVE.

AND IN CASE YOU HAVE NONE, PLEASE EXCUSE MY PRESUMPTION.

WE ARE OF THE DONNER PARISH. YOU ARE COMING WITH US TO SEE THE ANGEL PRINCESS.

THAT SOUNDS WONDERFUL. PERHAPS SHE CAN HELP US FIND OUR LOST COLLEAGUE. YOU SEE, WE HAVE TO GET HER TO THE GALACTIC COALITION H.Q. REAL SOON.

THE GALACTIC COALITION?! THE TREACHEROUS COALITION THAT SPREAD THE HOLY GIFT OF THE GODS ACROSS THE GALAXY LIKE THE VENEREAL DISEASE OF A WHORE?

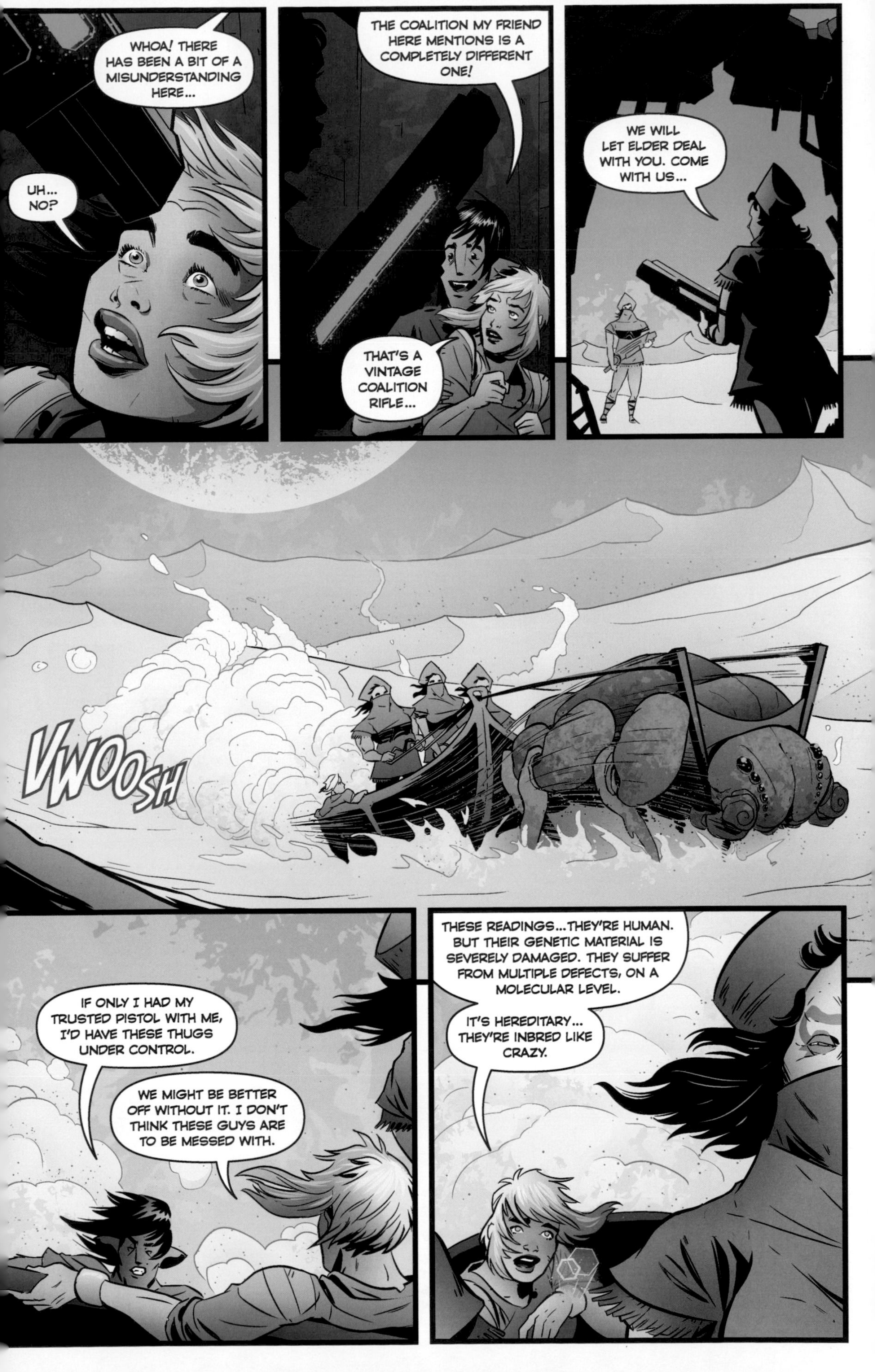
WHOA! THERE HAS BEEN A BIT OF A MISUNDERSTANDING HERE...
UH... NO?
THE COALITION MY FRIEND HERE MENTIONS IS A COMPLETELY DIFFERENT ONE!
THAT'S A VINTAGE COALITION RIFLE...
WE WILL LET ELDER DEAL WITH YOU. COME WITH US...
VWOOSH
IF ONLY I HAD MY TRUSTED PISTOL WITH ME, I'D HAVE THESE THUGS UNDER CONTROL.
WE MIGHT BE BETTER OFF WITHOUT IT. I DON'T THINK THESE GUYS ARE TO BE MESSED WITH.
THESE READINGS...THEY'RE HUMAN. BUT THEIR GENETIC MATERIAL IS SEVERELY DAMAGED. THEY SUFFER FROM MULTIPLE DEFECTS, ON A MOLECULAR LEVEL.
IT'S HEREDITARY... THEY'RE INBRED LIKE CRAZY.

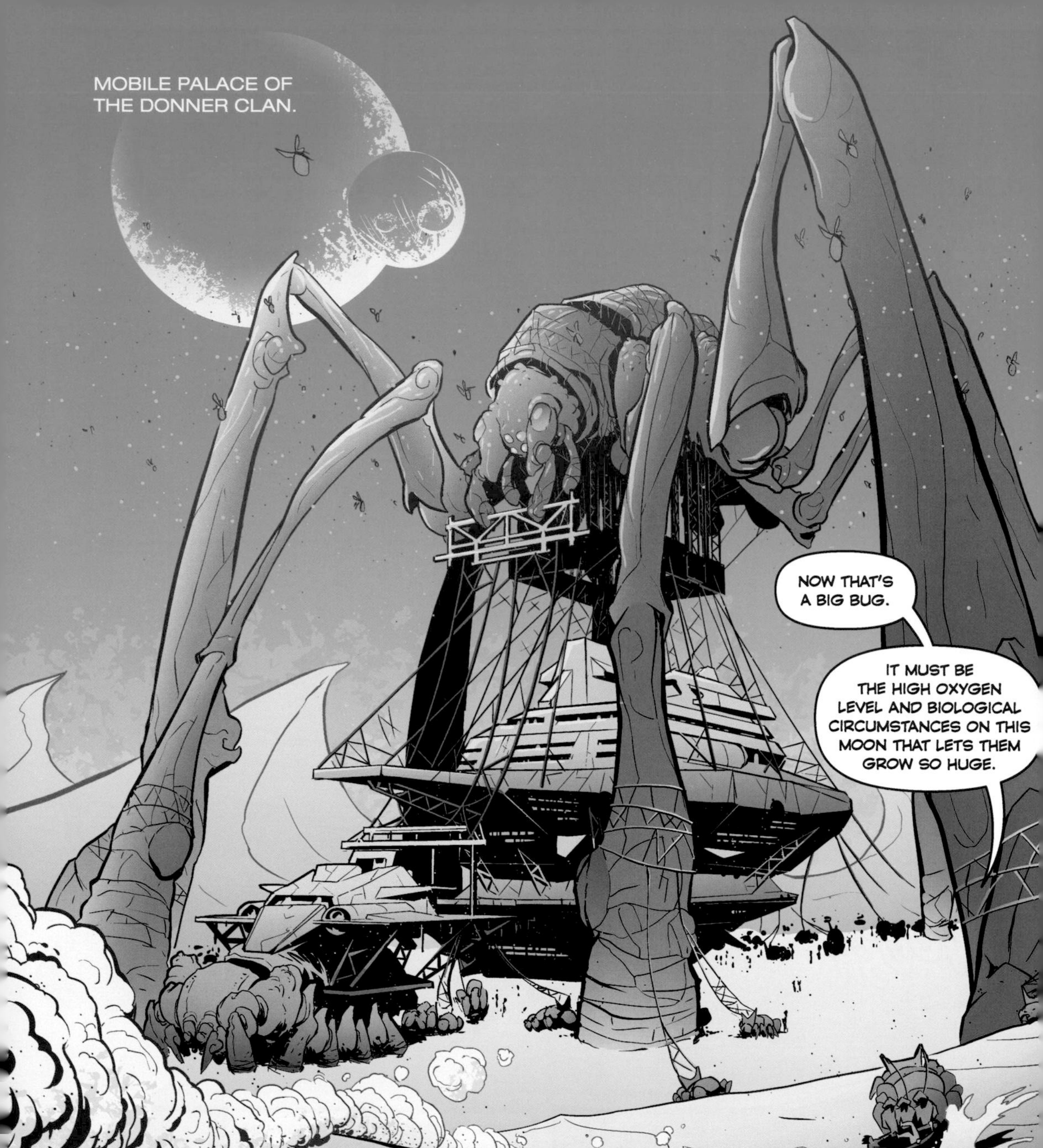
MOBILE PALACE OF
THE DONNER CLAN.
NOW THAT'S A BIG BUG.
IT MUST BE THE HIGH OXYGEN LEVEL AND BIOLOGICAL CIRCUMSTANCES ON THIS MOON THAT LETS THEM GROW SO HUGE.

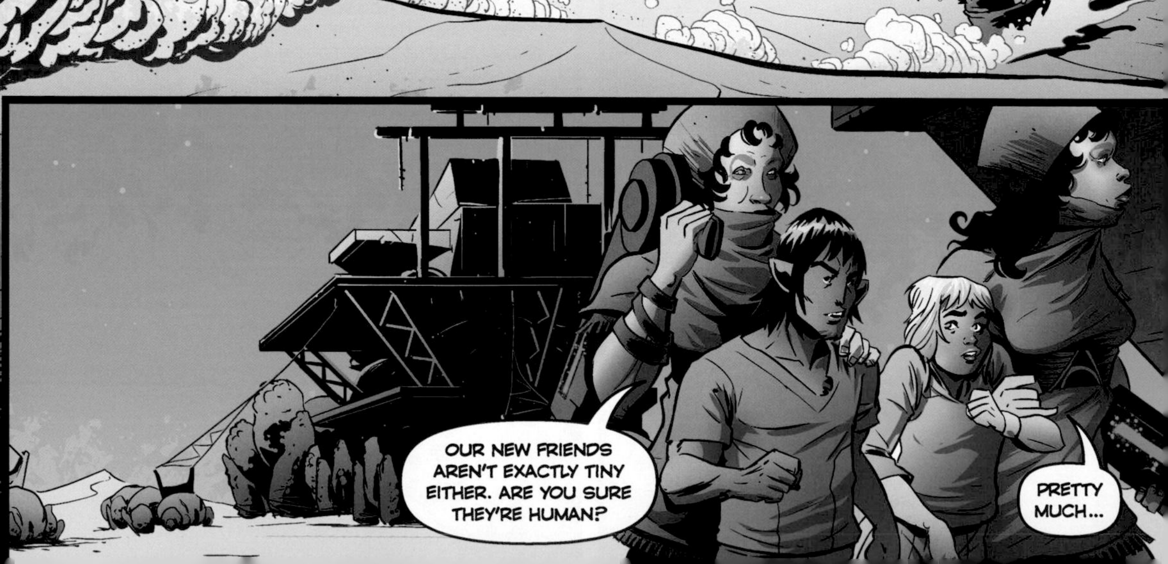
OUR NEW FRIENDS AREN'T EXACTLY TINY EITHER. ARE YOU SURE THEY'RE HUMAN?
PRETTY MUCH...

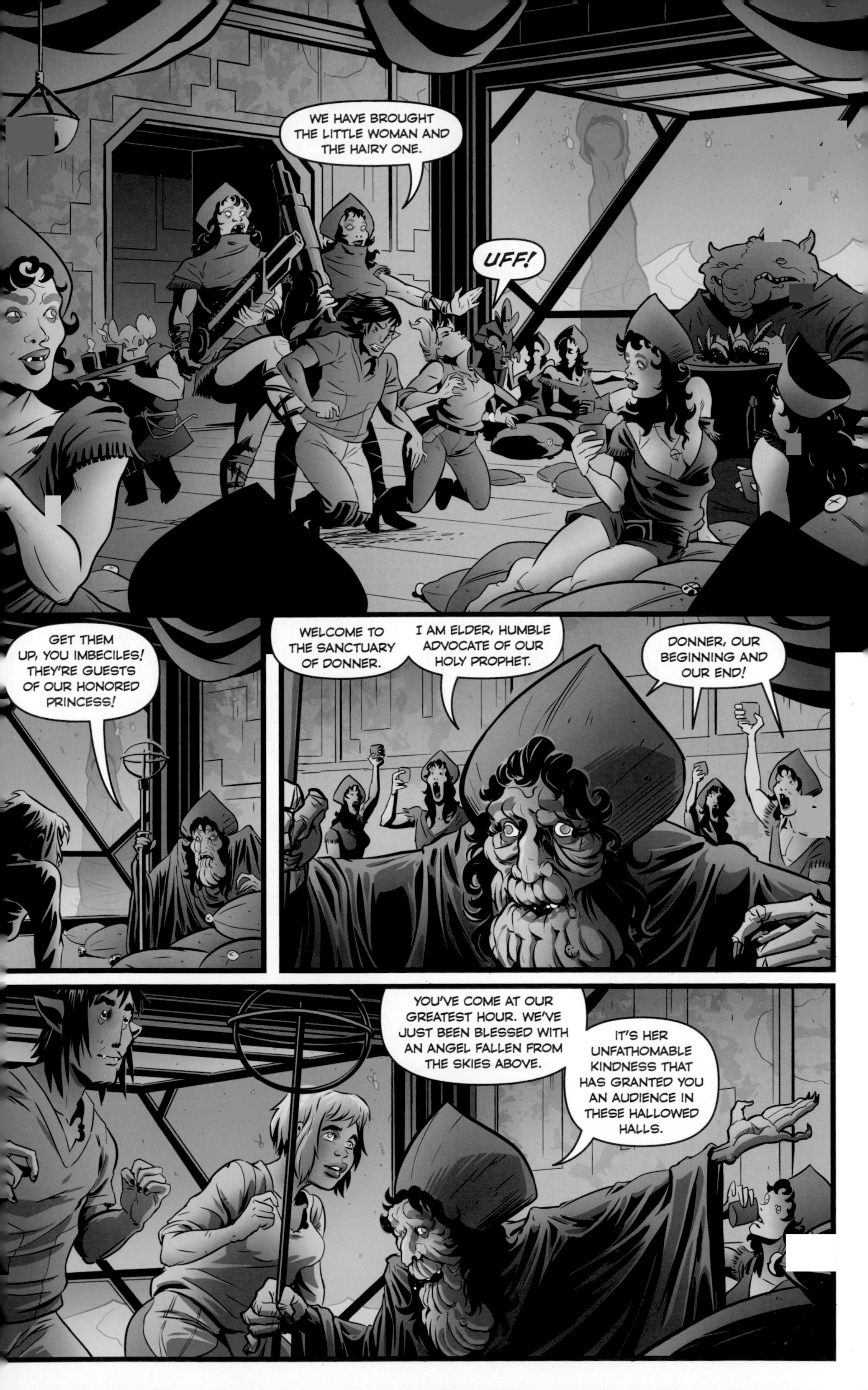
WE HAVE BROUGHT THE LITTLE WOMAN AND THE HAIRY ONE.
UFF!
GET THEM UP, YOU IMBECILES! THEY'RE GUESTS OF OUR HONORED PRINCESS!
WELCOME TO THE SANCTUARY OF DONNER.
I AM ELDER, HUMBLE ADVOCATE OF OUR HOLY PROPHET.
DONNER, OUR BEGINNING AND OUR END!
YOU'VE COME AT OUR GREATEST HOUR. WE'VE JUST BEEN BLESSED WITH AN ANGEL FALLEN FROM THE SKIES ABOVE.
IT'S HER UNFATHOMABLE KINDNESS THAT HAS GRANTED YOU AN AUDIENCE IN THESE HALLOWED HALLS.

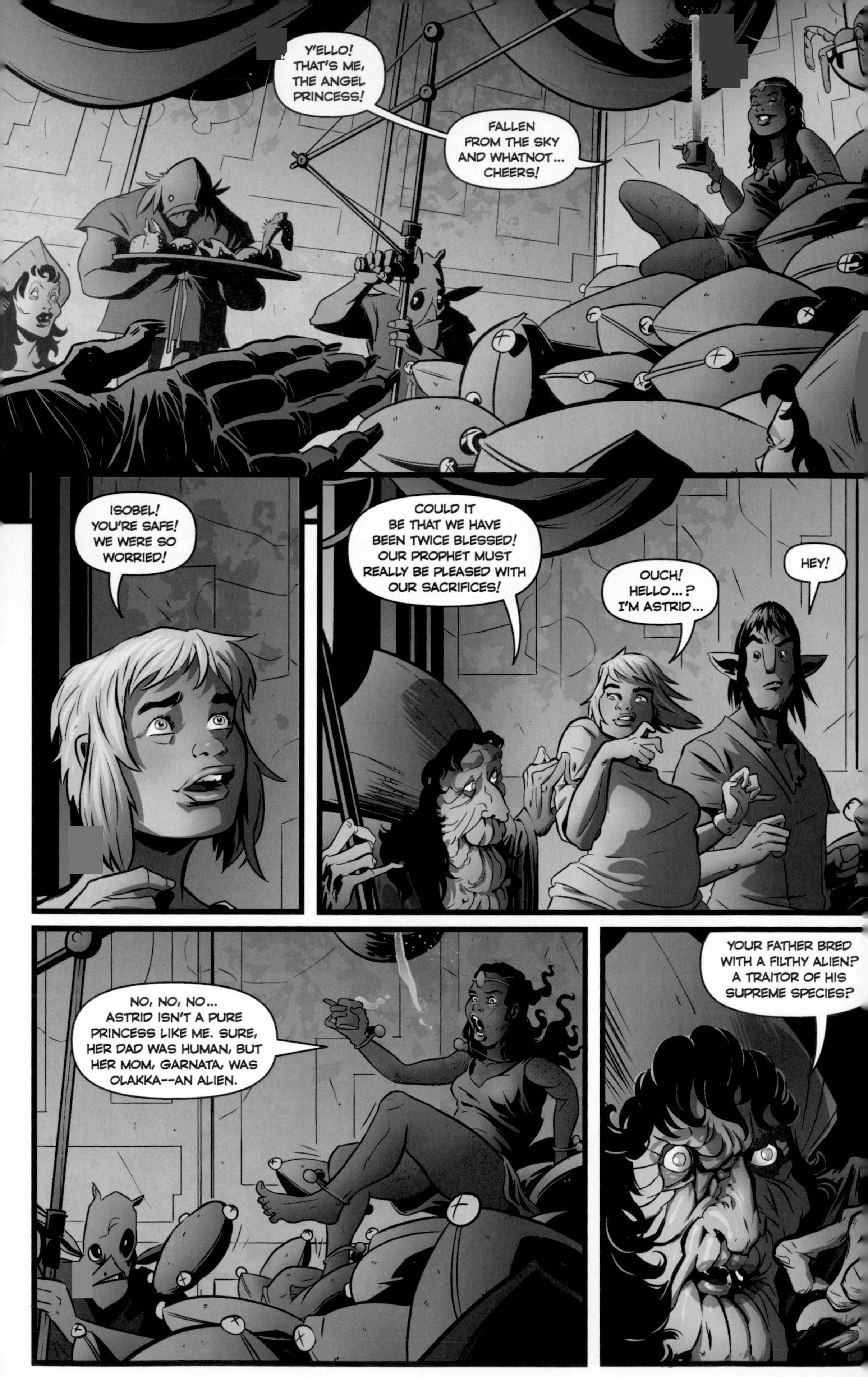
Y'ELLO! THAT'S ME, THE ANGEL PRINCESS!
FALLEN FROM THE SKY AND WHATNOT... CHEERS!
ISOBEL! YOU'RE SAFE! WE WERE SO WORRIED!
COULD IT BE THAT WE HAVE BEEN TWICE BLESSED! OUR PROPHET MUST REALLY BE PLEASED WITH OUR SACRIFICES!
OUCH! HELLO...? I'M ASTRID...
HEY!
NO, NO, NO... ASTRID ISN'T A PURE PRINCESS LIKE ME. SURE, HER DAD WAS HUMAN, BUT HER MOM, GARNATA, WAS OLAKKA--AN ALIEN.
YOUR FATHER BRED WITH A FILTHY ALIEN? A TRAITOR OF HIS SUPREME SPECIES?

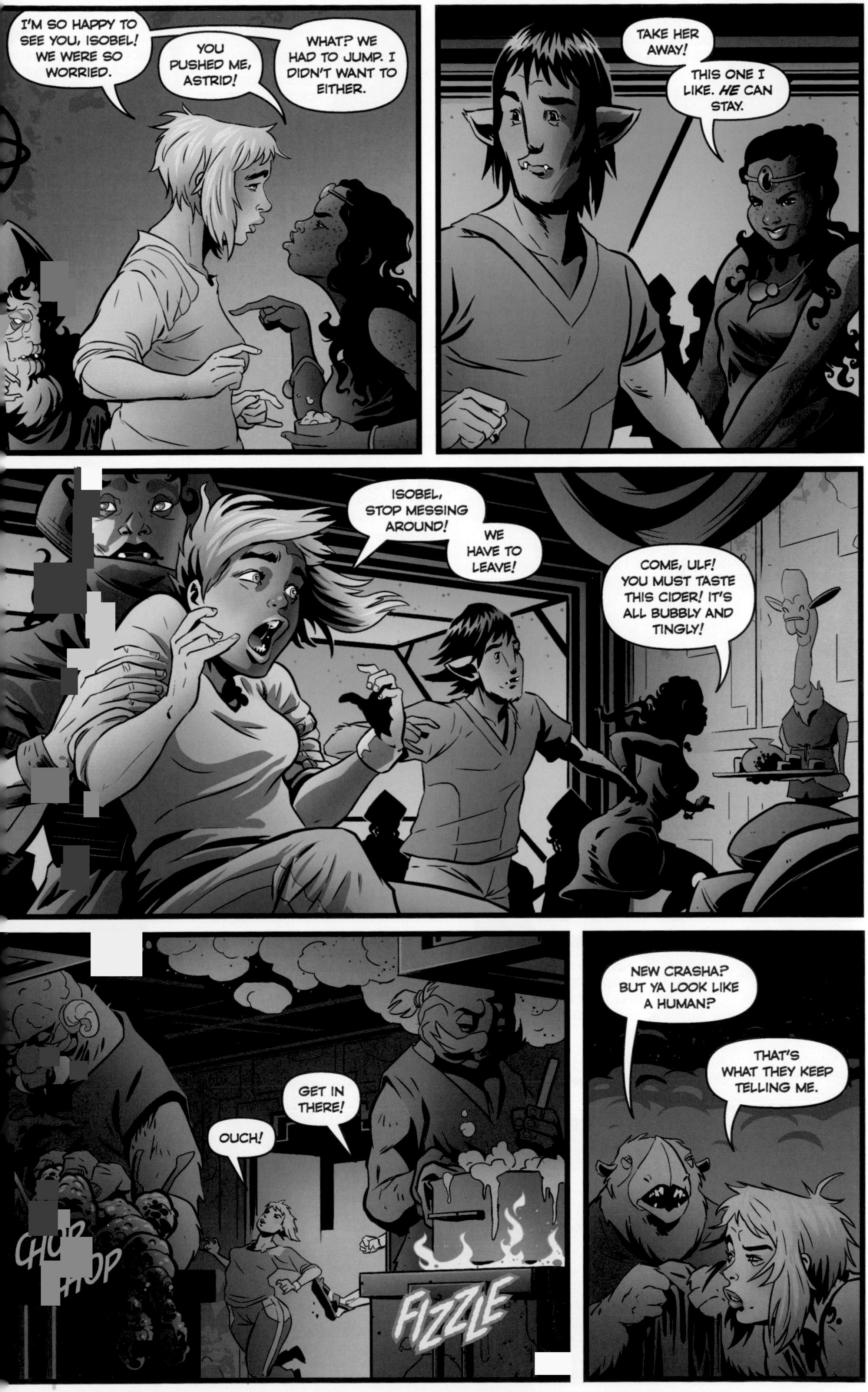
I'M SO HAPPY TO SEE YOU, ISOBEL! WE WERE SO WORRIED.
YOU PUSHED ME, ASTRID!
WHAT? WE HAD TO JUMP. I DIDN'T WANT TO EITHER.
TAKE HER AWAY!
THIS ONE I LIKE. *HE* CAN STAY.
ISOBEL, STOP MESSING AROUND!
WE HAVE TO LEAVE!
COME, ULF! YOU MUST TASTE THIS CIDER! IT'S ALL BUBBLY AND TINGLY!
GET IN THERE!
OUCH!
FIZZLE
NEW CRASHA? BUT YA LOOK LIKE A HUMAN?
THAT'S WHAT THEY KEEP TELLING ME.

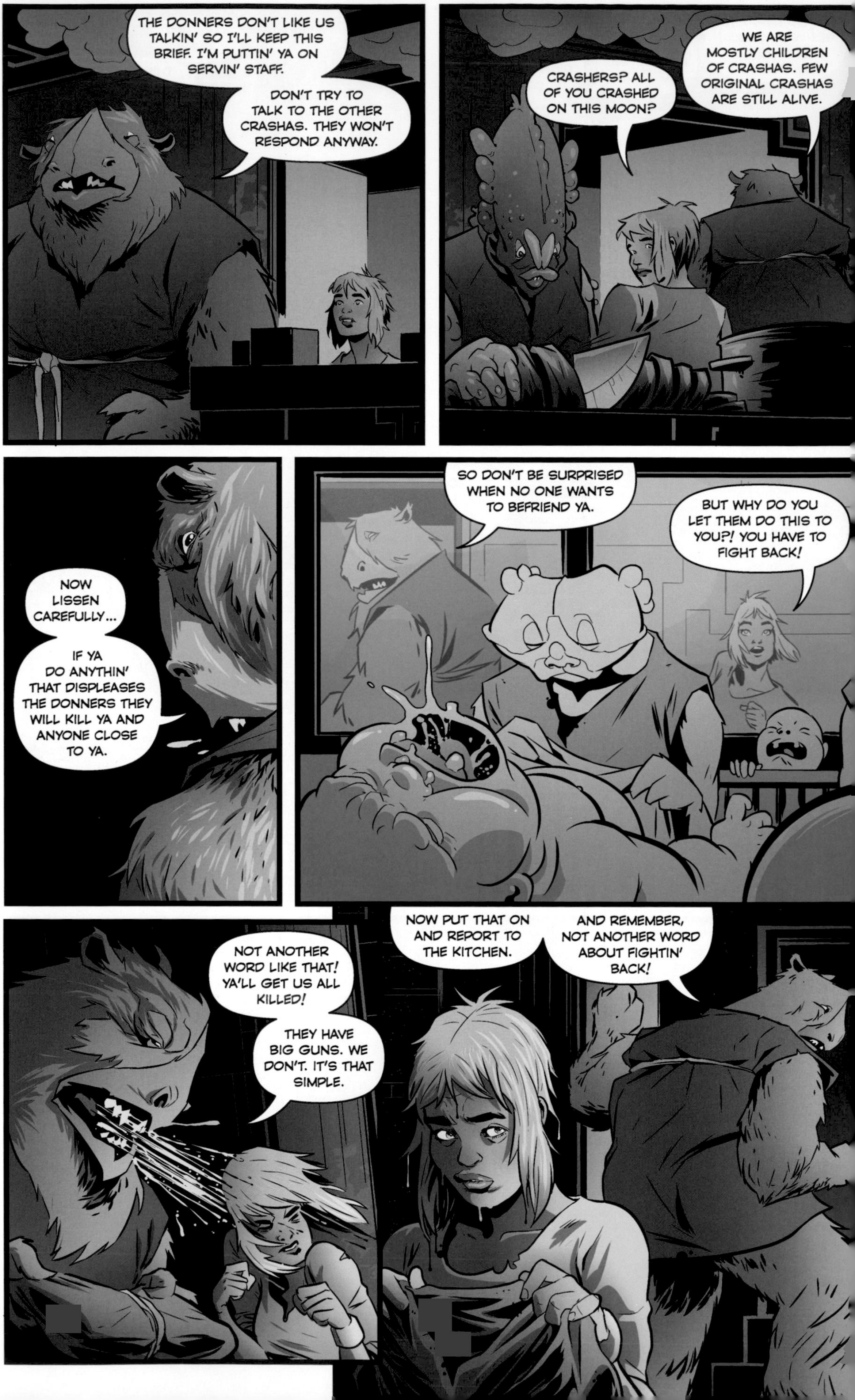
THE DONNERS DON'T LIKE US TALKIN' SO I'LL KEEP THIS BRIEF. I'M PUTTIN' YA ON SERVIN' STAFF.
DON'T TRY TO TALK TO THE OTHER CRASHAS. THEY WON'T RESPOND ANYWAY.
CRASHERS? ALL OF YOU CRASHED ON THIS MOON?
WE ARE MOSTLY CHILDREN OF CRASHAS. FEW ORIGINAL CRASHAS ARE STILL ALIVE.
NOW LISSEN CAREFULLY...
IF YA DO ANYTHIN' THAT DISPLEASES THE DONNERS THEY WILL KILL YA AND ANYONE CLOSE TO YA.
SO DON'T BE SURPRISED WHEN NO ONE WANTS TO BEFRIEND YA.
BUT WHY DO YOU LET THEM DO THIS TO YOU?! YOU HAVE TO FIGHT BACK!
NOT ANOTHER WORD LIKE THAT! YA'LL GET US ALL KILLED!
THEY HAVE BIG GUNS. WE DON'T. IT'S THAT SIMPLE.
NOW PUT THAT ON AND REPORT TO THE KITCHEN.
AND REMEMBER, NOT ANOTHER WORD ABOUT FIGHTIN' BACK!

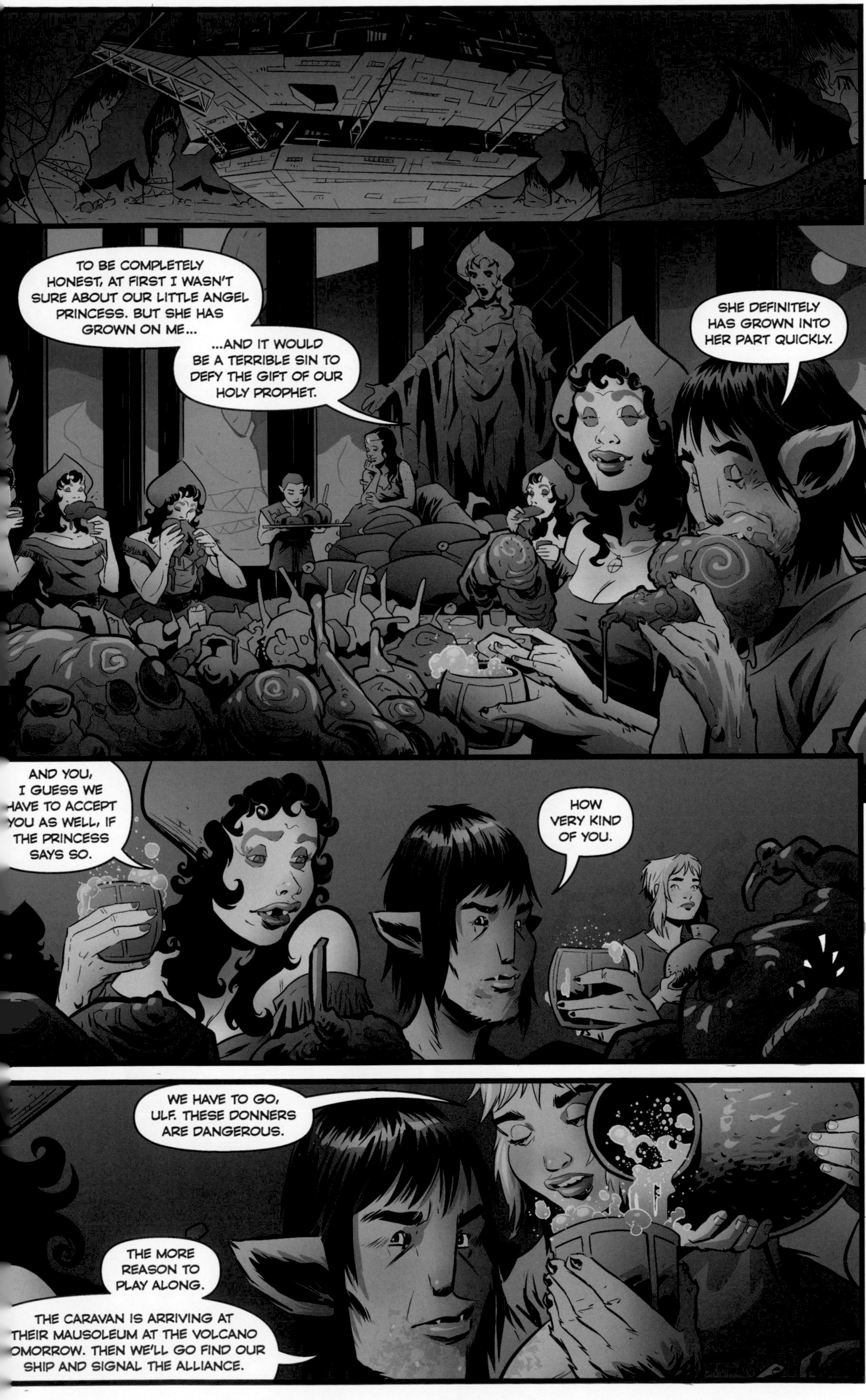
TO BE COMPLETELY HONEST, AT FIRST I WASN'T SURE ABOUT OUR LITTLE ANGEL PRINCESS. BUT SHE HAS GROWN ON ME...
...AND IT WOULD BE A TERRIBLE SIN TO DEFY THE GIFT OF OUR HOLY PROPHET.
SHE DEFINITELY HAS GROWN INTO HER PART QUICKLY.
AND YOU, I GUESS WE HAVE TO ACCEPT YOU AS WELL, IF THE PRINCESS SAYS SO.
HOW VERY KIND OF YOU.
WE HAVE TO GO, ULF. THESE DONNERS ARE DANGEROUS.
THE MORE REASON TO PLAY ALONG.
THE CARAVAN IS ARRIVING AT THEIR MAUSOLEUM AT THE VOLCANO TOMORROW. THEN WE'LL GO FIND OUR SHIP AND SIGNAL THE ALLIANCE.

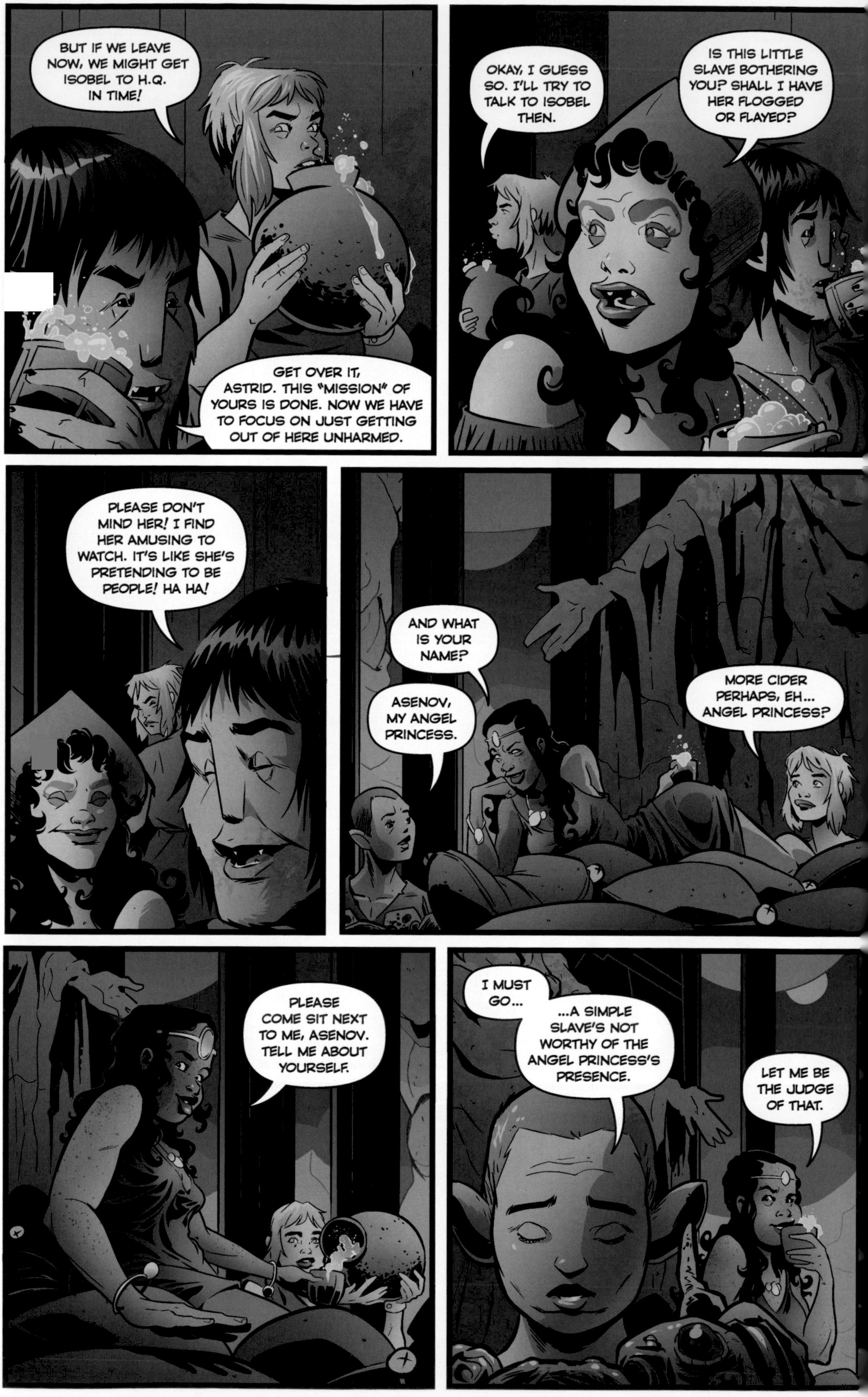
BUT IF WE LEAVE NOW, WE MIGHT GET ISOBEL TO H.Q. IN TIME!
GET OVER IT, ASTRID. THIS "MISSION" OF YOURS IS DONE. NOW WE HAVE TO FOCUS ON JUST GETTING OUT OF HERE UNHARMED.
OKAY, I GUESS SO. I'LL TRY TO TALK TO ISOBEL THEN.
IS THIS LITTLE SLAVE BOTHERING YOU? SHALL I HAVE HER FLOGGED OR FLAYED?
PLEASE DON'T MIND HER! I FIND HER AMUSING TO WATCH. IT'S LIKE SHE'S PRETENDING TO BE PEOPLE! HA HA!
AND WHAT IS YOUR NAME?
ASENOV, MY ANGEL PRINCESS.
MORE CIDER PERHAPS, EH... ANGEL PRINCESS?
PLEASE COME SIT NEXT TO ME, ASENOV. TELL ME ABOUT YOURSELF.
I MUST GO...
...A SIMPLE SLAVE'S NOT WORTHY OF THE ANGEL PRINCESS'S PRESENCE.
LET ME BE THE JUDGE OF THAT.

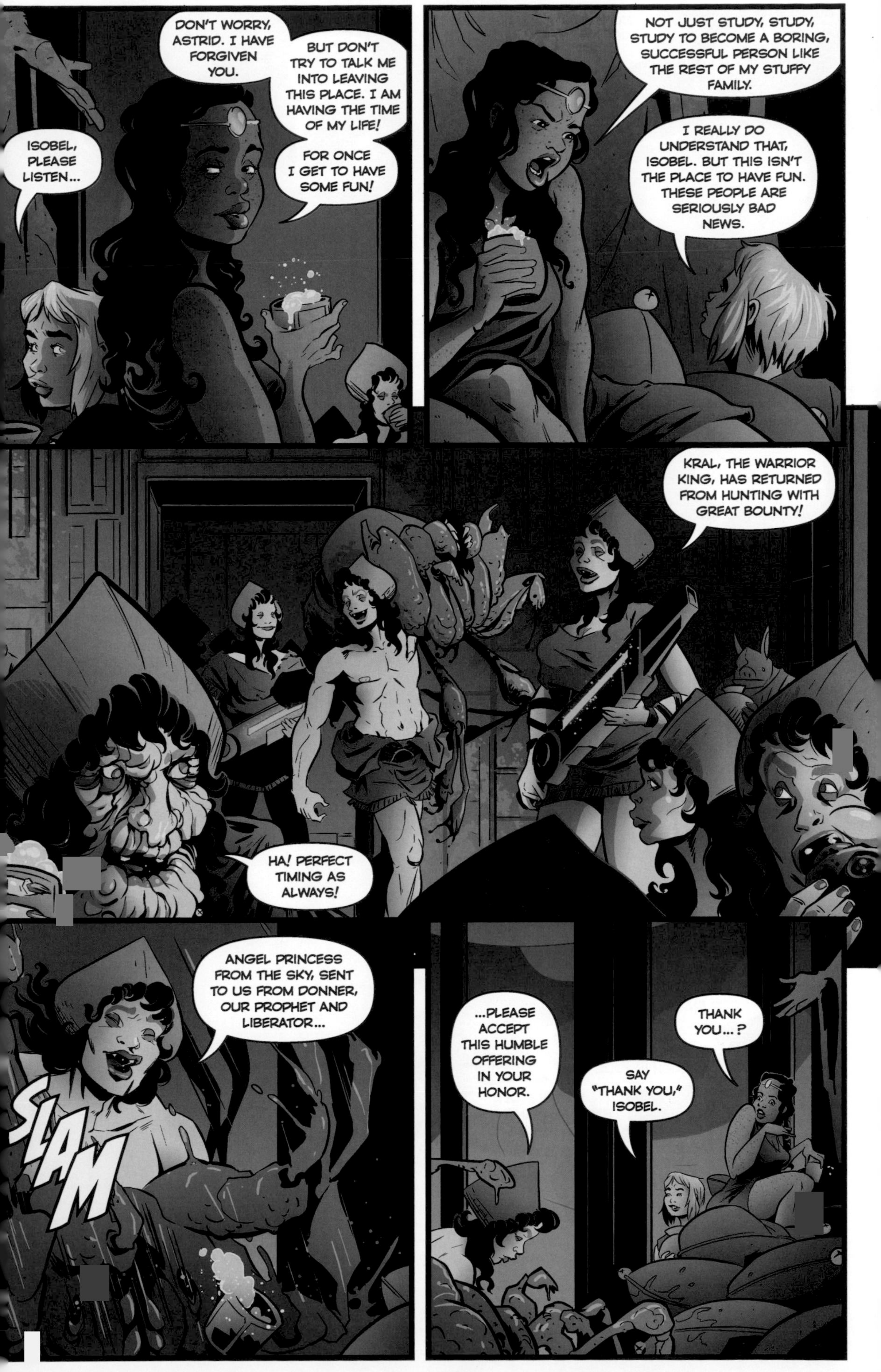

ISOBEL, PLEASE LISTEN...
DON'T WORRY, ASTRID. I HAVE FORGIVEN YOU.
BUT DON'T TRY TO TALK ME INTO LEAVING THIS PLACE. I AM HAVING THE TIME OF MY LIFE!
FOR ONCE I GET TO HAVE SOME FUN!
NOT JUST STUDY, STUDY, STUDY TO BECOME A BORING, SUCCESSFUL PERSON LIKE THE REST OF MY STUFFY FAMILY.
I REALLY DO UNDERSTAND THAT, ISOBEL. BUT THIS ISN'T THE PLACE TO HAVE FUN. THESE PEOPLE ARE SERIOUSLY BAD NEWS.
KRAL, THE WARRIOR KING, HAS RETURNED FROM HUNTING WITH GREAT BOUNTY!
HA! PERFECT TIMING AS ALWAYS!
ANGEL PRINCESS FROM THE SKY, SENT TO US FROM DONNER, OUR PROPHET AND LIBERATOR...
SLAM
...PLEASE ACCEPT THIS HUMBLE OFFERING IN YOUR HONOR.
SAY "THANK YOU," ISOBEL.
THANK YOU...?

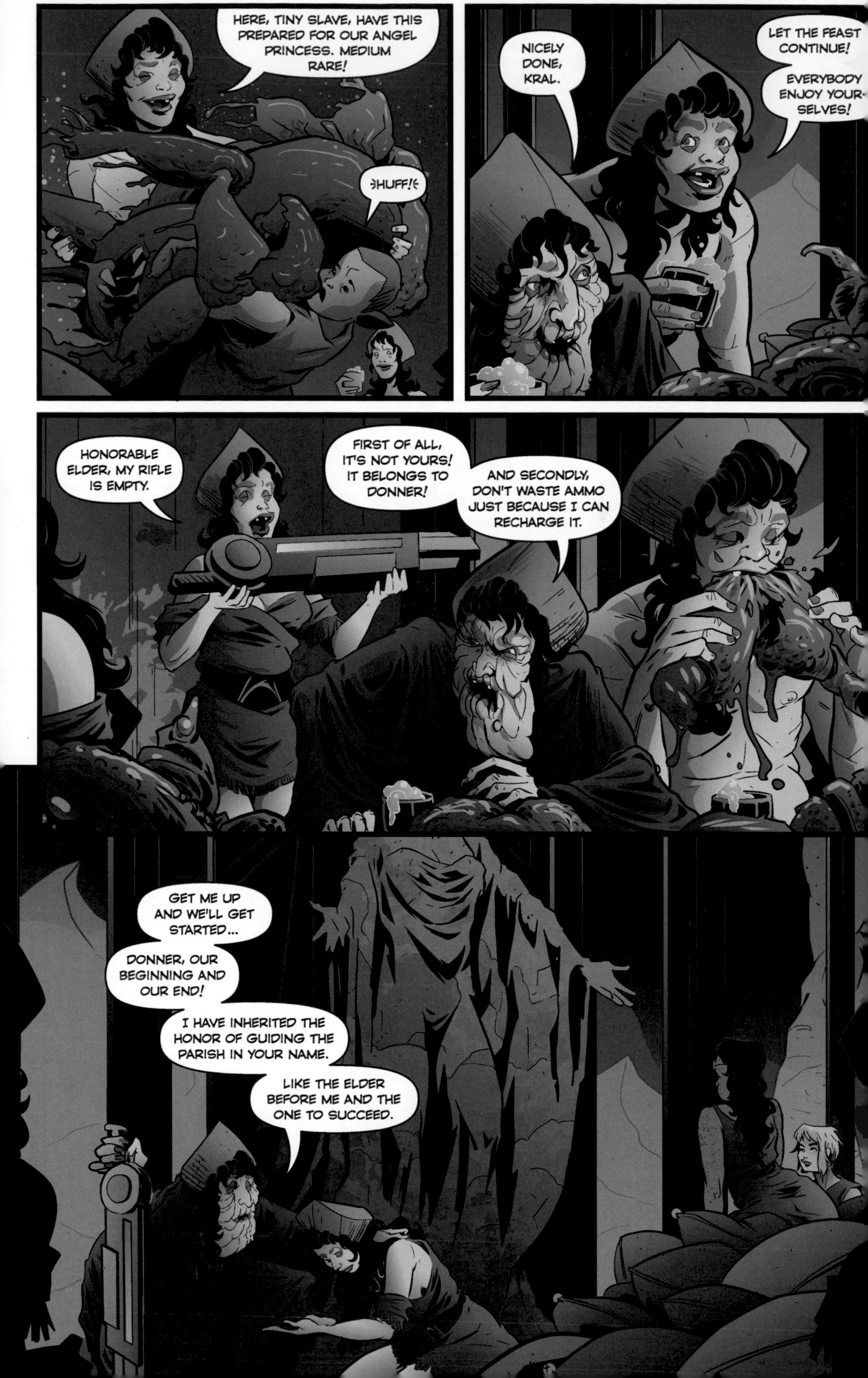
HERE, TINY SLAVE, HAVE THIS PREPARED FOR OUR ANGEL PRINCESS. MEDIUM RARE!
HUFF!
NICELY DONE, KRAL.
LET THE FEAST CONTINUE!
EVERYBODY ENJOY YOUR-SELVES!
HONORABLE ELDER, MY RIFLE IS EMPTY.
FIRST OF ALL, IT'S NOT YOURS! IT BELONGS TO DONNER!
AND SECONDLY, DON'T WASTE AMMO JUST BECAUSE I CAN RECHARGE IT.
GET ME UP AND WE'LL GET STARTED...
DONNER, OUR BEGINNING AND OUR END!
I HAVE INHERITED THE HONOR OF GUIDING THE PARISH IN YOUR NAME.
LIKE THE ELDER BEFORE ME AND THE ONE TO SUCCEED.

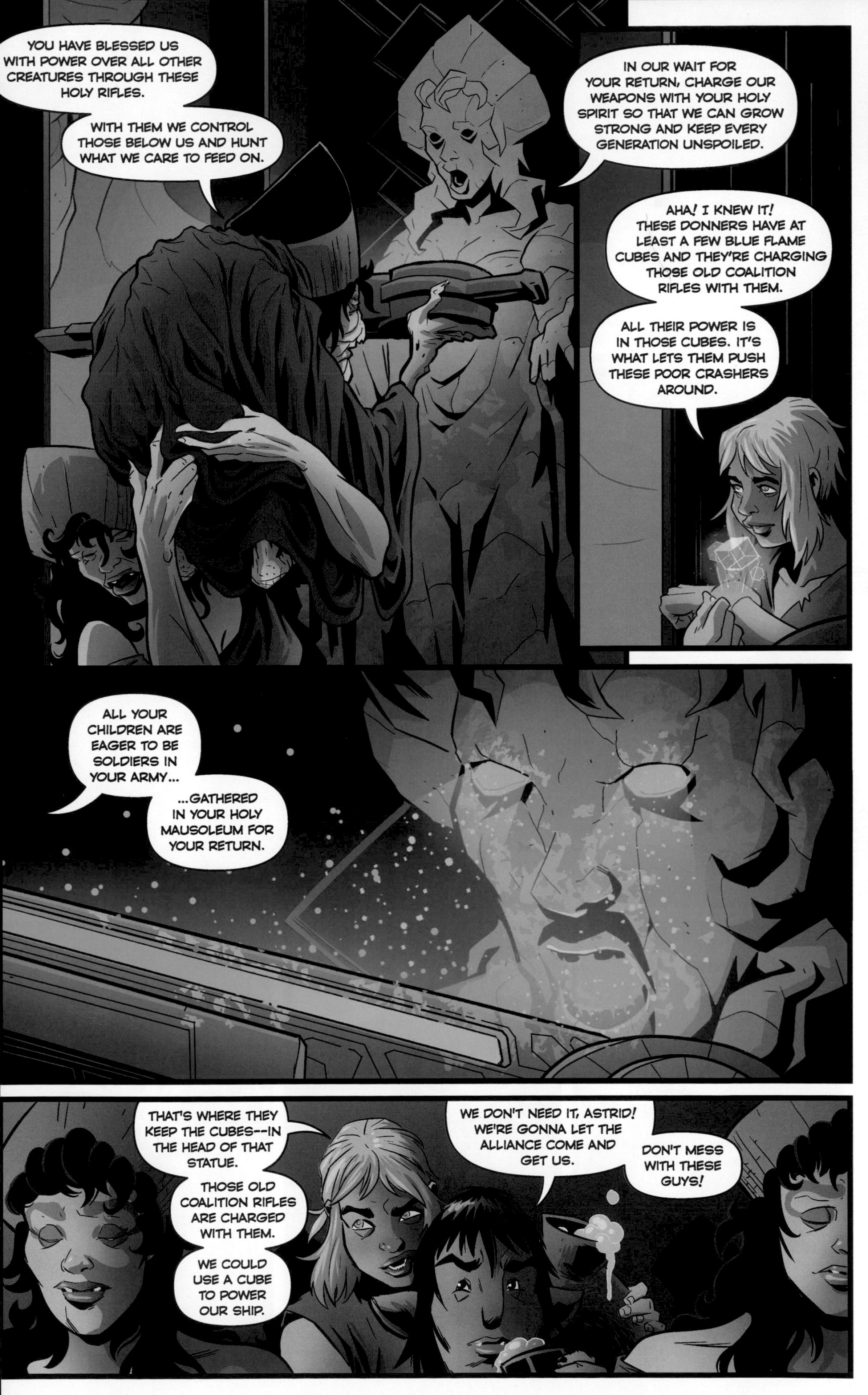
YOU HAVE BLESSED US WITH POWER OVER ALL OTHER CREATURES THROUGH THESE HOLY RIFLES.
WITH THEM WE CONTROL THOSE BELOW US AND HUNT WHAT WE CARE TO FEED ON.
IN OUR WAIT FOR YOUR RETURN, CHARGE OUR WEAPONS WITH YOUR HOLY SPIRIT SO THAT WE CAN GROW STRONG AND KEEP EVERY GENERATION UNSPOILED.
AHA! I KNEW IT! THESE DONNERS HAVE AT LEAST A FEW BLUE FLAME CUBES AND THEY'RE CHARGING THOSE OLD COALITION RIFLES WITH THEM.
ALL THEIR POWER IS IN THOSE CUBES. IT'S WHAT LETS THEM PUSH THESE POOR CRASHERS AROUND.
ALL YOUR CHILDREN ARE EAGER TO BE SOLDIERS IN YOUR ARMY...
...GATHERED IN YOUR HOLY MAUSOLEUM FOR YOUR RETURN.
THAT'S WHERE THEY KEEP THE CUBES--IN THE HEAD OF THAT STATUE.
THOSE OLD COALITION RIFLES ARE CHARGED WITH THEM.
WE COULD USE A CUBE TO POWER OUR SHIP.
WE DON'T NEED IT, ASTRID! WE'RE GONNA LET THE ALLIANCE COME AND GET US.
DON'T MESS WITH THESE GUYS!

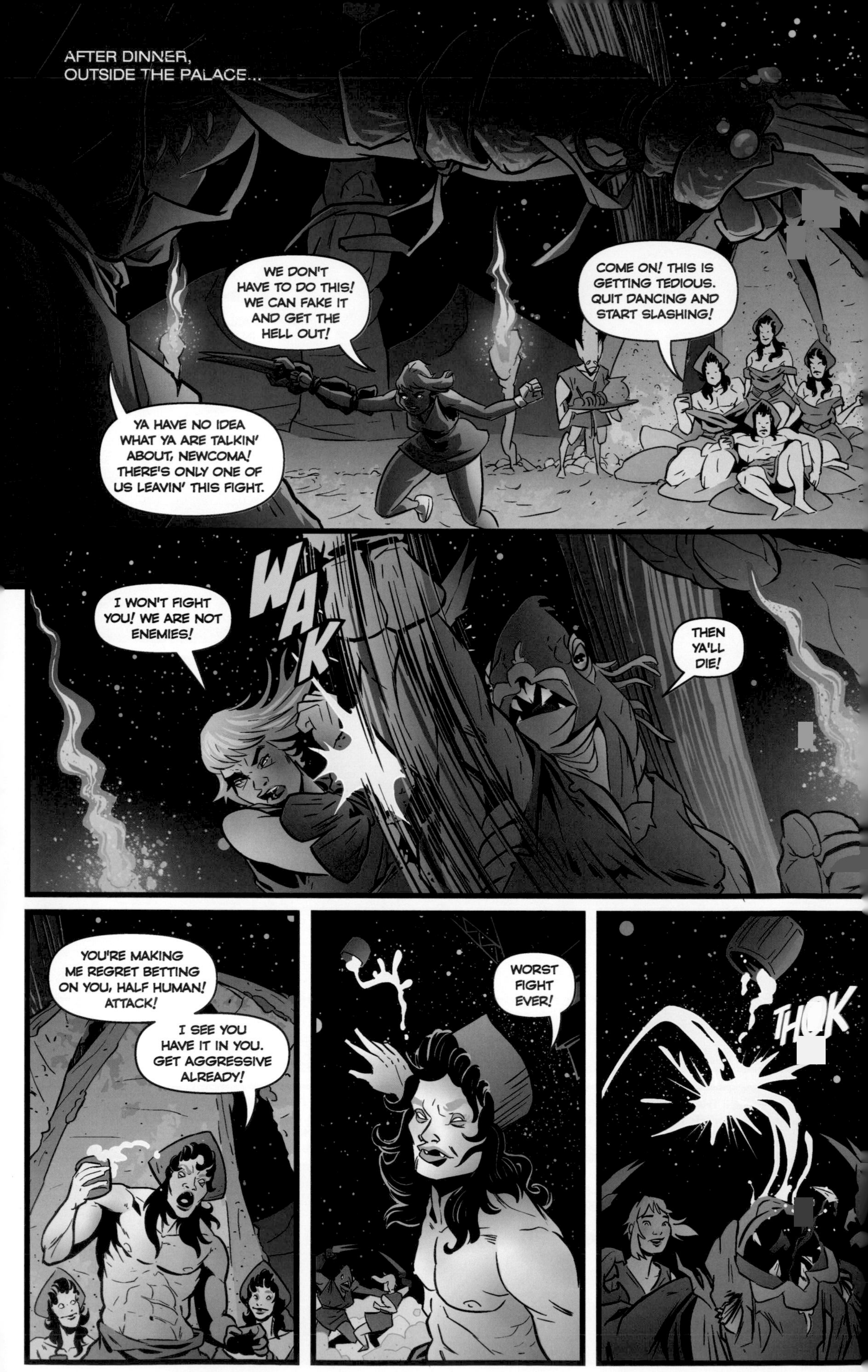
AFTER DINNER,
OUTSIDE THE PALACE...
WE DON'T HAVE TO DO THIS! WE CAN FAKE IT AND GET THE HELL OUT!
COME ON! THIS IS GETTING TEDIOUS. QUIT DANCING AND START SLASHING!
YA HAVE NO IDEA WHAT YA ARE TALKIN' ABOUT, NEWCOMA! THERE'S ONLY ONE OF US LEAVIN' THIS FIGHT.
WAK
I WON'T FIGHT YOU! WE ARE NOT ENEMIES!
THEN YA'LL DIE!
YOU'RE MAKING ME REGRET BETTING ON YOU, HALF HUMAN! ATTACK!
I SEE YOU HAVE IT IN YOU. GET AGGRESSIVE ALREADY!
WORST FIGHT EVER!
THOK

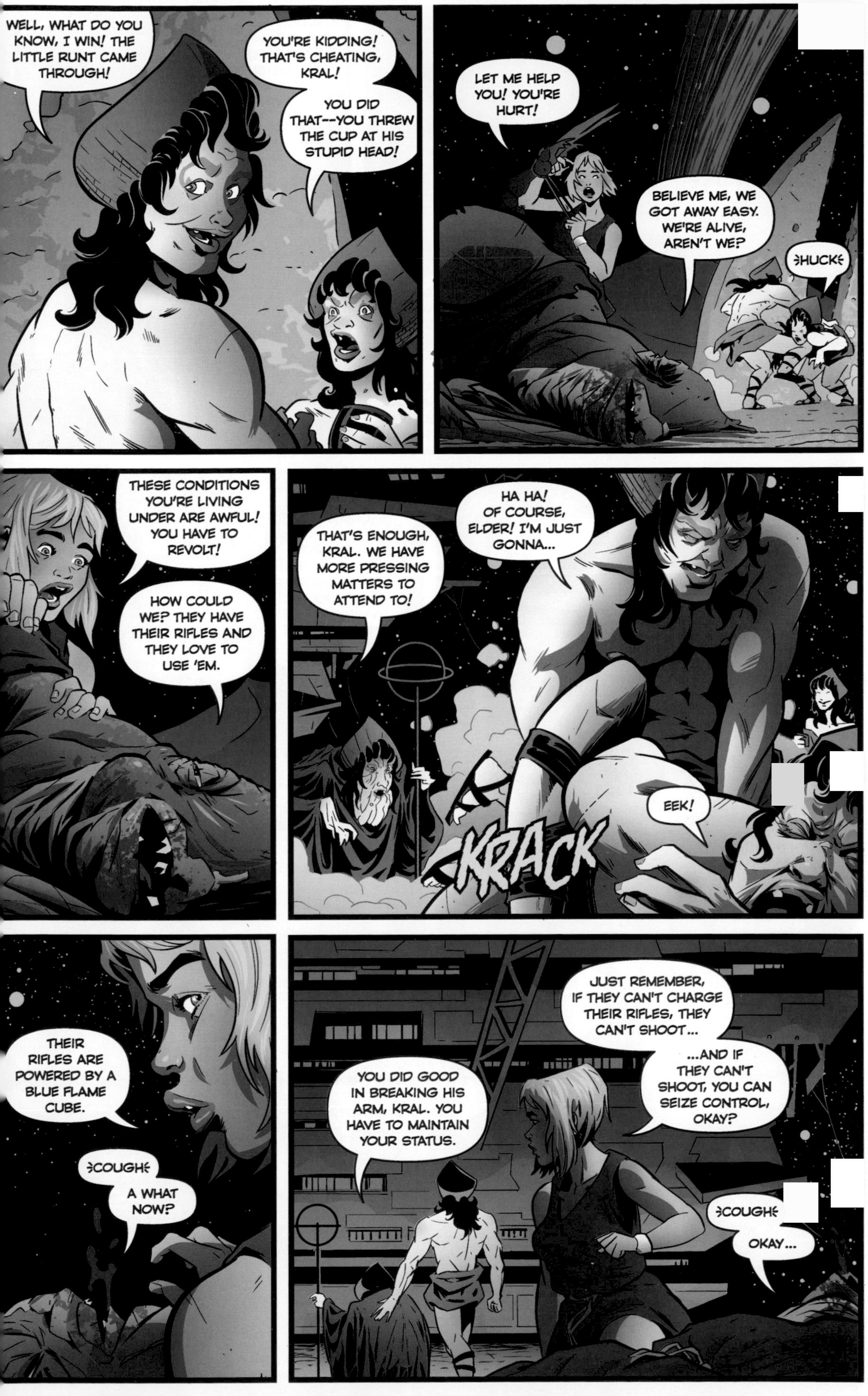
WELL, WHAT DO YOU KNOW, I WIN! THE LITTLE RUNT CAME THROUGH!
YOU'RE KIDDING! THAT'S CHEATING, KRAL!
YOU DID THAT--YOU THREW THE CUP AT HIS STUPID HEAD!
LET ME HELP YOU! YOU'RE HURT!
BELIEVE ME, WE GOT AWAY EASY. WE'RE ALIVE, AREN'T WE?
HUCK
THESE CONDITIONS YOU'RE LIVING UNDER ARE AWFUL! YOU HAVE TO REVOLT!
HOW COULD WE? THEY HAVE THEIR RIFLES AND THEY LOVE TO USE 'EM.
HA HA! OF COURSE, ELDER! I'M JUST GONNA...
THAT'S ENOUGH, KRAL. WE HAVE MORE PRESSING MATTERS TO ATTEND TO!
EEK!
KRACK
THEIR RIFLES ARE POWERED BY A BLUE FLAME CUBE.
COUGH
A WHAT NOW?
JUST REMEMBER, IF THEY CAN'T CHARGE THEIR RIFLES, THEY CAN'T SHOOT...
YOU DID GOOD IN BREAKING HIS ARM, KRAL. YOU HAVE TO MAINTAIN YOUR STATUS.
...AND IF THEY CAN'T SHOOT, YOU CAN SEIZE CONTROL, OKAY?
COUGH
OKAY...

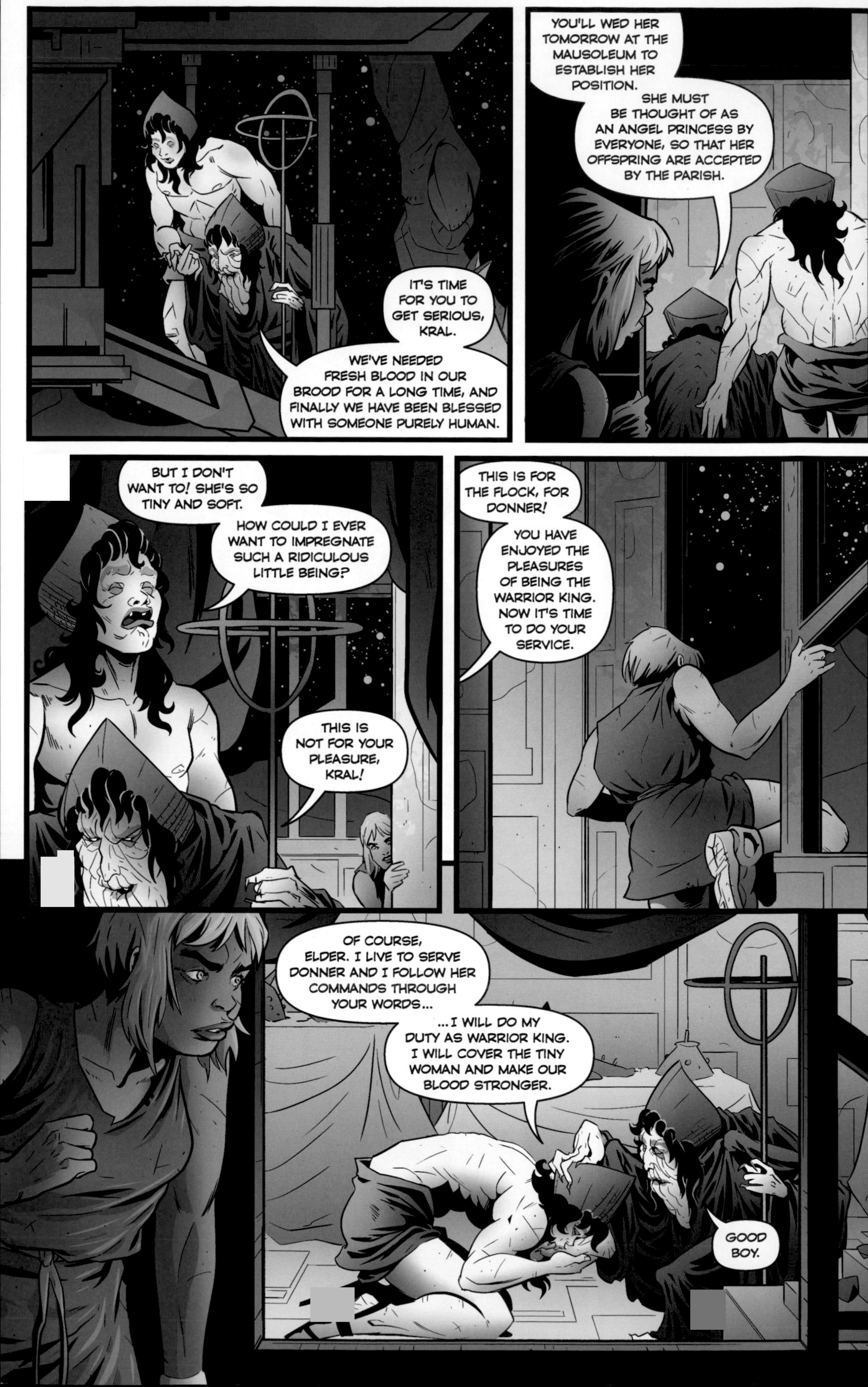
IT'S TIME FOR YOU TO GET SERIOUS, KRAL.
WE'VE NEEDED FRESH BLOOD IN OUR BROOD FOR A LONG TIME, AND FINALLY WE HAVE BEEN BLESSED WITH SOMEONE PURELY HUMAN.
YOU'LL WED HER TOMORROW AT THE MAUSOLEUM TO ESTABLISH HER POSITION.
SHE MUST BE THOUGHT OF AS AN ANGEL PRINCESS BY EVERYONE, SO THAT HER OFFSPRING ARE ACCEPTED BY THE PARISH.
BUT I DON'T WANT TO! SHE'S SO TINY AND SOFT.
HOW COULD I EVER WANT TO IMPREGNATE SUCH A RIDICULOUS LITTLE BEING?
THIS IS NOT FOR YOUR PLEASURE, KRAL!
THIS IS FOR THE FLOCK, FOR DONNER!
YOU HAVE ENJOYED THE PLEASURES OF BEING THE WARRIOR KING. NOW IT'S TIME TO DO YOUR SERVICE.
OF COURSE, ELDER. I LIVE TO SERVE DONNER AND I FOLLOW HER COMMANDS THROUGH YOUR WORDS...
...I WILL DO MY DUTY AS WARRIOR KING. I WILL COVER THE TINY WOMAN AND MAKE OUR BLOOD STRONGER.
GOOD BOY.

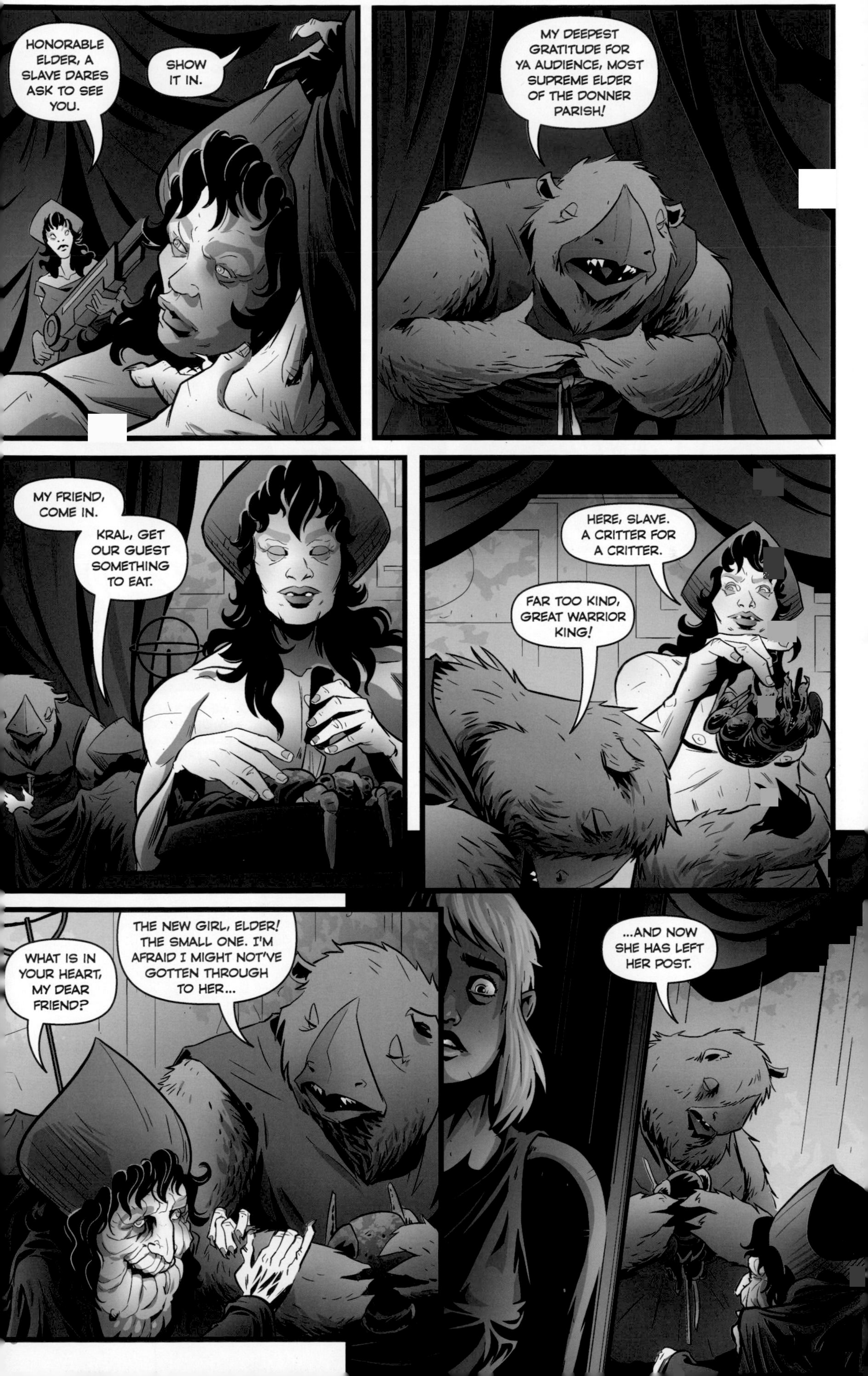
HONORABLE ELDER, A SLAVE DARES ASK TO SEE YOU.
SHOW IT IN.
MY DEEPEST GRATITUDE FOR YA AUDIENCE, MOST SUPREME ELDER OF THE DONNER PARISH!
MY FRIEND, COME IN.
KRAL, GET OUR GUEST SOMETHING TO EAT.
HERE, SLAVE. A CRITTER FOR A CRITTER.
FAR TOO KIND, GREAT WARRIOR KING!
WHAT IS IN YOUR HEART, MY DEAR FRIEND?
THE NEW GIRL, ELDER! THE SMALL ONE. I'M AFRAID I MIGHT NOT'VE GOTTEN THROUGH TO HER...
...AND NOW SHE HAS LEFT HER POST.

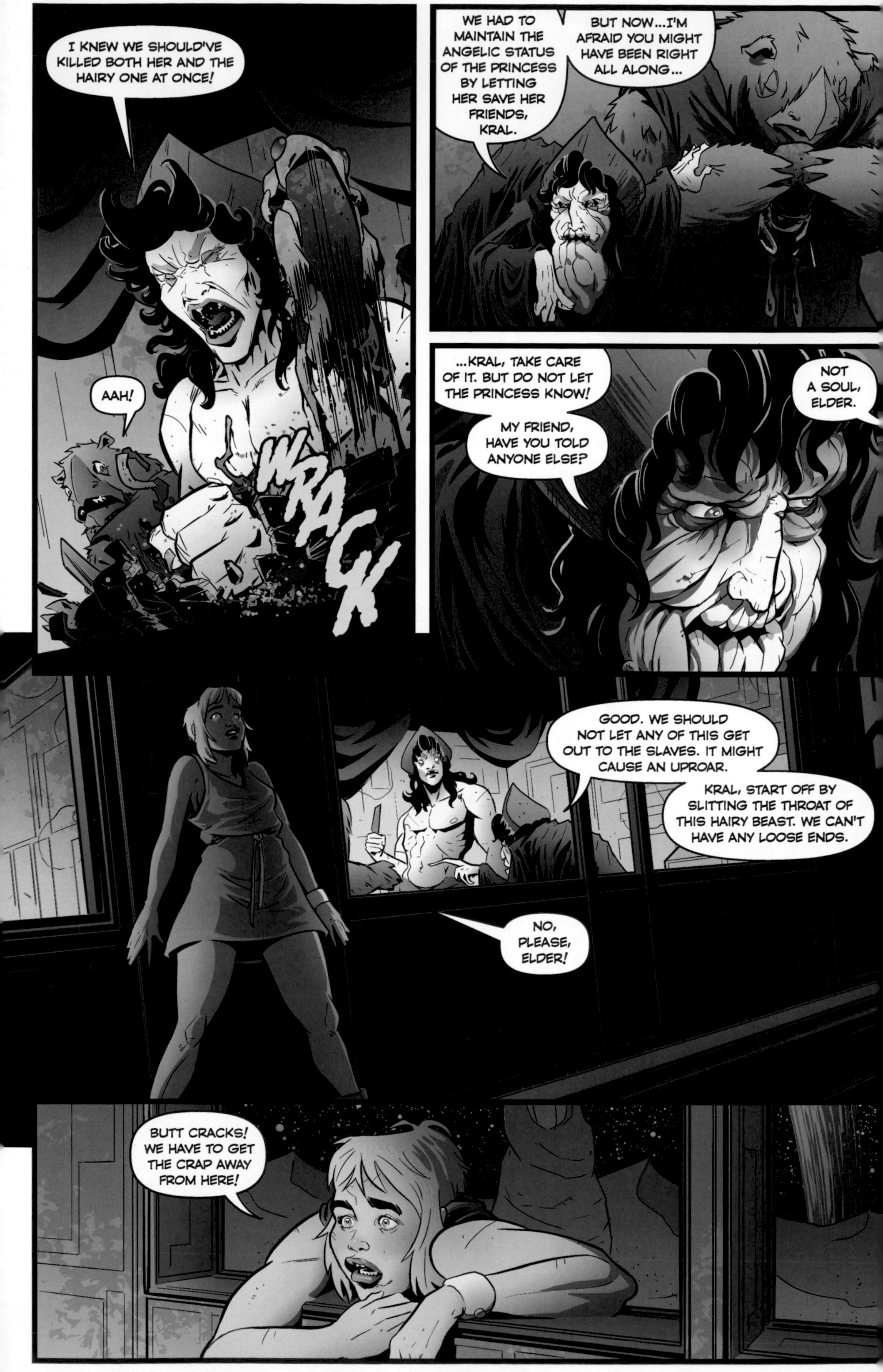
I KNEW WE SHOULD'VE KILLED BOTH HER AND THE HAIRY ONE AT ONCE!
AAH!
WRACK
WE HAD TO MAINTAIN THE ANGELIC STATUS OF THE PRINCESS BY LETTING HER SAVE HER FRIENDS, KRAL.
BUT NOW...I'M AFRAID YOU MIGHT HAVE BEEN RIGHT ALL ALONG...
...KRAL, TAKE CARE OF IT. BUT DO NOT LET THE PRINCESS KNOW!
MY FRIEND, HAVE YOU TOLD ANYONE ELSE?
NOT A SOUL, ELDER.
GOOD. WE SHOULD NOT LET ANY OF THIS GET OUT TO THE SLAVES. IT MIGHT CAUSE AN UPROAR.
KRAL, START OFF BY SLITTING THE THROAT OF THIS HAIRY BEAST. WE CAN'T HAVE ANY LOOSE ENDS.
NO, PLEASE, ELDER!
BUTT CRACKS! WE HAVE TO GET THE CRAP AWAY FROM HERE!

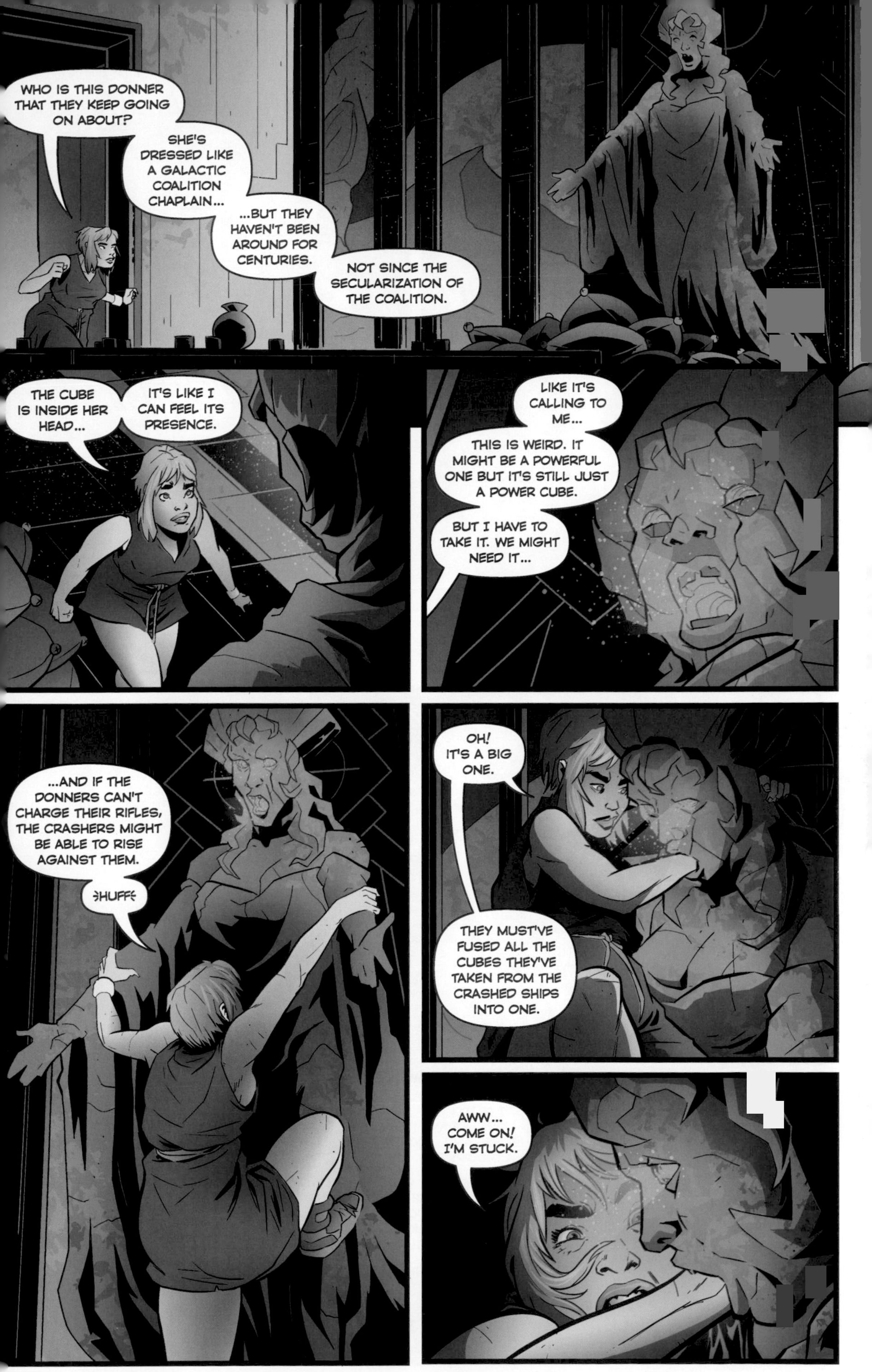
WHO IS THIS DONNER THAT THEY KEEP GOING ON ABOUT?
SHE'S DRESSED LIKE A GALACTIC COALITION CHAPLAIN...
...BUT THEY HAVEN'T BEEN AROUND FOR CENTURIES.
NOT SINCE THE SECULARIZATION OF THE COALITION.
THE CUBE IS INSIDE HER HEAD...
IT'S LIKE I CAN FEEL ITS PRESENCE.
LIKE IT'S CALLING TO ME...
THIS IS WEIRD. IT MIGHT BE A POWERFUL ONE BUT IT'S STILL JUST A POWER CUBE.
BUT I HAVE TO TAKE IT. WE MIGHT NEED IT...
...AND IF THE DONNERS CAN'T CHARGE THEIR RIFLES, THE CRASHERS MIGHT BE ABLE TO RISE AGAINST THEM.
HUFF
OH! IT'S A BIG ONE.
THEY MUST'VE FUSED ALL THE CUBES THEY'VE TAKEN FROM THE CRASHED SHIPS INTO ONE.
AWW... COME ON! I'M STUCK.

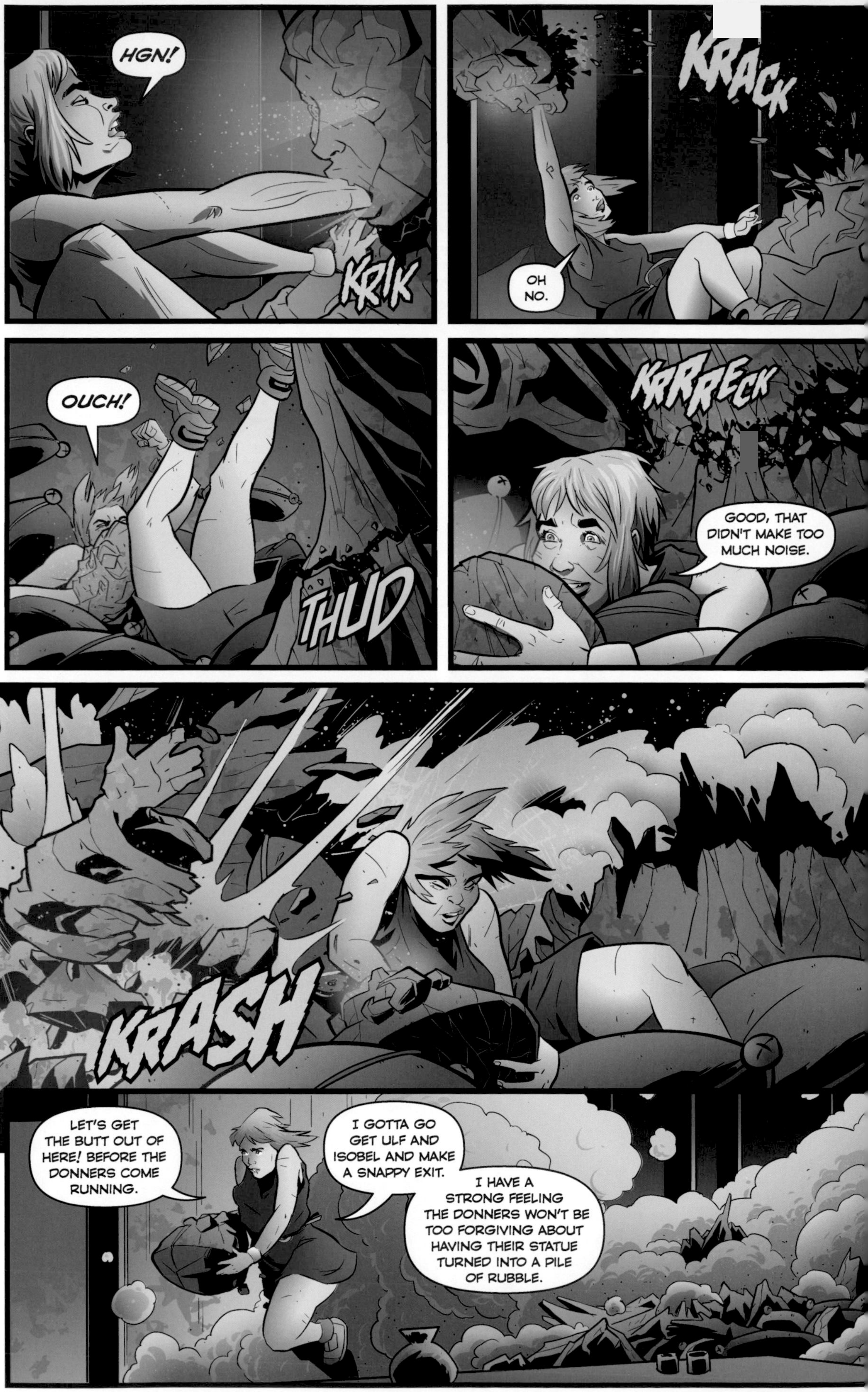
HGN!
KRIK
KRACK
OH NO.
OUCH!
THUD
KRRREck
GOOD, THAT DIDN'T MAKE TOO MUCH NOISE.
KRASH
LET'S GET THE BUTT OUT OF HERE! BEFORE THE DONNERS COME RUNNING.
I GOTTA GO GET ULF AND ISOBEL AND MAKE A SNAPPY EXIT.
I HAVE A STRONG FEELING THE DONNERS WON'T BE TOO FORGIVING ABOUT HAVING THEIR STATUE TURNED INTO A PILE OF RUBBLE.

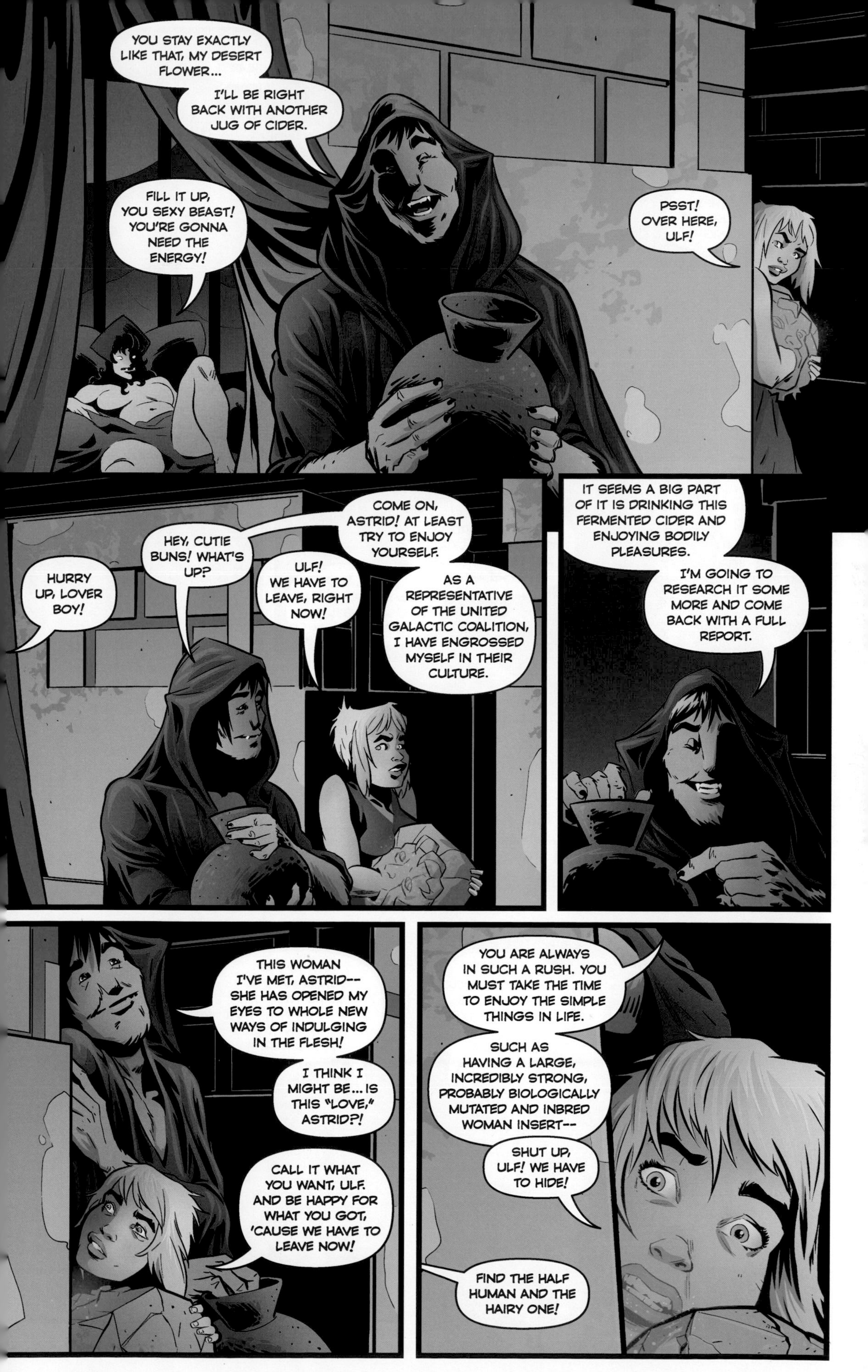
YOU STAY EXACTLY LIKE THAT, MY DESERT FLOWER...
I'LL BE RIGHT BACK WITH ANOTHER JUG OF CIDER.
FILL IT UP, YOU SEXY BEAST! YOU'RE GONNA NEED THE ENERGY!
PSST! OVER HERE, ULF!
HURRY UP, LOVER BOY!
HEY, CUTIE BUNS! WHAT'S UP?
ULF! WE HAVE TO LEAVE, RIGHT NOW!
COME ON, ASTRID! AT LEAST TRY TO ENJOY YOURSELF.
AS A REPRESENTATIVE OF THE UNITED GALACTIC COALITION, I HAVE ENGROSSED MYSELF IN THEIR CULTURE.
IT SEEMS A BIG PART OF IT IS DRINKING THIS FERMENTED CIDER AND ENJOYING BODILY PLEASURES.
I'M GOING TO RESEARCH IT SOME MORE AND COME BACK WITH A FULL REPORT.
THIS WOMAN I'VE MET, ASTRID-- SHE HAS OPENED MY EYES TO WHOLE NEW WAYS OF INDULGING IN THE FLESH!
I THINK I MIGHT BE... IS THIS "LOVE," ASTRID?!
CALL IT WHAT YOU WANT, ULF. AND BE HAPPY FOR WHAT YOU GOT, 'CAUSE WE HAVE TO LEAVE NOW!
YOU ARE ALWAYS IN SUCH A RUSH. YOU MUST TAKE THE TIME TO ENJOY THE SIMPLE THINGS IN LIFE.
SUCH AS HAVING A LARGE, INCREDIBLY STRONG, PROBABLY BIOLOGICALLY MUTATED AND INBRED WOMAN INSERT--
SHUT UP, ULF! WE HAVE TO HIDE!
FIND THE HALF HUMAN AND THE HAIRY ONE!

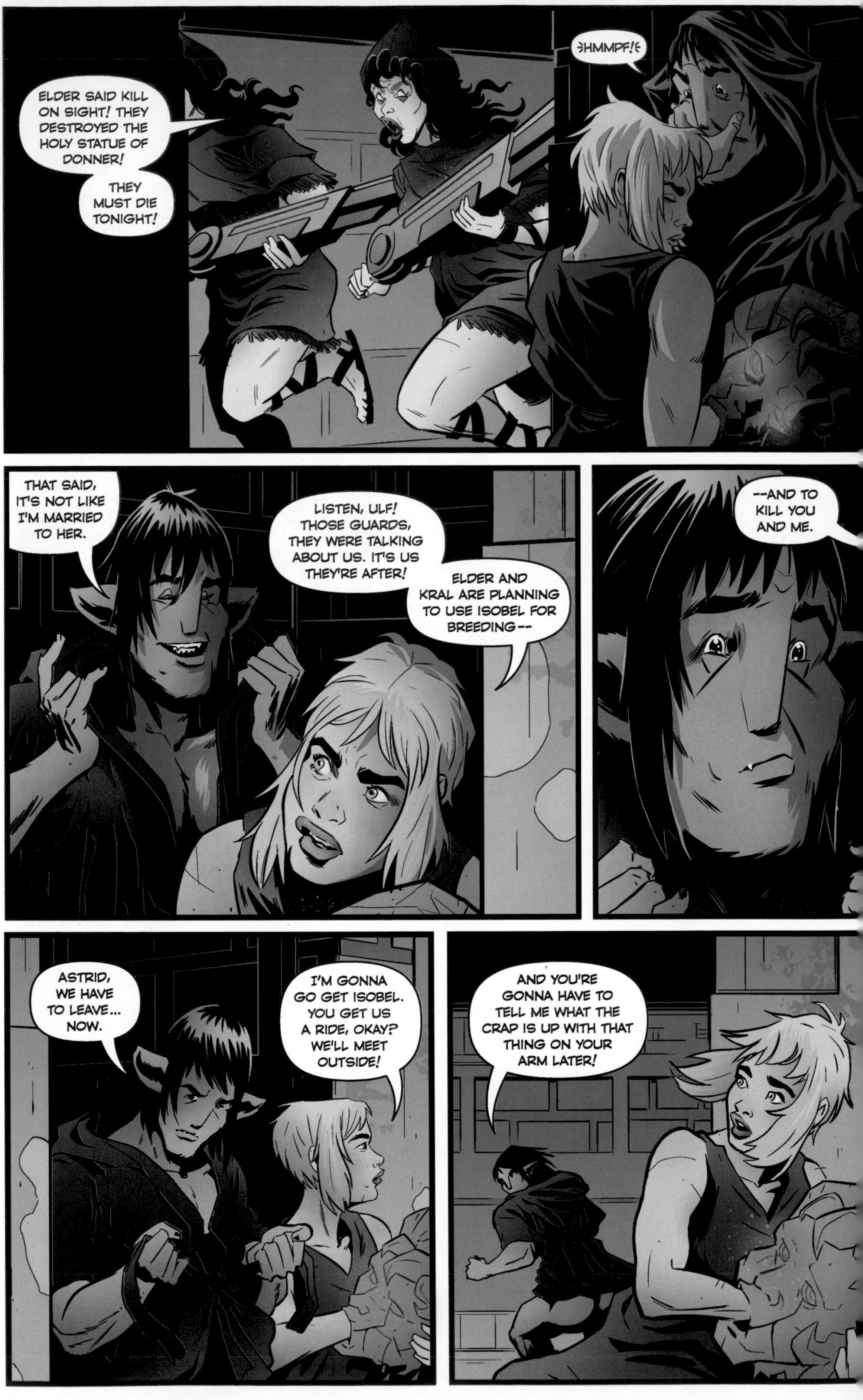
ELDER SAID KILL ON SIGHT! THEY DESTROYED THE HOLY STATUE OF DONNER!
THEY MUST DIE TONIGHT!
HMMPF!
THAT SAID, IT'S NOT LIKE I'M MARRIED TO HER.
LISTEN, ULF! THOSE GUARDS, THEY WERE TALKING ABOUT US. IT'S US THEY'RE AFTER!
ELDER AND KRAL ARE PLANNING TO USE ISOBEL FOR BREEDING--
--AND TO KILL YOU AND ME.
ASTRID, WE HAVE TO LEAVE... NOW.
I'M GONNA GO GET ISOBEL. YOU GET US A RIDE, OKAY? WE'LL MEET OUTSIDE!
AND YOU'RE GONNA HAVE TO TELL ME WHAT THE CRAP IS UP WITH THAT THING ON YOUR ARM LATER!

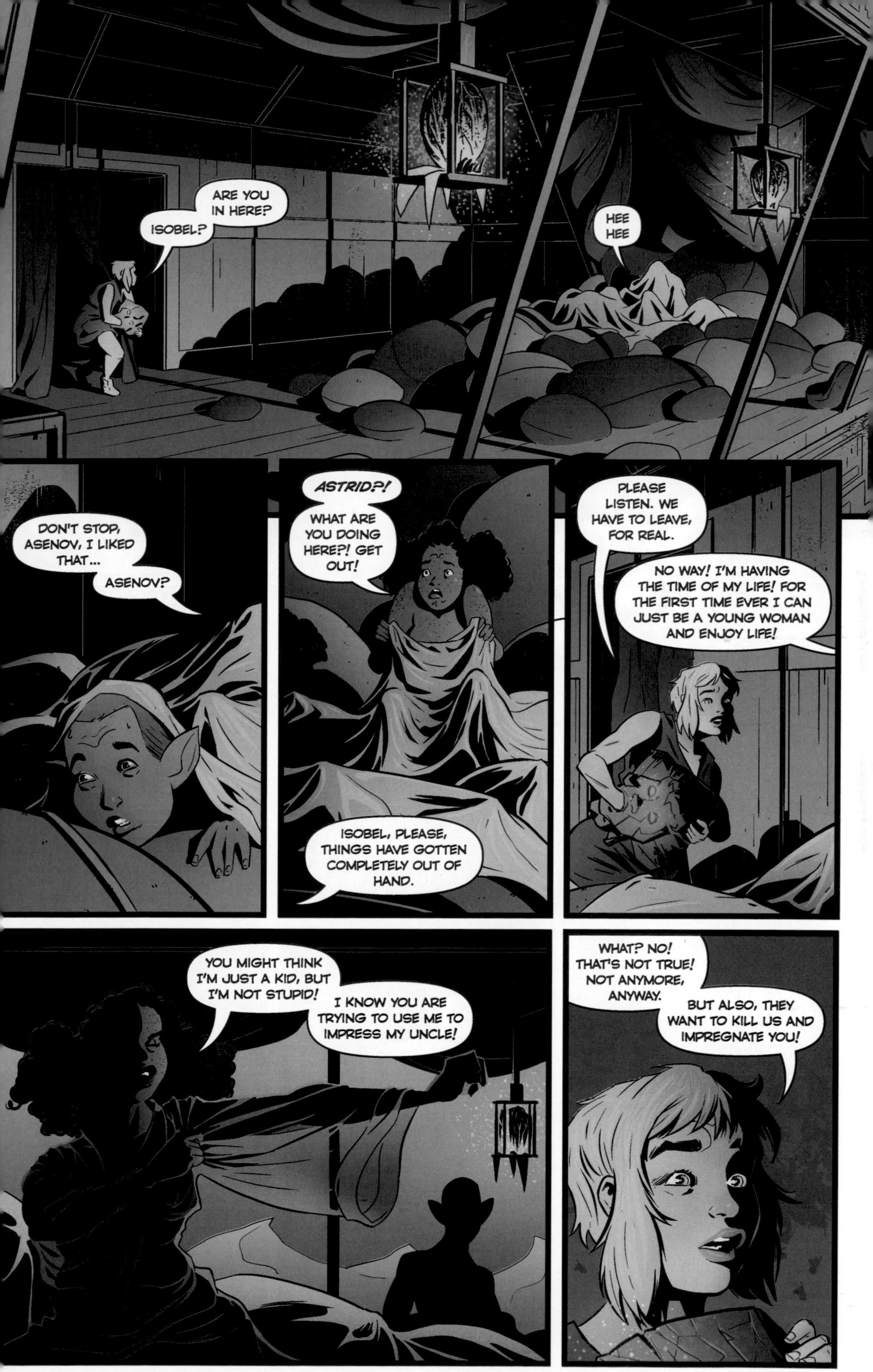
ISOBEL?
ARE YOU IN HERE?
HEE HEE
DON'T STOP, ASENOV, I LIKED THAT...
ASENOV?
ASTRID?!
WHAT ARE YOU DOING HERE?! GET OUT!
ISOBEL, PLEASE, THINGS HAVE GOTTEN COMPLETELY OUT OF HAND.
PLEASE LISTEN. WE HAVE TO LEAVE, FOR REAL.
NO WAY! I'M HAVING THE TIME OF MY LIFE! FOR THE FIRST TIME EVER I CAN JUST BE A YOUNG WOMAN AND ENJOY LIFE!
YOU MIGHT THINK I'M JUST A KID, BUT I'M NOT STUPID!
I KNOW YOU ARE TRYING TO USE ME TO IMPRESS MY UNCLE!
WHAT? NO! THAT'S NOT TRUE! NOT ANYMORE, ANYWAY.
BUT ALSO, THEY WANT TO KILL US AND IMPREGNATE YOU!

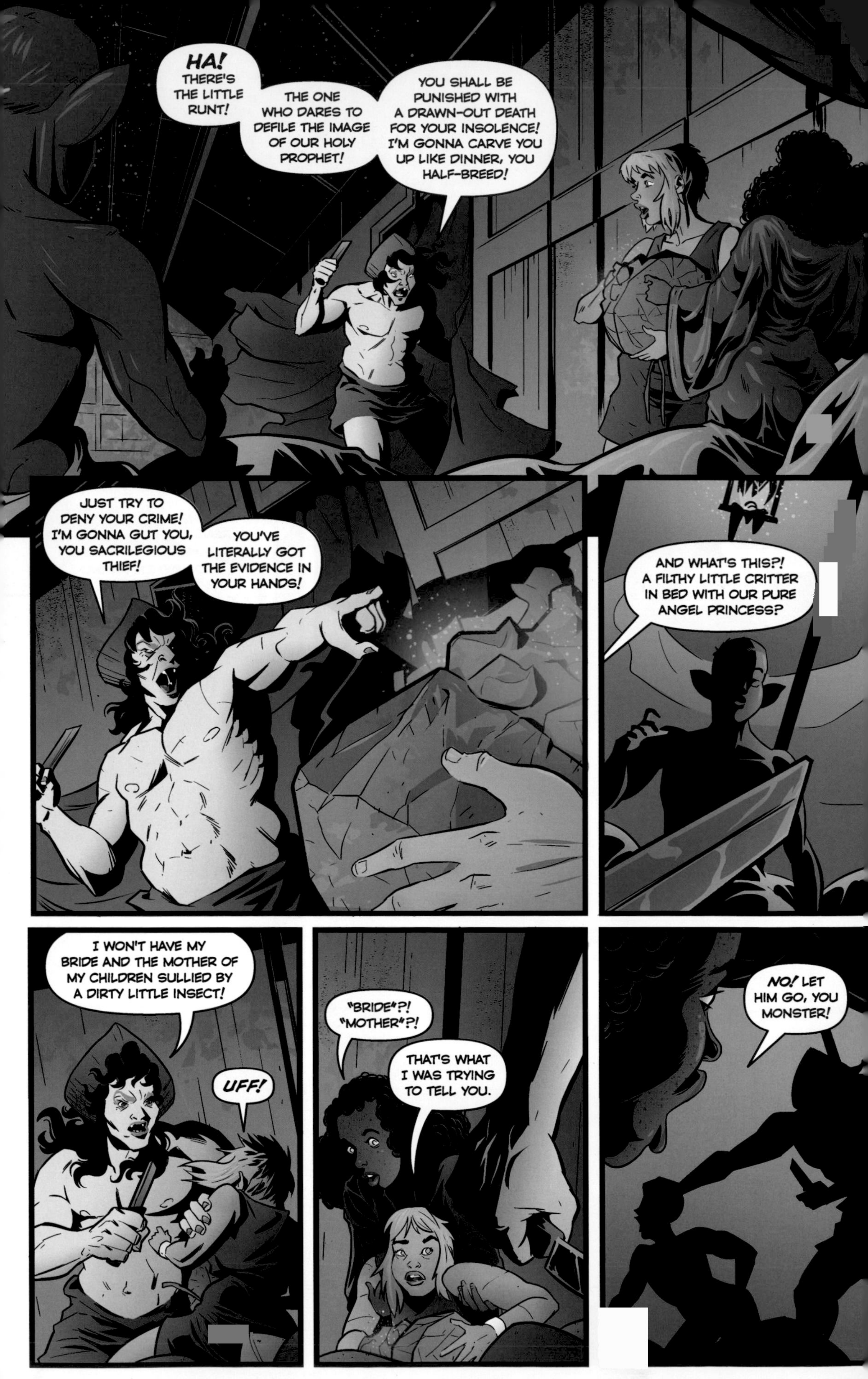
HA! THERE'S THE LITTLE RUNT!
THE ONE WHO DARES TO DEFILE THE IMAGE OF OUR HOLY PROPHET!
YOU SHALL BE PUNISHED WITH A DRAWN-OUT DEATH FOR YOUR INSOLENCE! I'M GONNA CARVE YOU UP LIKE DINNER, YOU HALF-BREED!
JUST TRY TO DENY YOUR CRIME! I'M GONNA GUT YOU, YOU SACRILEGIOUS THIEF!
YOU'VE LITERALLY GOT THE EVIDENCE IN YOUR HANDS!
AND WHAT'S THIS?! A FILTHY LITTLE CRITTER IN BED WITH OUR PURE ANGEL PRINCESS?
I WON'T HAVE MY BRIDE AND THE MOTHER OF MY CHILDREN SULLIED BY A DIRTY LITTLE INSECT!
UFF!
"BRIDE"?! "MOTHER"?!
THAT'S WHAT I WAS TRYING TO TELL YOU.
NO! LET HIM GO, YOU MONSTER!

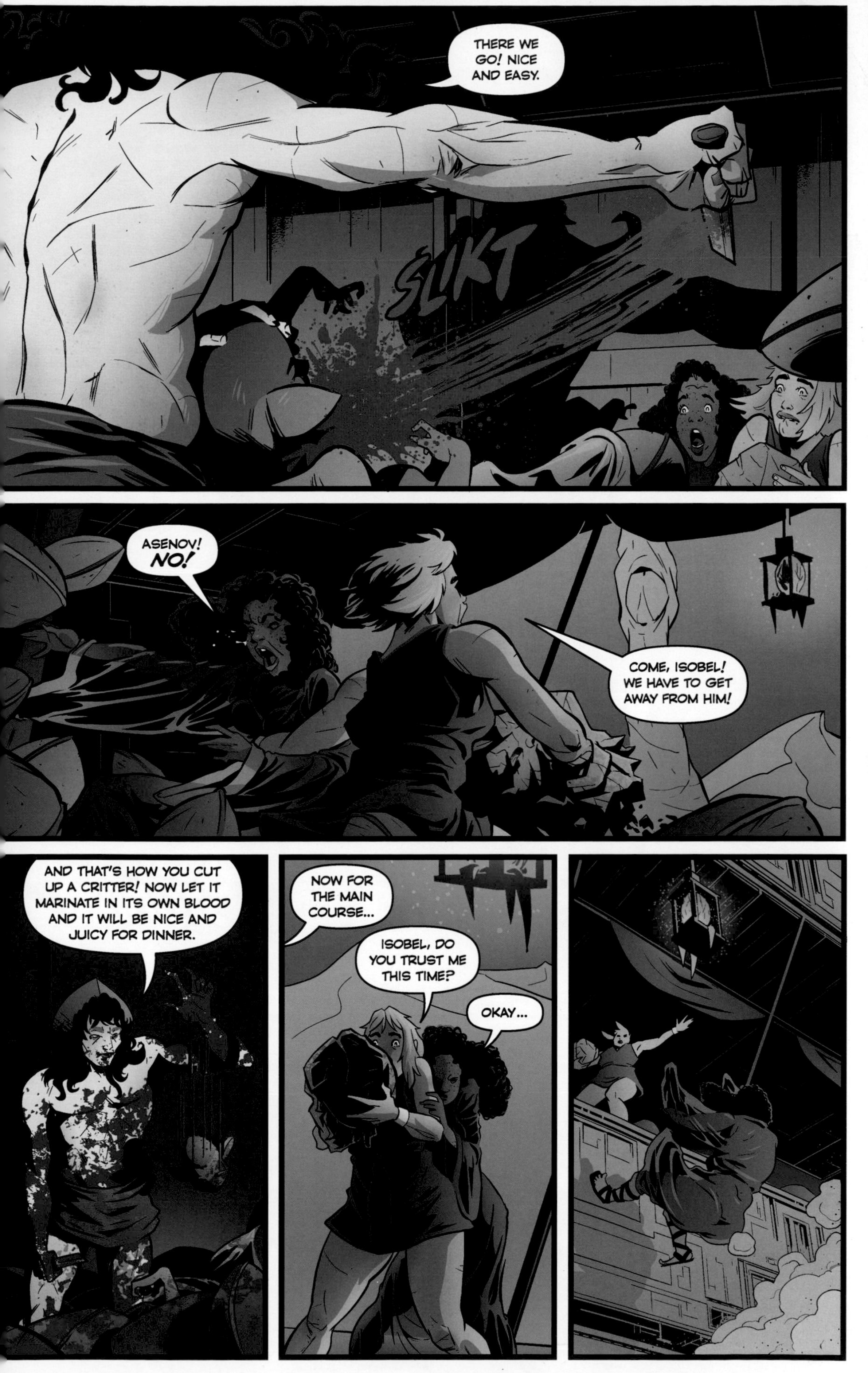
THERE WE GO! NICE AND EASY.
SLIKT
ASENOV! NO!
COME, ISOBEL! WE HAVE TO GET AWAY FROM HIM!
AND THAT'S HOW YOU CUT UP A CRITTER! NOW LET IT MARINATE IN ITS OWN BLOOD AND IT WILL BE NICE AND JUICY FOR DINNER.
NOW FOR THE MAIN COURSE...
ISOBEL, DO YOU TRUST ME THIS TIME?
OKAY...

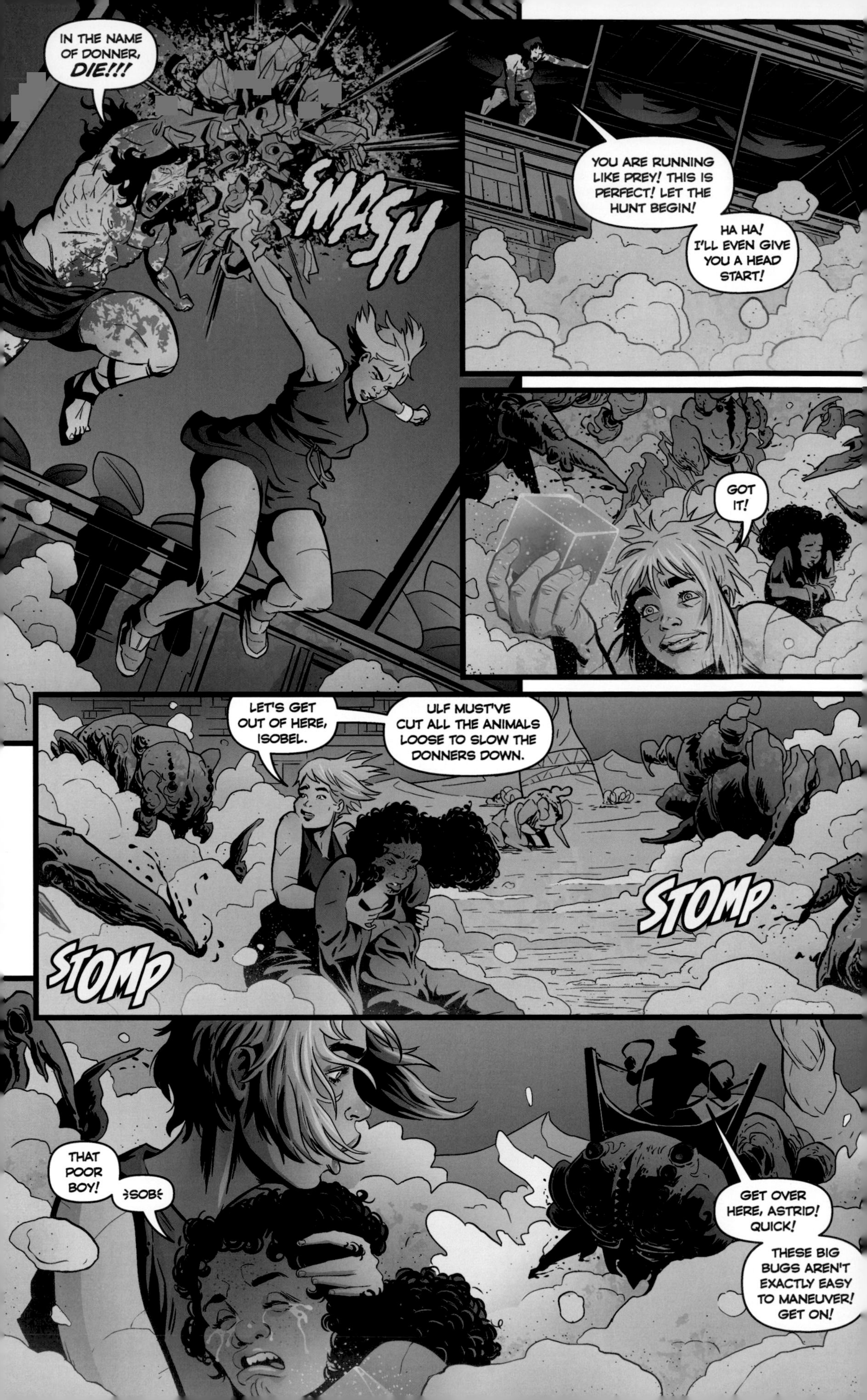
IN THE NAME OF DONNER, DIE!!!
SMASH
YOU ARE RUNNING LIKE PREY! THIS IS PERFECT! LET THE HUNT BEGIN!
HA HA! I'LL EVEN GIVE YOU A HEAD START!
GOT IT!
LET'S GET OUT OF HERE, ISOBEL.
ULF MUST'VE CUT ALL THE ANIMALS LOOSE TO SLOW THE DONNERS DOWN.
STOMP
STOMP
THAT POOR BOY!
SOB
GET OVER HERE, ASTRID! QUICK!
THESE BIG BUGS AREN'T EXACTLY EASY TO MANEUVER! GET ON!

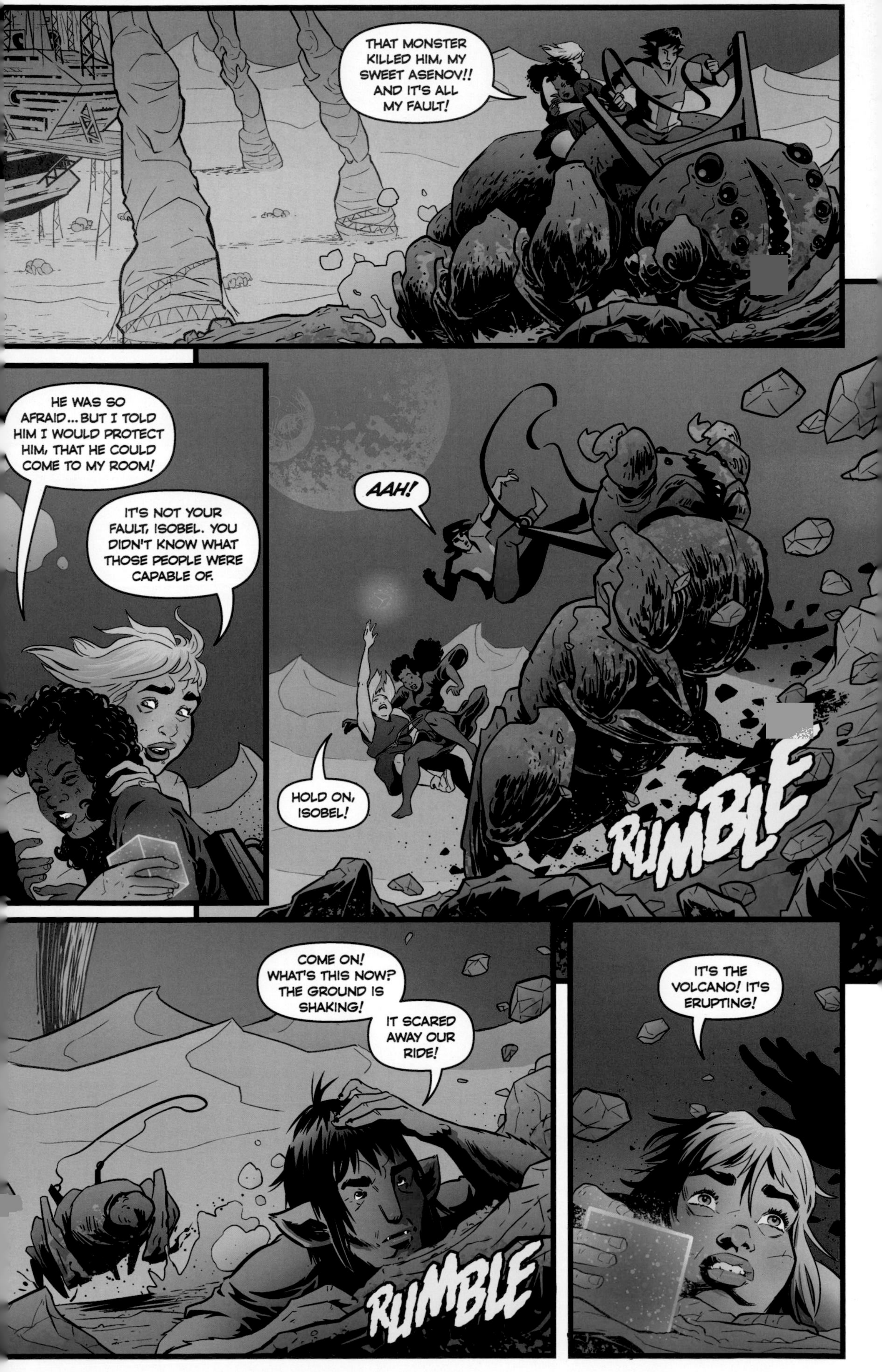
THAT MONSTER KILLED HIM, MY SWEET ASENOV!! AND IT'S ALL MY FAULT!
HE WAS SO AFRAID... BUT I TOLD HIM I WOULD PROTECT HIM, THAT HE COULD COME TO MY ROOM!
IT'S NOT YOUR FAULT, ISOBEL. YOU DIDN'T KNOW WHAT THOSE PEOPLE WERE CAPABLE OF.
AAH!
HOLD ON, ISOBEL!
RUMBLE
COME ON! WHAT'S THIS NOW? THE GROUND IS SHAKING!
IT SCARED AWAY OUR RIDE!
RUMBLE
IT'S THE VOLCANO! IT'S ERUPTING!

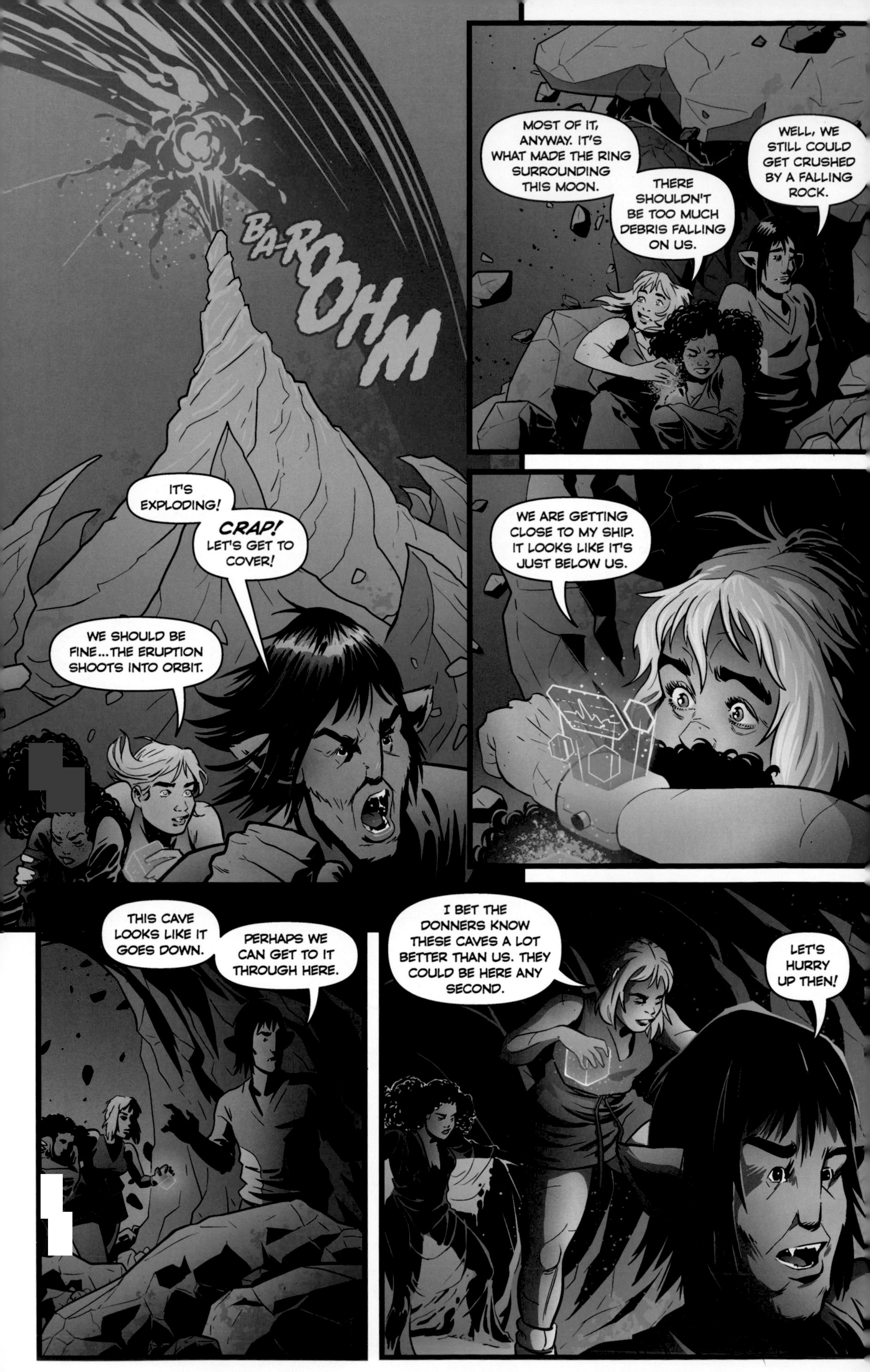
BA-ROOOHM
IT'S EXPLODING!
CRAP! LET'S GET TO COVER!
WE SHOULD BE FINE...THE ERUPTION SHOOTS INTO ORBIT.
MOST OF IT, ANYWAY. IT'S WHAT MADE THE RING SURROUNDING THIS MOON.
THERE SHOULDN'T BE TOO MUCH DEBRIS FALLING ON US.
WELL, WE STILL COULD GET CRUSHED BY A FALLING ROCK.
WE ARE GETTING CLOSE TO MY SHIP. IT LOOKS LIKE IT'S JUST BELOW US.
THIS CAVE LOOKS LIKE IT GOES DOWN.
PERHAPS WE CAN GET TO IT THROUGH HERE.
I BET THE DONNERS KNOW THESE CAVES A LOT BETTER THAN US. THEY COULD BE HERE ANY SECOND.
LET'S HURRY UP THEN!

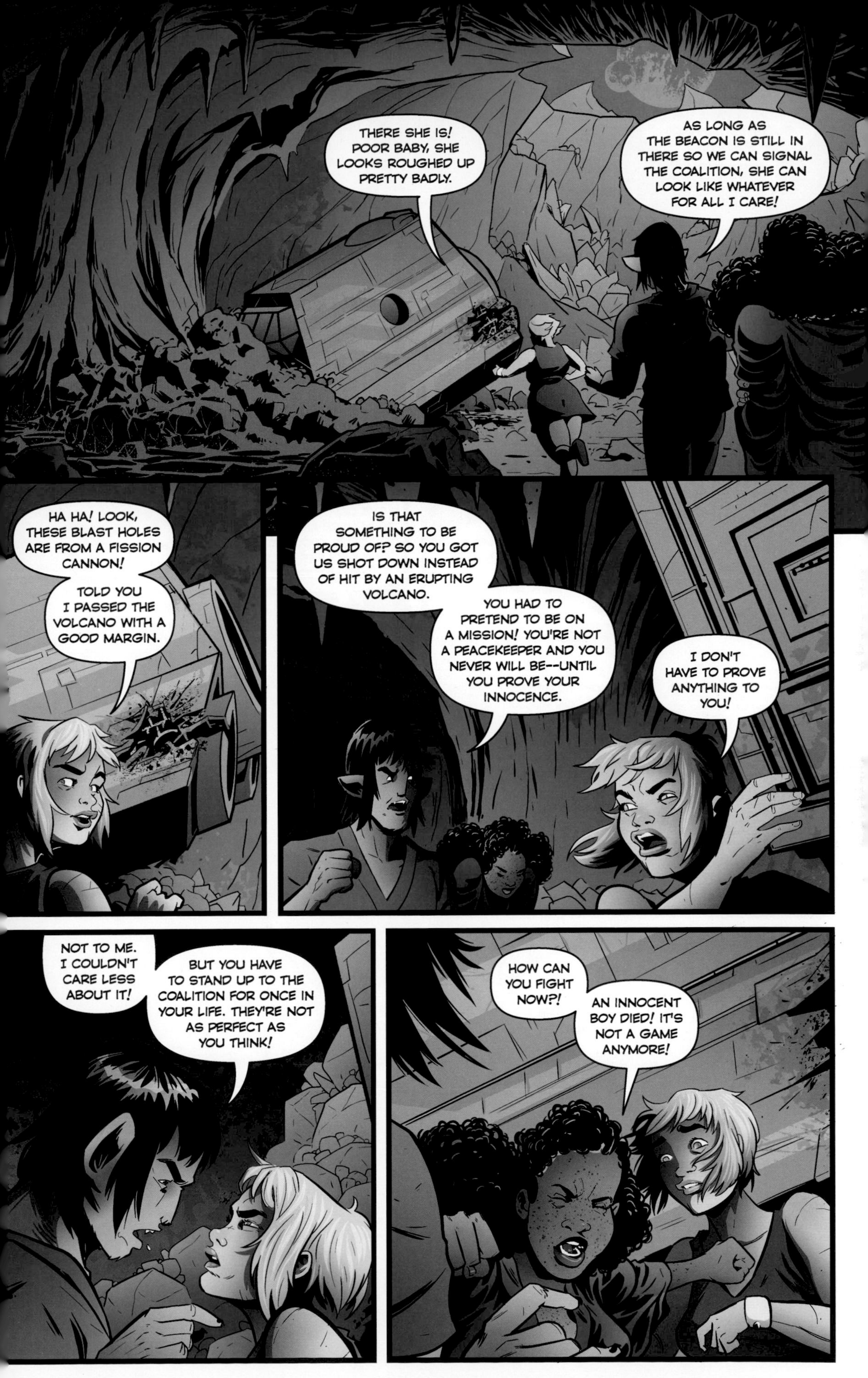
THERE SHE IS! POOR BABY, SHE LOOKS ROUGHED UP PRETTY BADLY.
AS LONG AS THE BEACON IS STILL IN THERE SO WE CAN SIGNAL THE COALITION, SHE CAN LOOK LIKE WHATEVER FOR ALL I CARE!
HA HA! LOOK, THESE BLAST HOLES ARE FROM A FISSION CANNON!
TOLD YOU I PASSED THE VOLCANO WITH A GOOD MARGIN.
IS THAT SOMETHING TO BE PROUD OF? SO YOU GOT US SHOT DOWN INSTEAD OF HIT BY AN ERUPTING VOLCANO.
YOU HAD TO PRETEND TO BE ON A MISSION! YOU'RE NOT A PEACEKEEPER AND YOU NEVER WILL BE--UNTIL YOU PROVE YOUR INNOCENCE.
I DON'T HAVE TO PROVE ANYTHING TO YOU!
NOT TO ME. I COULDN'T CARE LESS ABOUT IT!
BUT YOU HAVE TO STAND UP TO THE COALITION FOR ONCE IN YOUR LIFE. THEY'RE NOT AS PERFECT AS YOU THINK!
HOW CAN YOU FIGHT NOW?!
AN INNOCENT BOY DIED! IT'S NOT A GAME ANYMORE!

WHAT WE HAVE TO DO NOW IS WORK TOGETHER, IF WE'RE GONNA HAVE THE SLIGHTEST CHANCE OF SURVIVING.

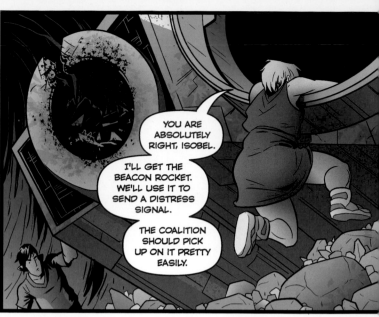

YOU ARE ABSOLUTELY RIGHT, ISOBEL.

I'LL GET THE BEACON ROCKET. WE'LL USE IT TO SEND A DISTRESS SIGNAL.

THE COALITION SHOULD PICK UP ON IT PRETTY EASILY.

HERE, ULF...

...CLIMB UP THAT HOLE IN THE CAVE ROOF. JUST AIM IT STRAIGHT UP AND PRESS THE BUTTON.

WATCH IT, ASTRID. I KNOW HOW TO SET UP A BEACON ROCKET.

JUST AS I THOUGHT. THE DONNERS HAVE BEEN HERE AND TAKEN OUR CUBE TOO. LUCKILY WE STOLE IT BACK, WITH INTEREST.

THIS HERE IS SEVERAL POWER CUBES FUSED INTO ONE AWESOME SUPERCUBE.

I'M GETTING FED UP WITH ASTRID NOT STANDING UP FOR HERSELF TO THE GALACTIC COALITION.

IF SHE REALLY DIDN'T CHEAT, THAT MEANS THE COALITION IS WRONG. SHE HAS TO REALIZE THAT THEY'RE NOT INFALLIBLE.

SHE THINKS SO HIGHLY OF THE COALITION, HAVING GROWN UP INSIDE IT, SHE CAN'T EVEN SEE THAT THEY CAN BE WRONG ABOUT HER EVEN WHEN SHE KNOWS SHE'S INNOCENT.

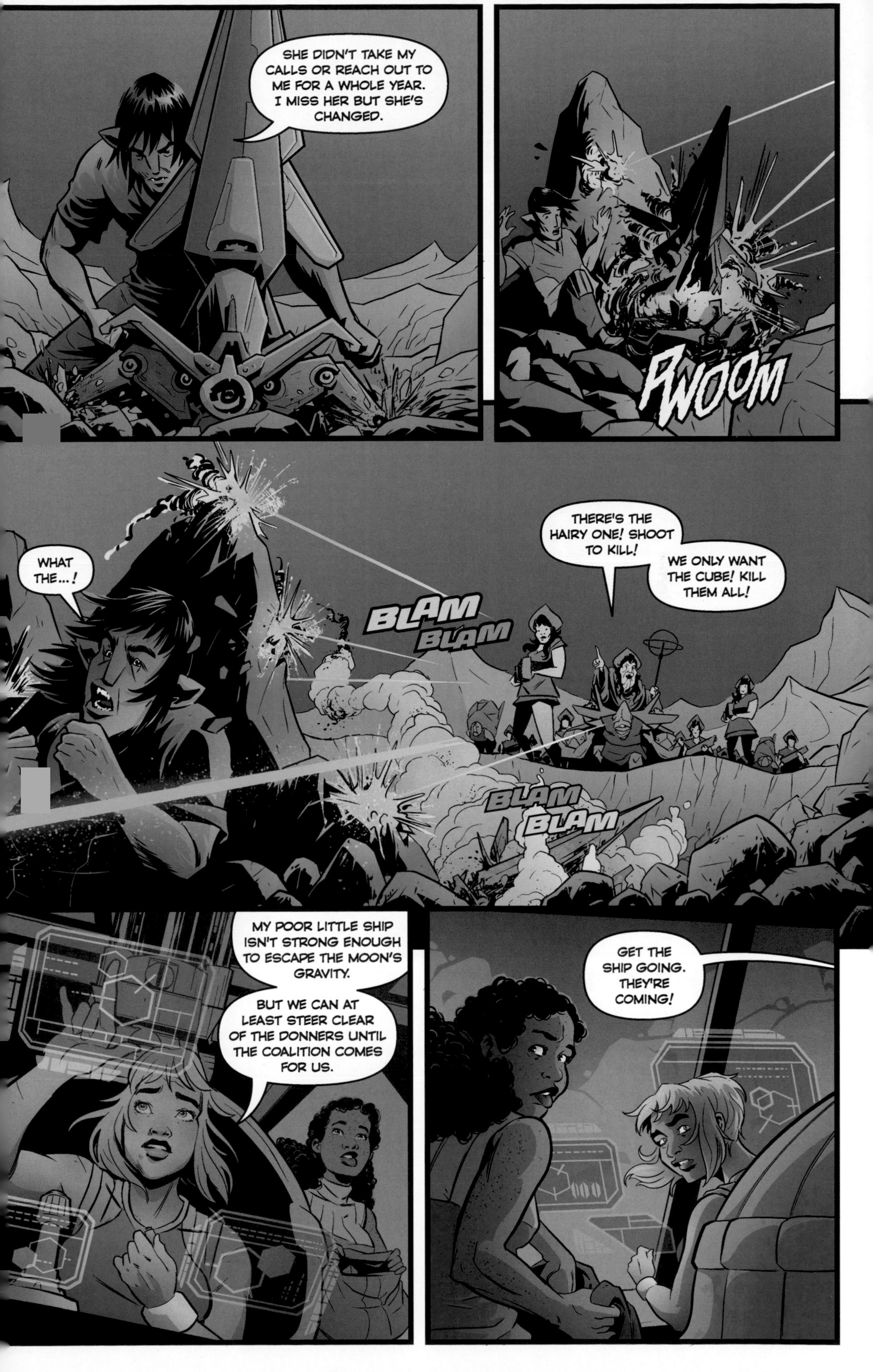
SHE DIDN'T TAKE MY CALLS OR REACH OUT TO ME FOR A WHOLE YEAR. I MISS HER BUT SHE'S CHANGED.
PWOOM
WHAT THE...!
BLAM
BLAM
THERE'S THE HAIRY ONE! SHOOT TO KILL!
WE ONLY WANT THE CUBE! KILL THEM ALL!
BLAM
BLAM
MY POOR LITTLE SHIP ISN'T STRONG ENOUGH TO ESCAPE THE MOON'S GRAVITY.
BUT WE CAN AT LEAST STEER CLEAR OF THE DONNERS UNTIL THE COALITION COMES FOR US.
GET THE SHIP GOING. THEY'RE COMING!

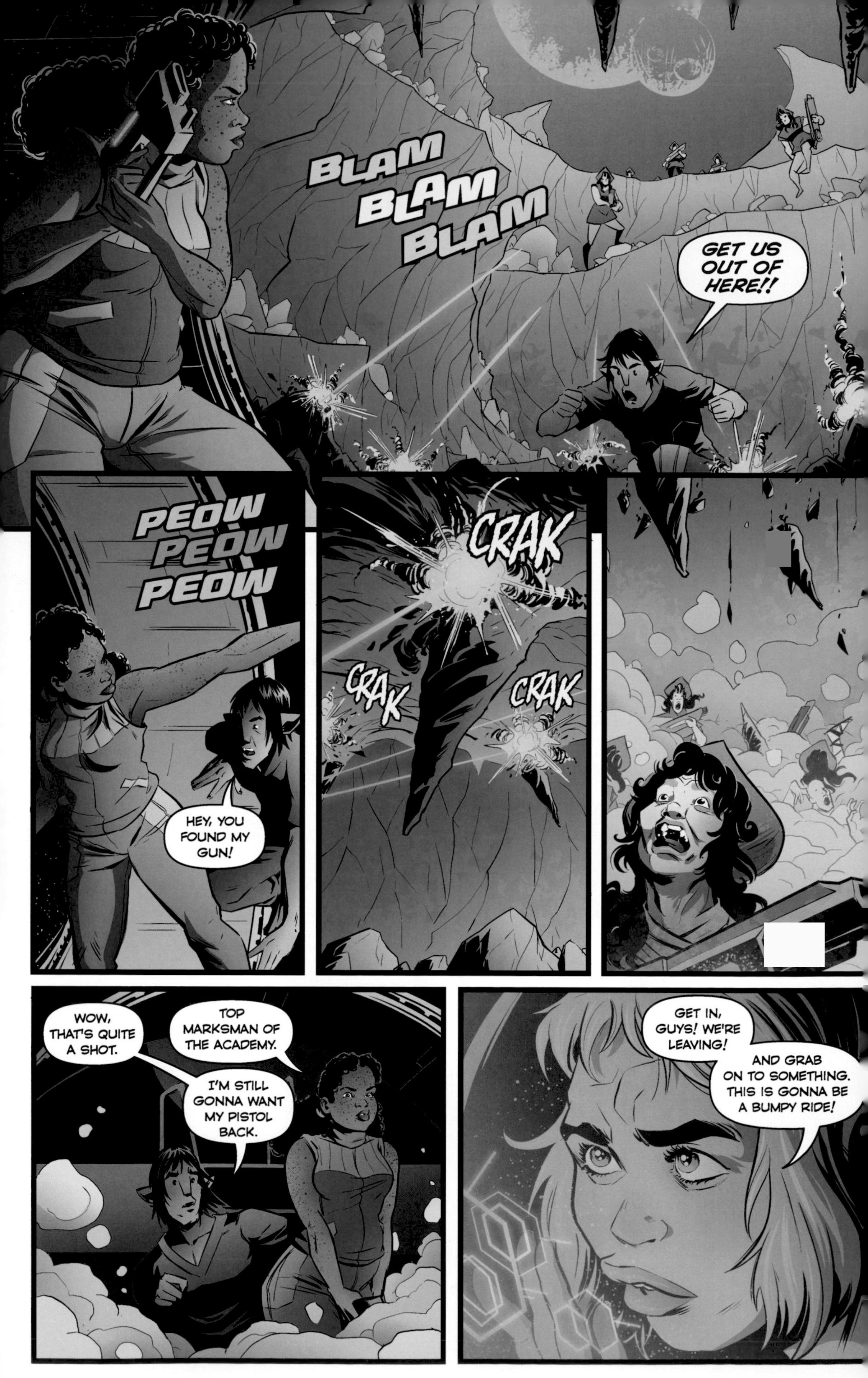
BLAM
BLAM
BLAM
GET US OUT OF HERE!!
PEOW
PEOW
PEOW
HEY, YOU FOUND MY GUN!
CRAK
CRAK
CRAK
WOW, THAT'S QUITE A SHOT.
TOP MARKSMAN OF THE ACADEMY.
I'M STILL GONNA WANT MY PISTOL BACK.
GET IN, GUYS! WE'RE LEAVING!
AND GRAB ON TO SOMETHING. THIS IS GONNA BE A BUMPY RIDE!

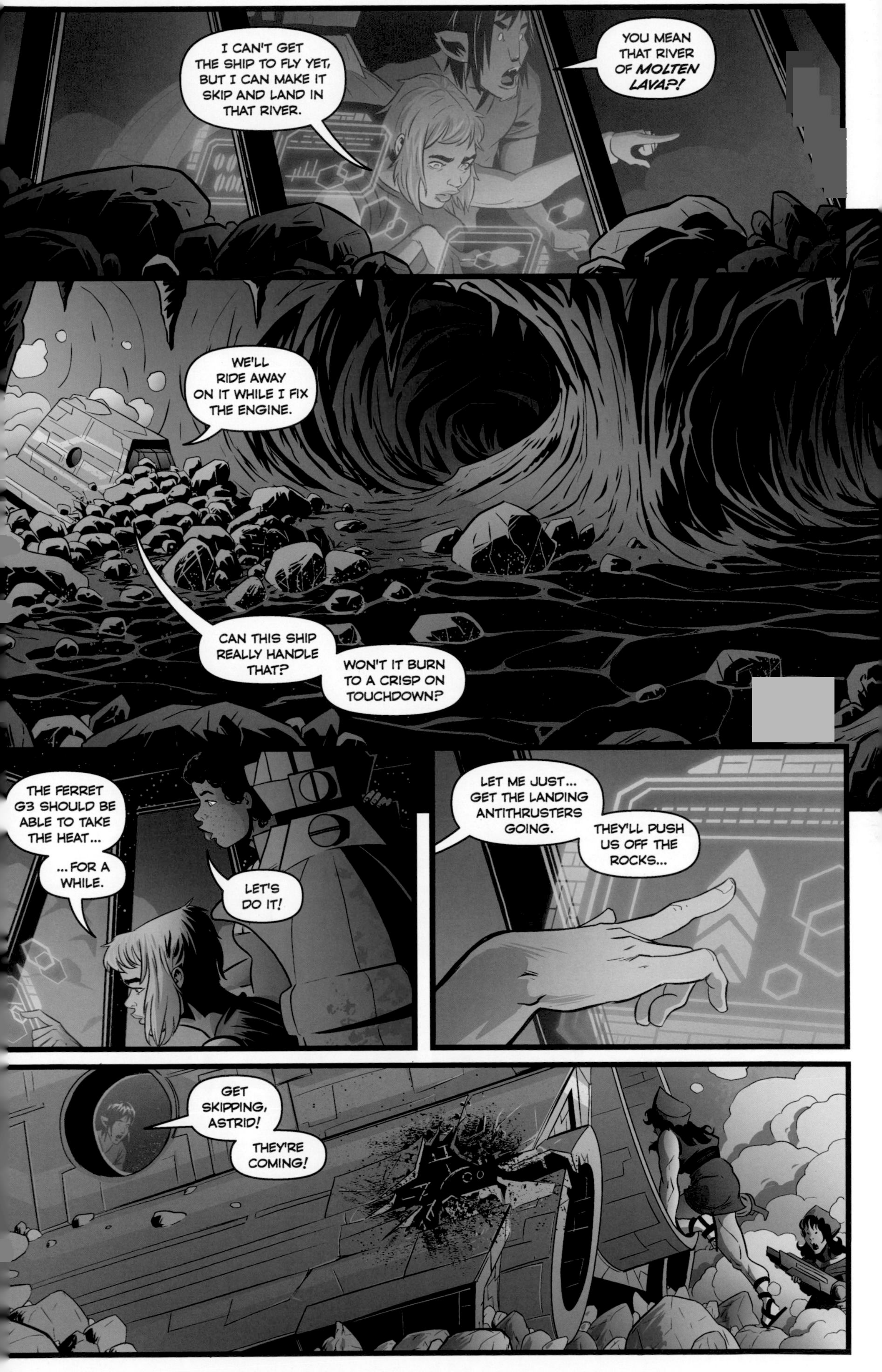
I CAN'T GET THE SHIP TO FLY YET, BUT I CAN MAKE IT SKIP AND LAND IN THAT RIVER.
YOU MEAN THAT RIVER OF *MOLTEN LAVA?!*
WE'LL RIDE AWAY ON IT WHILE I FIX THE ENGINE.
CAN THIS SHIP REALLY HANDLE THAT?
WON'T IT BURN TO A CRISP ON TOUCHDOWN?
THE FERRET G3 SHOULD BE ABLE TO TAKE THE HEAT...
...FOR A WHILE.
LET'S DO IT!
LET ME JUST... GET THE LANDING ANTITHRUSTERS GOING.
THEY'LL PUSH US OFF THE ROCKS...
GET SKIPPING, ASTRID!
THEY'RE COMING!

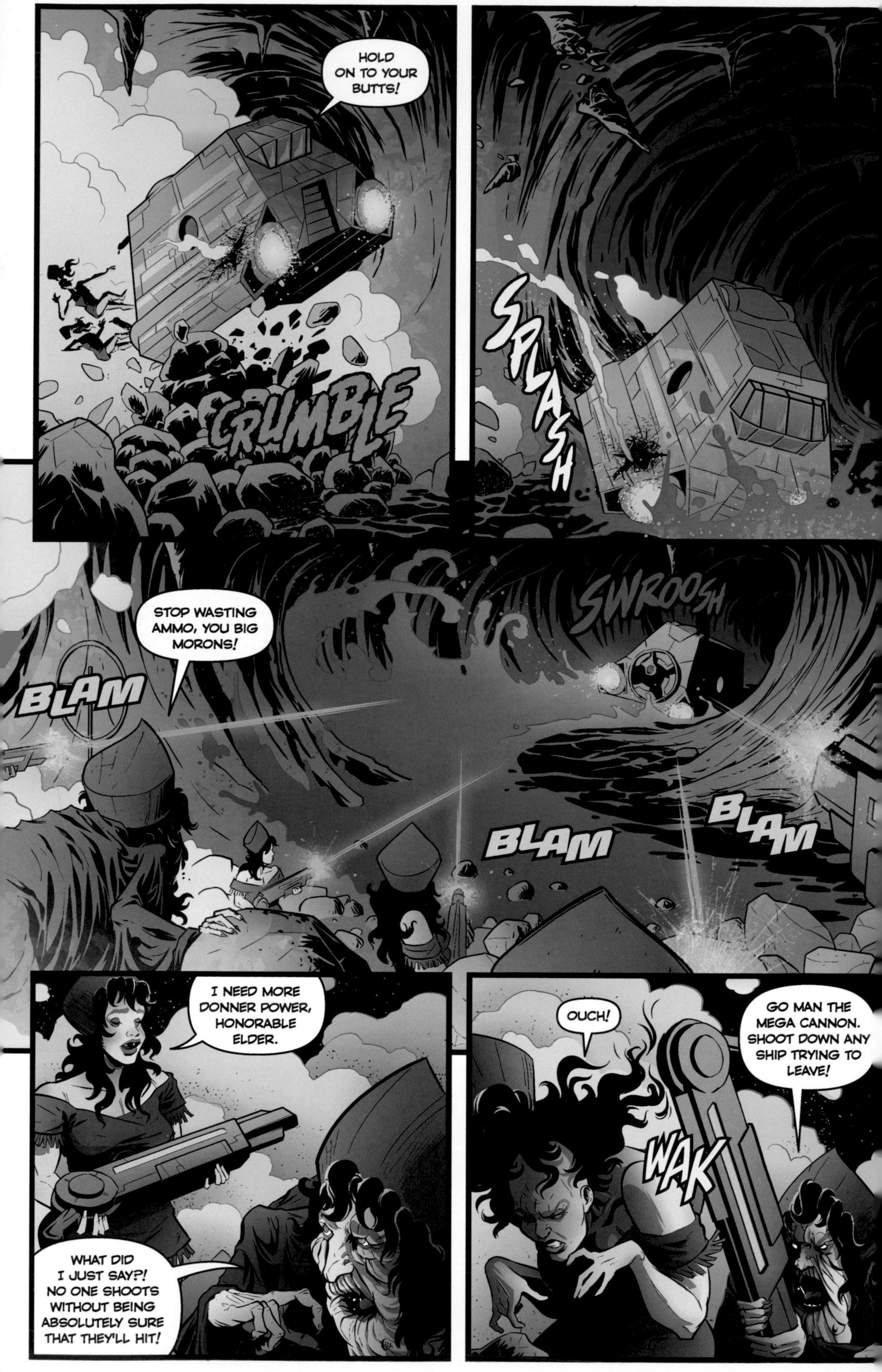
HOLD ON TO YOUR BUTTS!
CRUMBLE
SPLASH
SWROOSH
STOP WASTING AMMO, YOU BIG MORONS!
BLAM
BLAM
BLAM
I NEED MORE DONNER POWER, HONORABLE ELDER.
WHAT DID I JUST SAY?! NO ONE SHOOTS WITHOUT BEING ABSOLUTELY SURE THAT THEY'LL HIT!
OUCH!
GO MAN THE MEGA CANNON. SHOOT DOWN ANY SHIP TRYING TO LEAVE!
WAK

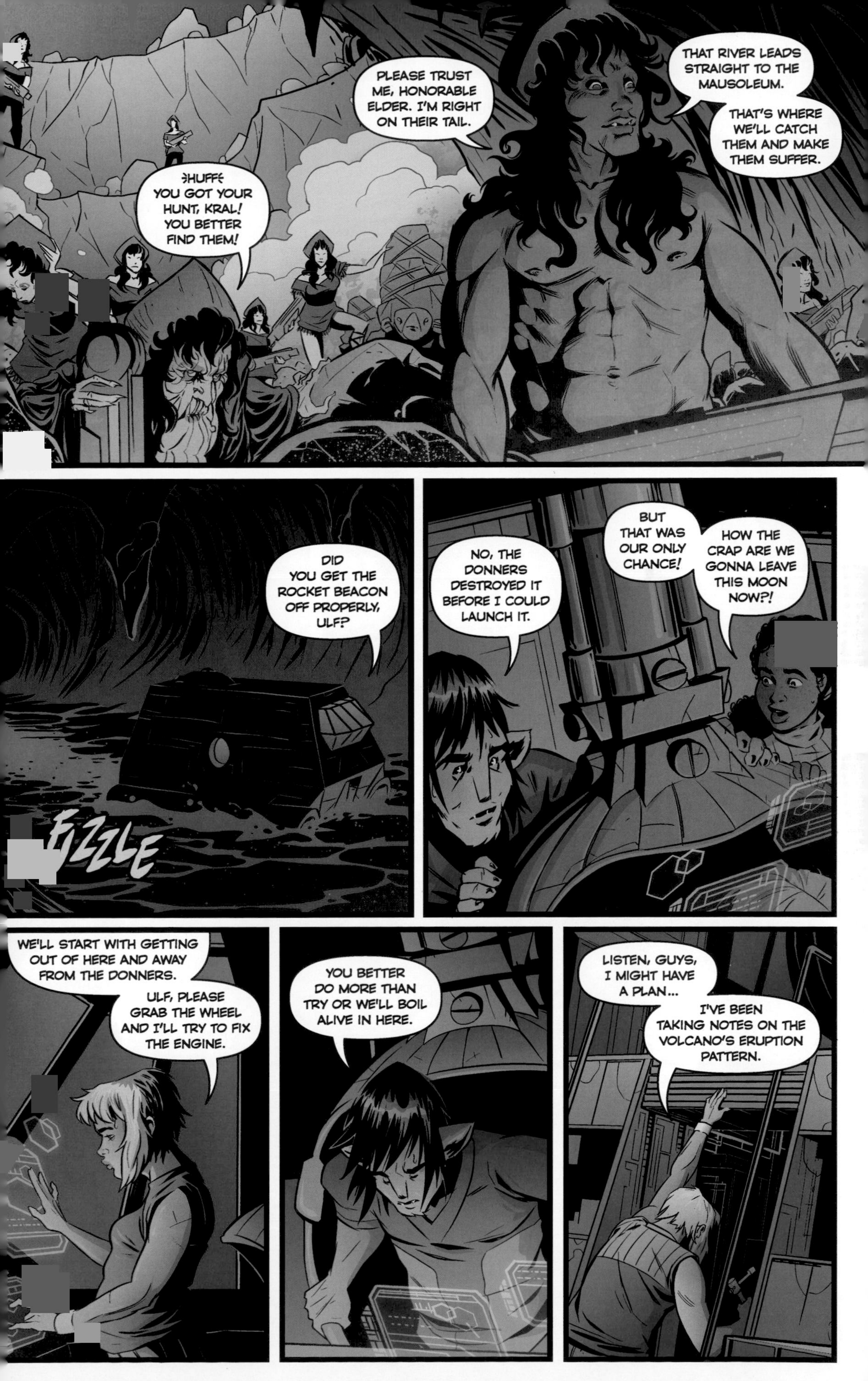
PLEASE TRUST ME, HONORABLE ELDER. I'M RIGHT ON THEIR TAIL.
THAT RIVER LEADS STRAIGHT TO THE MAUSOLEUM.
THAT'S WHERE WE'LL CATCH THEM AND MAKE THEM SUFFER.
ƎHUFFƐ YOU GOT YOUR HUNT, KRAL! YOU BETTER FIND THEM!
DID YOU GET THE ROCKET BEACON OFF PROPERLY, ULF?
FIZZLE
NO, THE DONNERS DESTROYED IT BEFORE I COULD LAUNCH IT.
BUT THAT WAS OUR ONLY CHANCE!
HOW THE CRAP ARE WE GONNA LEAVE THIS MOON NOW?!
WE'LL START WITH GETTING OUT OF HERE AND AWAY FROM THE DONNERS.
ULF, PLEASE GRAB THE WHEEL AND I'LL TRY TO FIX THE ENGINE.
YOU BETTER DO MORE THAN TRY OR WE'LL BOIL ALIVE IN HERE.
LISTEN, GUYS, I MIGHT HAVE A PLAN...
I'VE BEEN TAKING NOTES ON THE VOLCANO'S ERUPTION PATTERN.

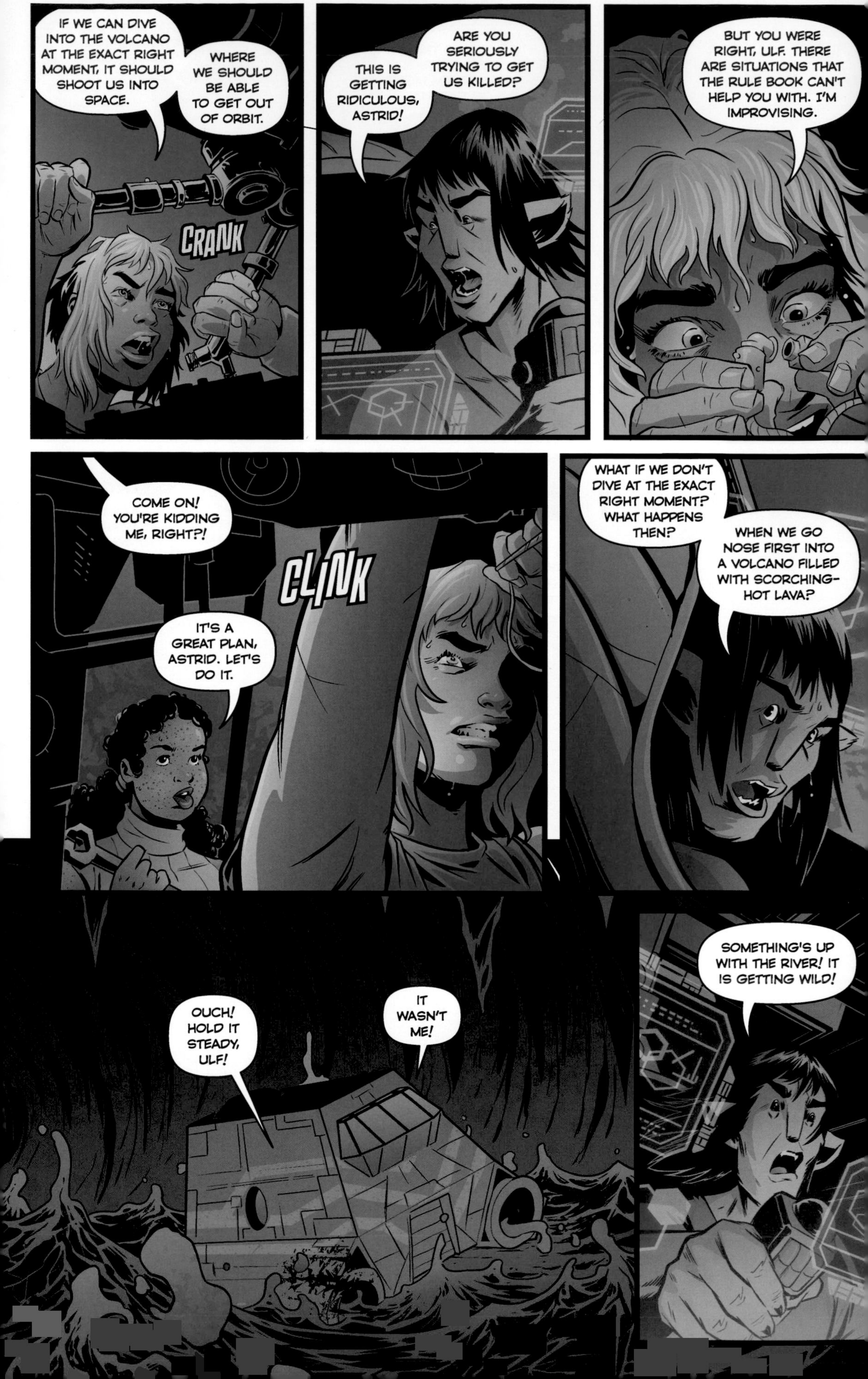
IF WE CAN DIVE INTO THE VOLCANO AT THE EXACT RIGHT MOMENT, IT SHOULD SHOOT US INTO SPACE.
WHERE WE SHOULD BE ABLE TO GET OUT OF ORBIT.
CRANK
ARE YOU SERIOUSLY TRYING TO GET US KILLED?
THIS IS GETTING RIDICULOUS, ASTRID!
BUT YOU WERE RIGHT, ULF. THERE ARE SITUATIONS THAT THE RULE BOOK CAN'T HELP YOU WITH. I'M IMPROVISING.
COME ON! YOU'RE KIDDING ME, RIGHT?!
CLINK
IT'S A GREAT PLAN, ASTRID. LET'S DO IT.
WHAT IF WE DON'T DIVE AT THE EXACT RIGHT MOMENT? WHAT HAPPENS THEN?
WHEN WE GO NOSE FIRST INTO A VOLCANO FILLED WITH SCORCHING-HOT LAVA?
OUCH! HOLD IT STEADY, ULF!
IT WASN'T ME!
SOMETHING'S UP WITH THE RIVER! IT IS GETTING WILD!

[redacted]

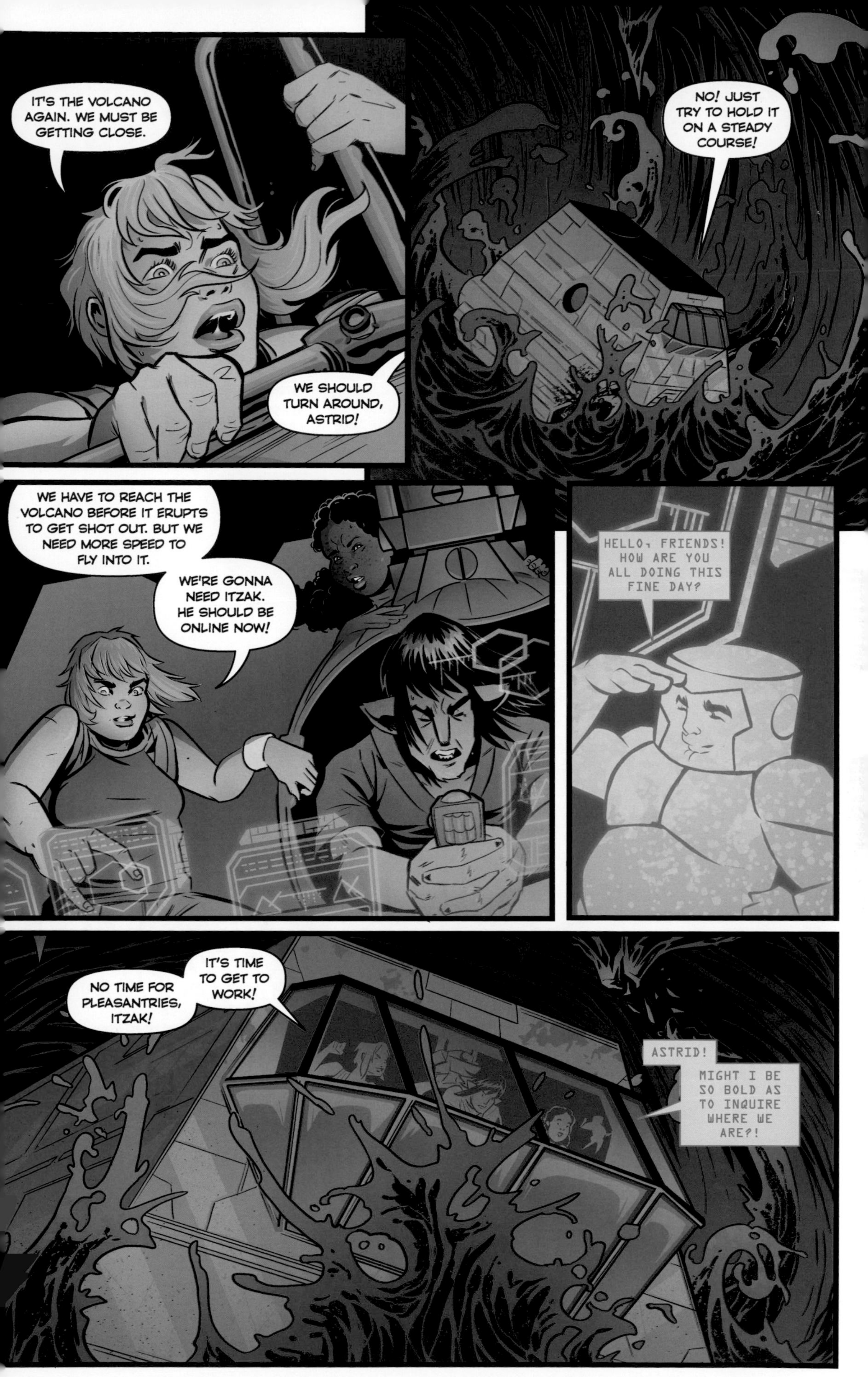
IT'S THE VOLCANO AGAIN. WE MUST BE GETTING CLOSE.
WE SHOULD TURN AROUND, ASTRID!
NO! JUST TRY TO HOLD IT ON A STEADY COURSE!
WE HAVE TO REACH THE VOLCANO BEFORE IT ERUPTS TO GET SHOT OUT. BUT WE NEED MORE SPEED TO FLY INTO IT.
WE'RE GONNA NEED ITZAK. HE SHOULD BE ONLINE NOW!
HELLO, FRIENDS! HOW ARE YOU ALL DOING THIS FINE DAY?
NO TIME FOR PLEASANTRIES, ITZAK!
IT'S TIME TO GET TO WORK!
ASTRID!
MIGHT I BE SO BOLD AS TO INQUIRE WHERE WE ARE?!

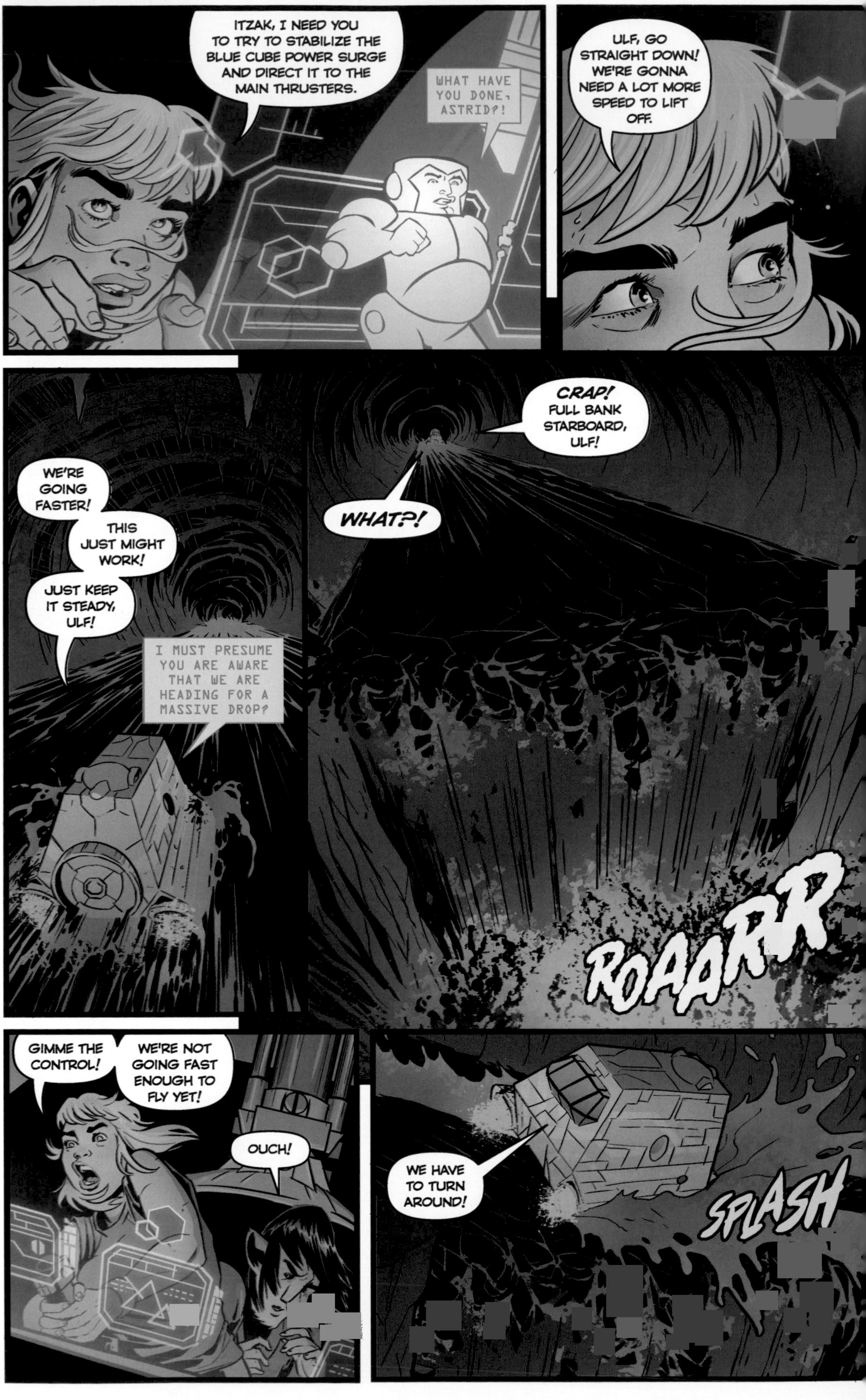
ITZAK, I NEED YOU TO TRY TO STABILIZE THE BLUE CUBE POWER SURGE AND DIRECT IT TO THE MAIN THRUSTERS.
WHAT HAVE YOU DONE, ASTRID?!
ULF, GO STRAIGHT DOWN! WE'RE GONNA NEED A LOT MORE SPEED TO LIFT OFF.
WE'RE GOING FASTER!
THIS JUST MIGHT WORK!
JUST KEEP IT STEADY, ULF!
I MUST PRESUME YOU ARE AWARE THAT WE ARE HEADING FOR A MASSIVE DROP?
CRAP! FULL BANK STARBOARD, ULF!
WHAT?!
ROAARR
GIMME THE CONTROL!
WE'RE NOT GOING FAST ENOUGH TO FLY YET!
OUCH!
WE HAVE TO TURN AROUND!
SPLASH

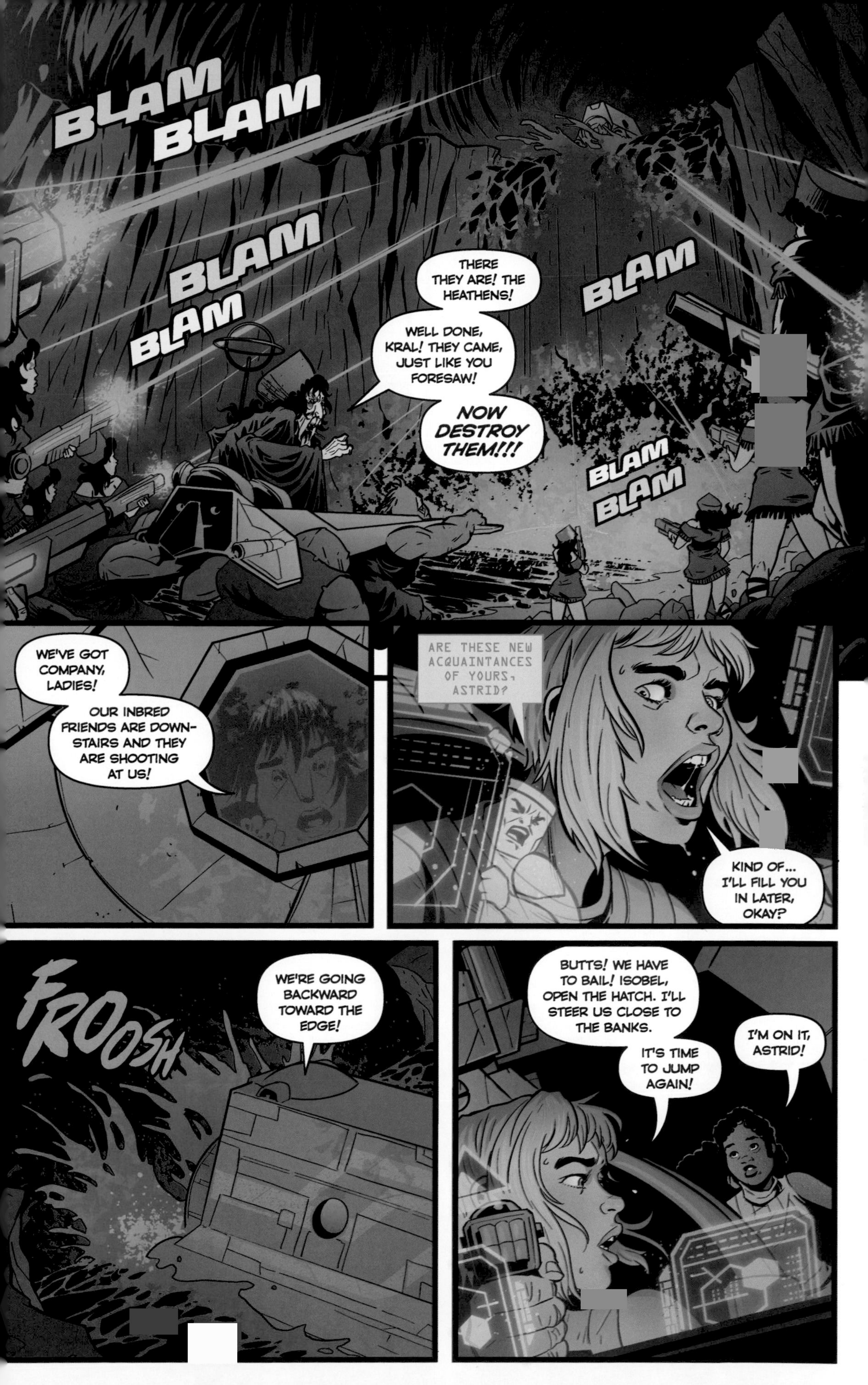
BLAM BLAM
BLAM BLAM
THERE THEY ARE! THE HEATHENS!
WELL DONE, KRAL! THEY CAME, JUST LIKE YOU FORESAW!
NOW DESTROY THEM!!!
BLAM
BLAM BLAM
WE'VE GOT COMPANY, LADIES!
OUR INBRED FRIENDS ARE DOWN-STAIRS AND THEY ARE SHOOTING AT US!
ARE THESE NEW ACQUAINTANCES OF YOURS, ASTRID?
KIND OF... I'LL FILL YOU IN LATER, OKAY?
FROOSH
WE'RE GOING BACKWARD TOWARD THE EDGE!
BUTTS! WE HAVE TO BAIL! ISOBEL, OPEN THE HATCH. I'LL STEER US CLOSE TO THE BANKS.
IT'S TIME TO JUMP AGAIN!
I'M ON IT, ASTRID!

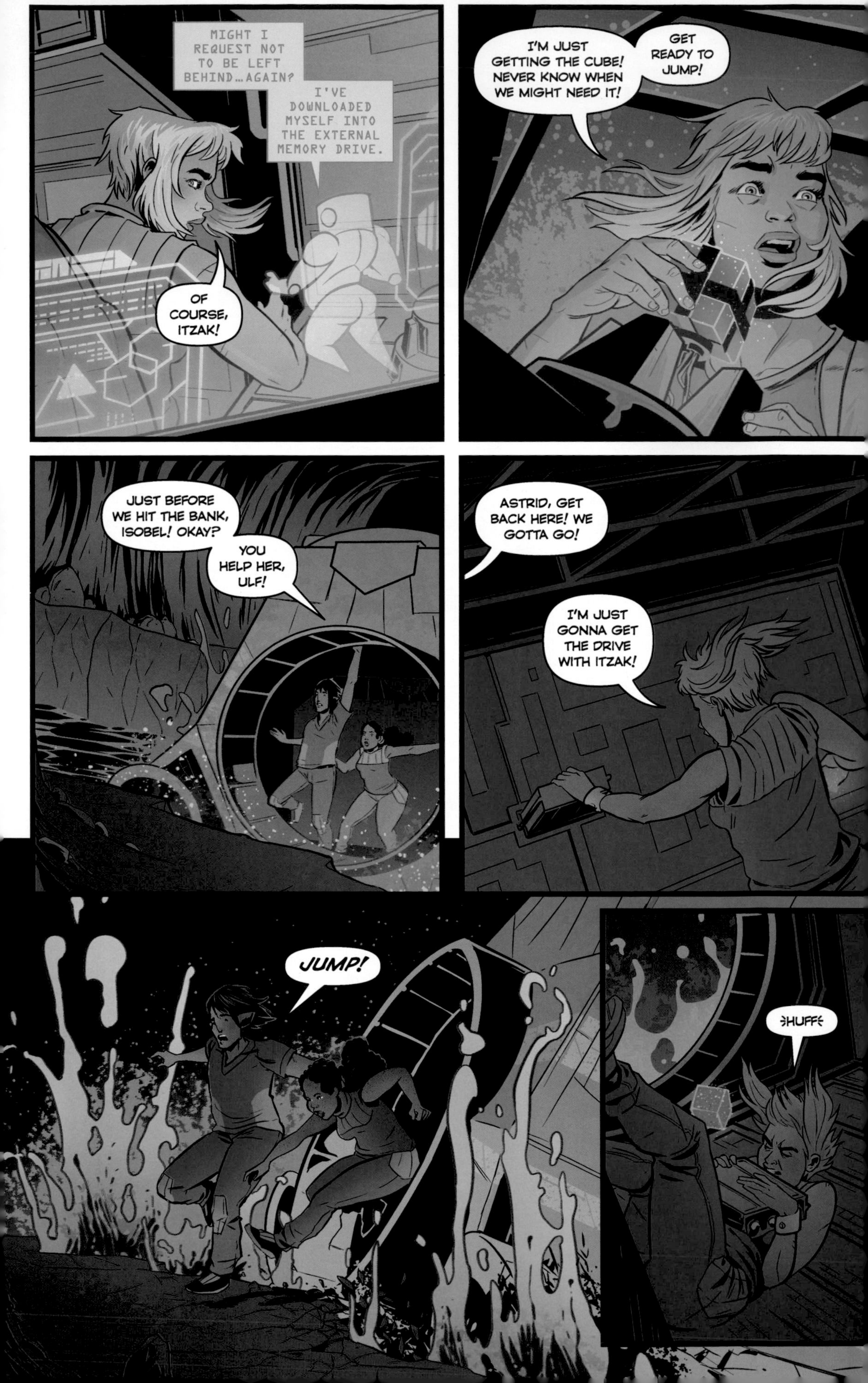
MIGHT I REQUEST NOT TO BE LEFT BEHIND...AGAIN?
I'VE DOWNLOADED MYSELF INTO THE EXTERNAL MEMORY DRIVE.
OF COURSE, ITZAK!
I'M JUST GETTING THE CUBE! NEVER KNOW WHEN WE MIGHT NEED IT!
GET READY TO JUMP!
JUST BEFORE WE HIT THE BANK, ISOBEL! OKAY?
YOU HELP HER, ULF!
ASTRID, GET BACK HERE! WE GOTTA GO!
I'M JUST GONNA GET THE DRIVE WITH ITZAK!
JUMP!
HUFF

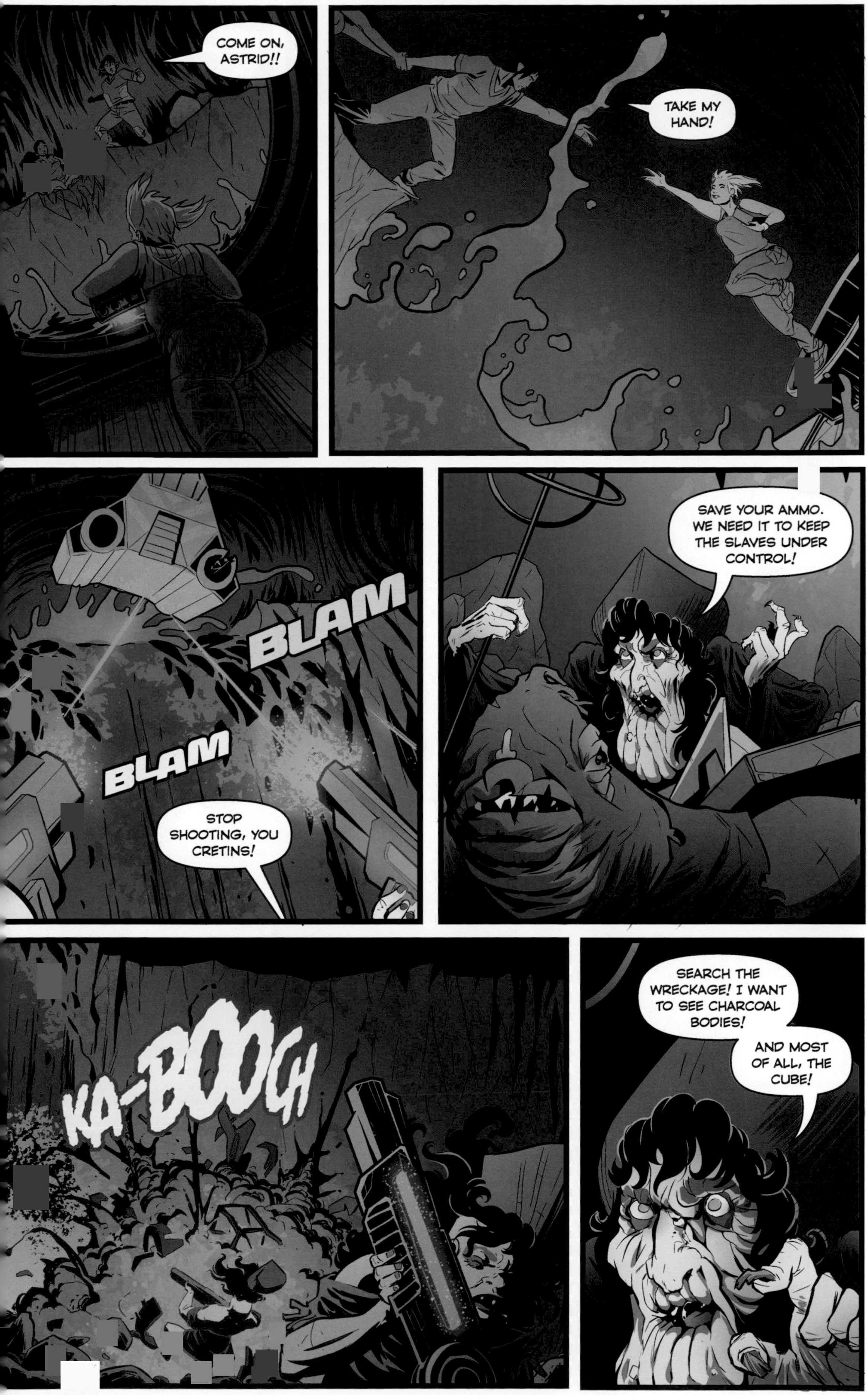
COME ON, ASTRID!!
TAKE MY HAND!
BLAM
BLAM
STOP SHOOTING, YOU CRETINS!
SAVE YOUR AMMO. WE NEED IT TO KEEP THE SLAVES UNDER CONTROL!
KA-BOOCH
SEARCH THE WRECKAGE! I WANT TO SEE CHARCOAL BODIES!
AND MOST OF ALL, THE CUBE!

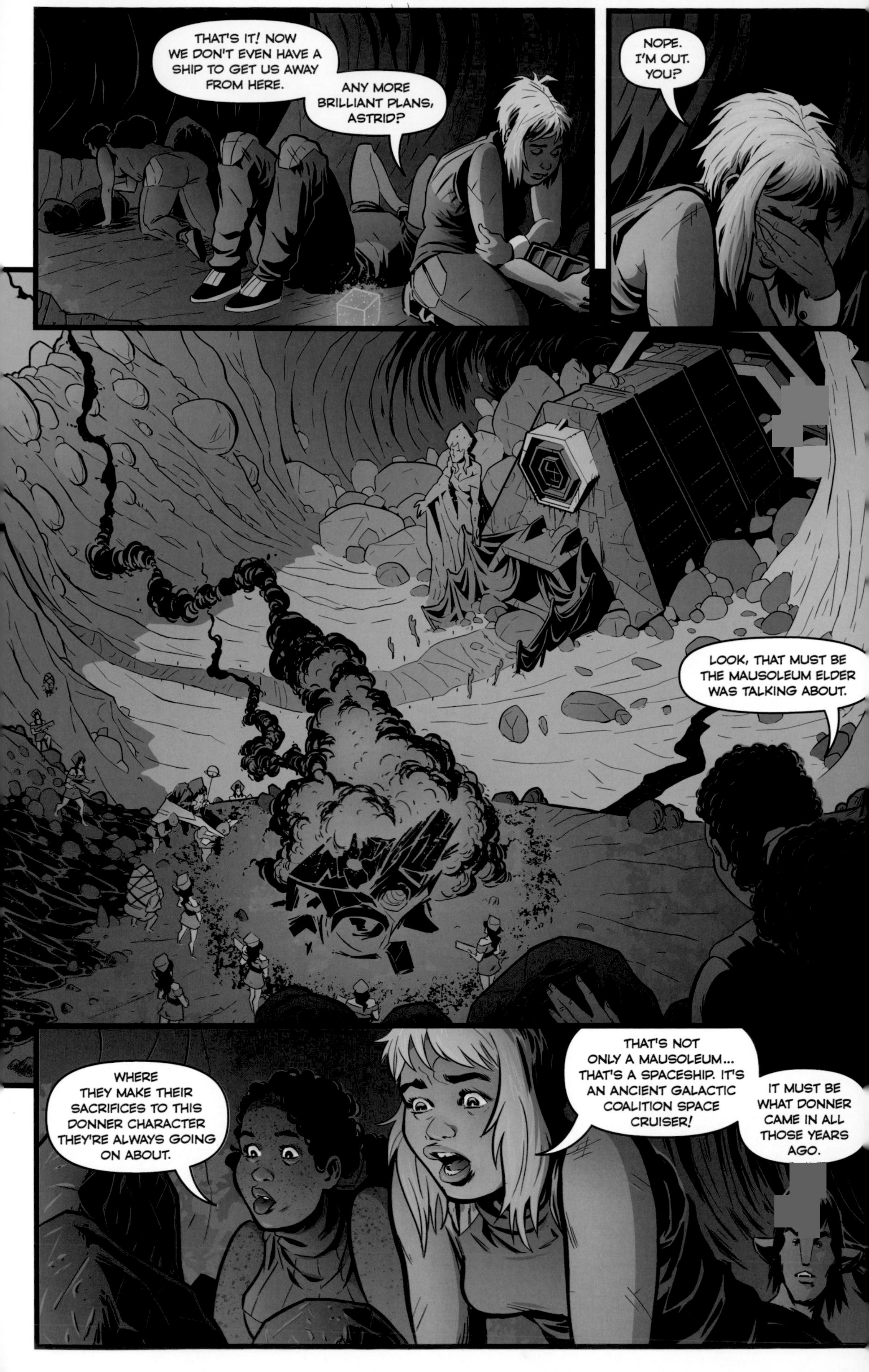
THAT'S IT! NOW WE DON'T EVEN HAVE A SHIP TO GET US AWAY FROM HERE.
ANY MORE BRILLIANT PLANS, ASTRID?
NOPE. I'M OUT. YOU?
LOOK, THAT MUST BE THE MAUSOLEUM ELDER WAS TALKING ABOUT.
WHERE THEY MAKE THEIR SACRIFICES TO THIS DONNER CHARACTER THEY'RE ALWAYS GOING ON ABOUT.
THAT'S NOT ONLY A MAUSOLEUM... THAT'S A SPACESHIP. IT'S AN ANCIENT GALACTIC COALITION SPACE CRUISER!
IT MUST BE WHAT DONNER CAME IN ALL THOSE YEARS AGO.

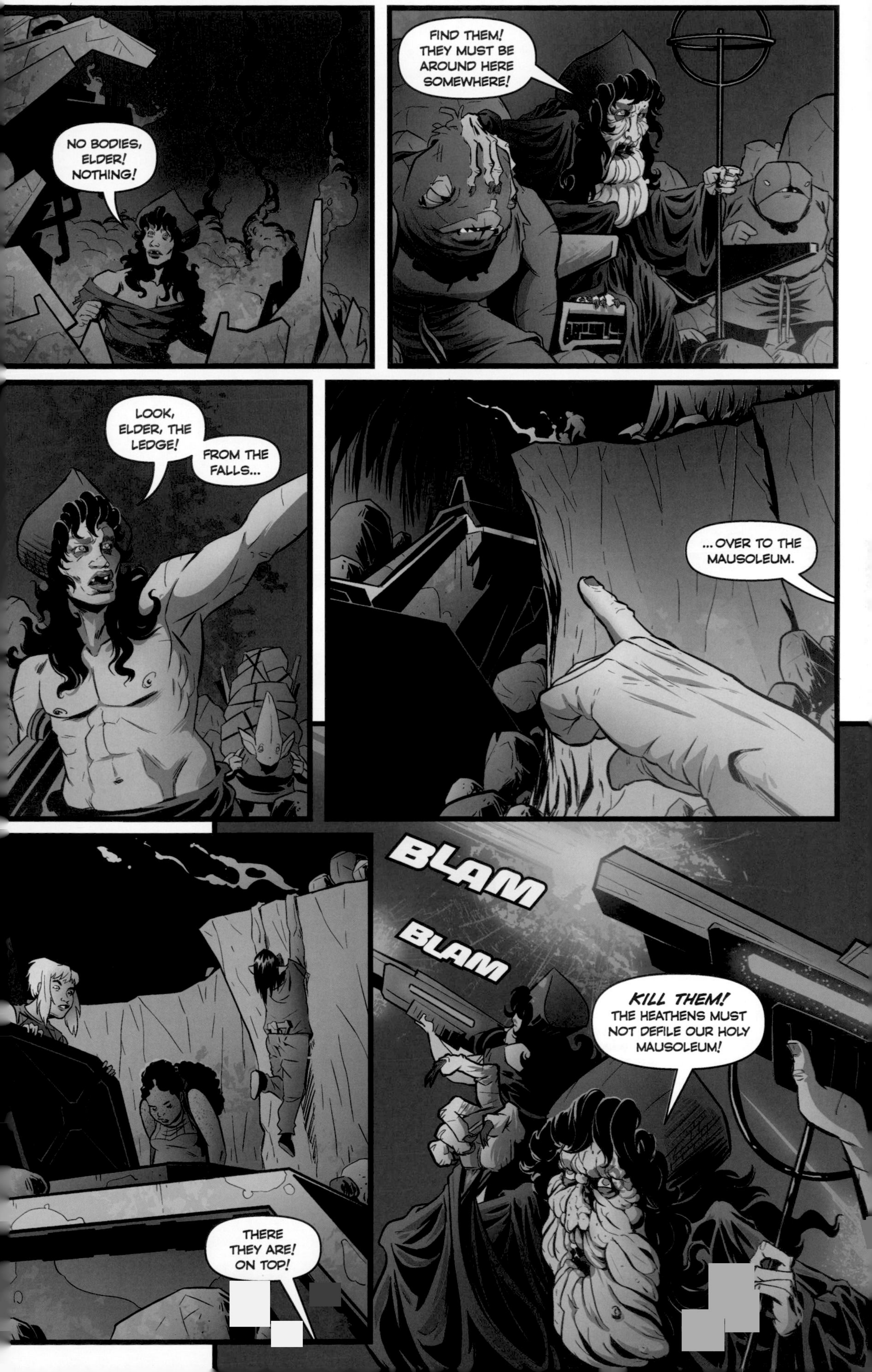
NO BODIES, ELDER! NOTHING!
FIND THEM! THEY MUST BE AROUND HERE SOMEWHERE!
LOOK, ELDER, THE LEDGE!
FROM THE FALLS...
...OVER TO THE MAUSOLEUM.
THERE THEY ARE! ON TOP!
BLAM
BLAM
KILL THEM! THE HEATHENS MUST NOT DEFILE OUR HOLY MAUSOLEUM!

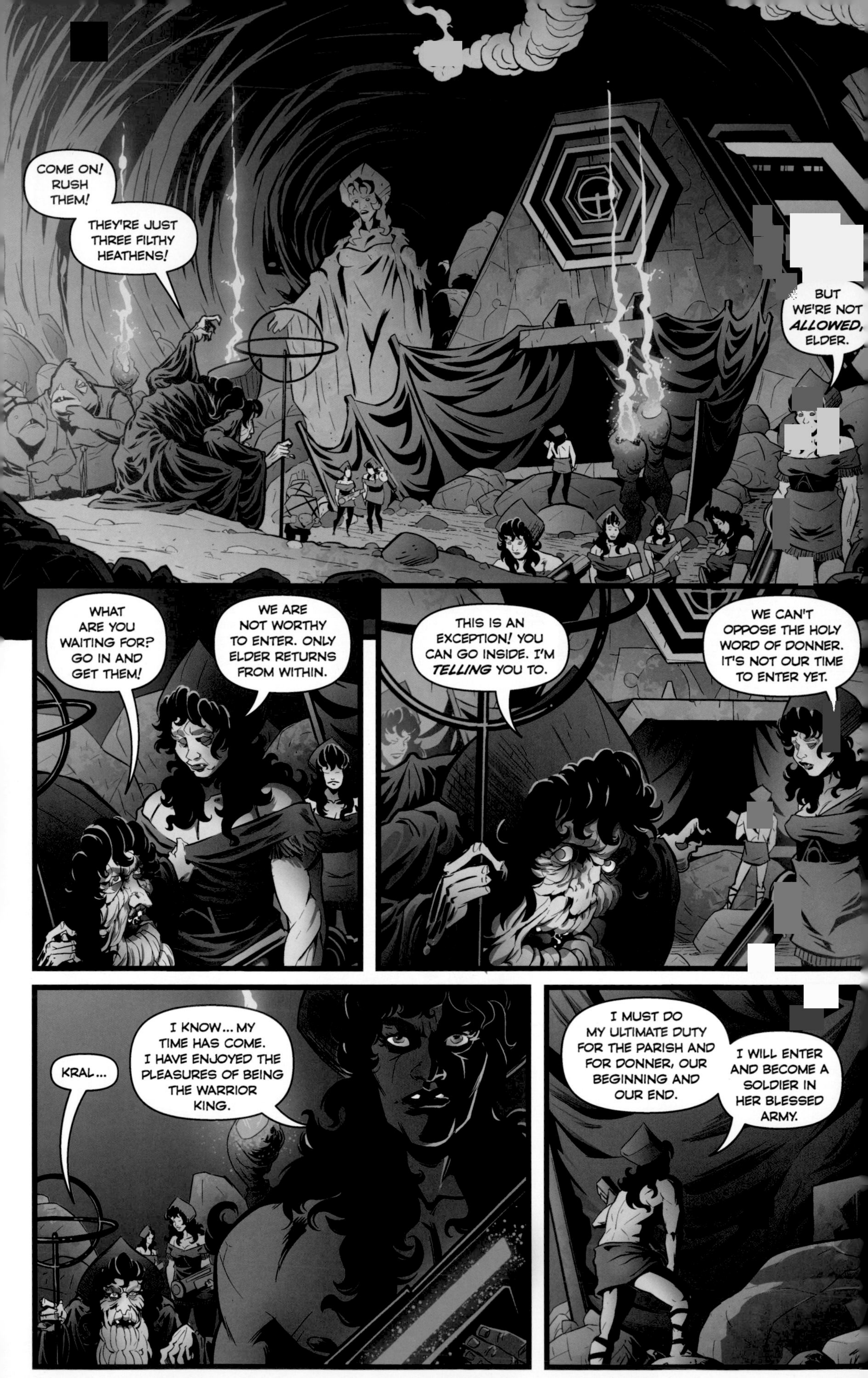
COME ON! RUSH THEM!
THEY'RE JUST THREE FILTHY HEATHENS!
BUT WE'RE NOT ALLOWED, ELDER.
WHAT ARE YOU WAITING FOR? GO IN AND GET THEM!
WE ARE NOT WORTHY TO ENTER. ONLY ELDER RETURNS FROM WITHIN.
THIS IS AN EXCEPTION! YOU CAN GO INSIDE. I'M TELLING YOU TO.
WE CAN'T OPPOSE THE HOLY WORD OF DONNER. IT'S NOT OUR TIME TO ENTER YET.
KRAL...
I KNOW... MY TIME HAS COME. I HAVE ENJOYED THE PLEASURES OF BEING THE WARRIOR KING.
I MUST DO MY ULTIMATE DUTY FOR THE PARISH AND FOR DONNER, OUR BEGINNING AND OUR END.
I WILL ENTER AND BECOME A SOLDIER IN HER BLESSED ARMY.

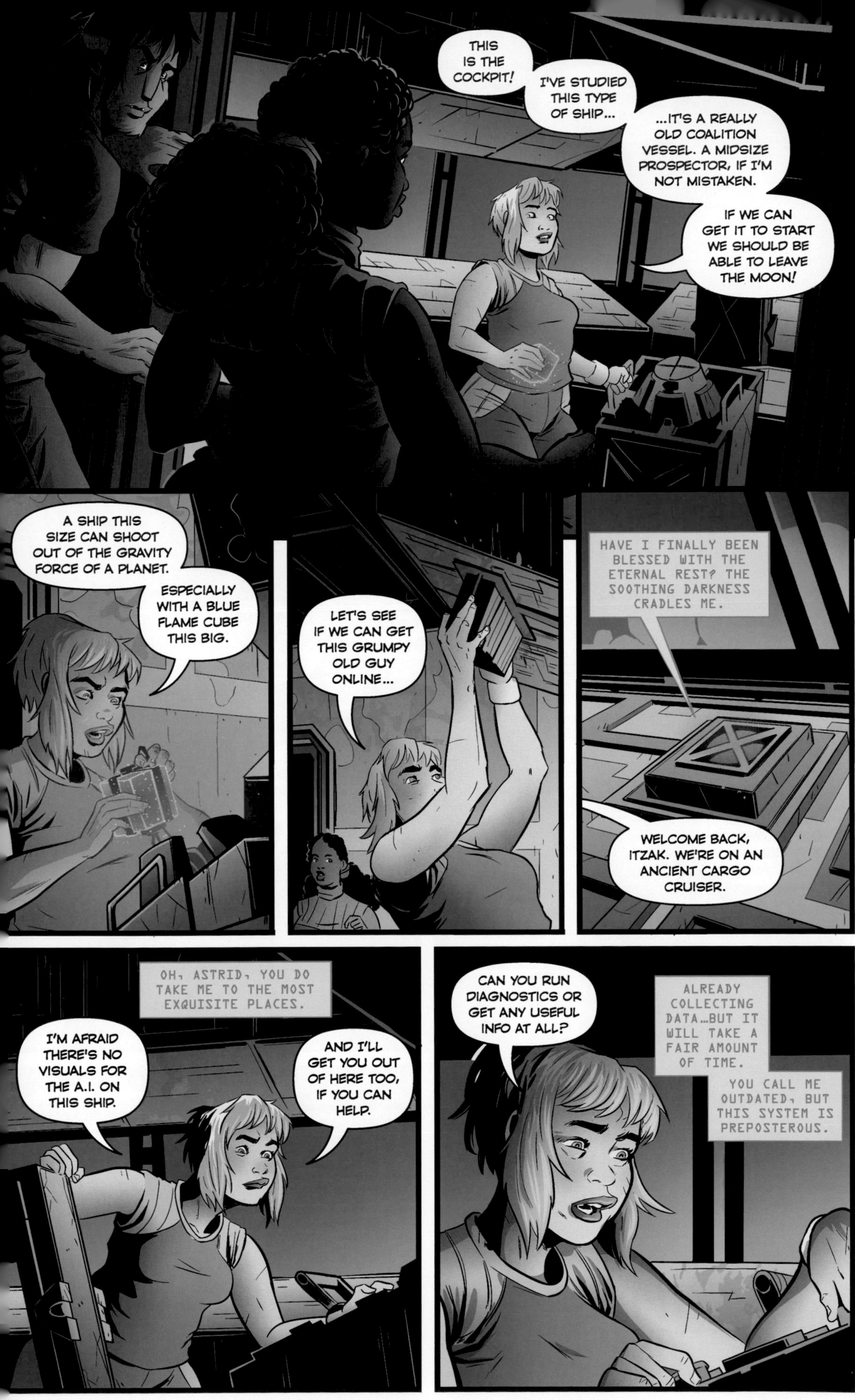
THIS IS THE COCKPIT!
I'VE STUDIED THIS TYPE OF SHIP...
...IT'S A REALLY OLD COALITION VESSEL. A MIDSIZE PROSPECTOR, IF I'M NOT MISTAKEN.
IF WE CAN GET IT TO START WE SHOULD BE ABLE TO LEAVE THE MOON!
A SHIP THIS SIZE CAN SHOOT OUT OF THE GRAVITY FORCE OF A PLANET.
ESPECIALLY WITH A BLUE FLAME CUBE THIS BIG.
LET'S SEE IF WE CAN GET THIS GRUMPY OLD GUY ONLINE...
HAVE I FINALLY BEEN BLESSED WITH THE ETERNAL REST? THE SOOTHING DARKNESS CRADLES ME.
WELCOME BACK, ITZAK. WE'RE ON AN ANCIENT CARGO CRUISER.
OH, ASTRID, YOU DO TAKE ME TO THE MOST EXQUISITE PLACES.
I'M AFRAID THERE'S NO VISUALS FOR THE A.I. ON THIS SHIP.
AND I'LL GET YOU OUT OF HERE TOO, IF YOU CAN HELP.
CAN YOU RUN DIAGNOSTICS OR GET ANY USEFUL INFO AT ALL?
ALREADY COLLECTING DATA...BUT IT WILL TAKE A FAIR AMOUNT OF TIME.
YOU CALL ME OUTDATED, BUT THIS SYSTEM IS PREPOSTEROUS.

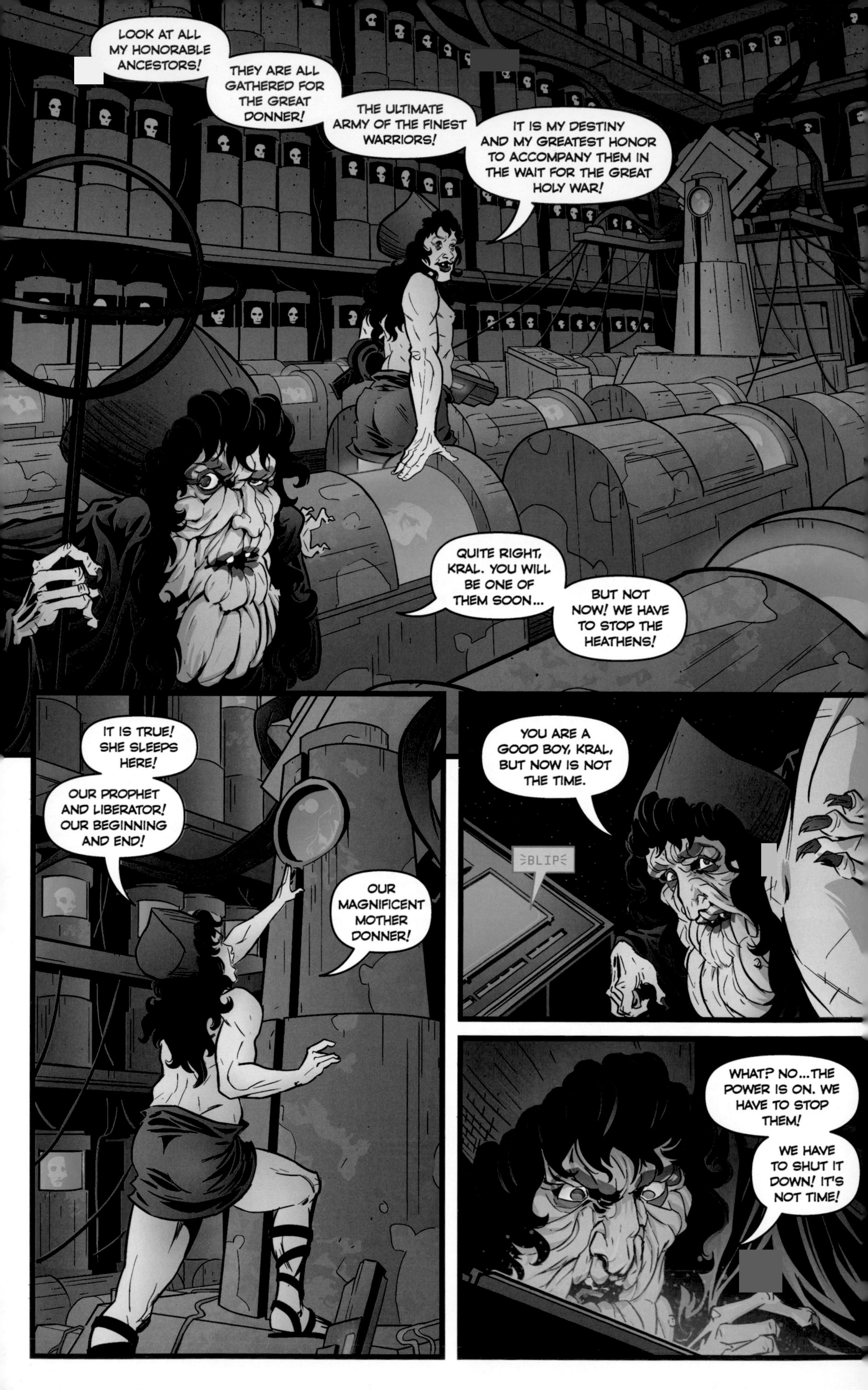

LOOK AT ALL MY HONORABLE ANCESTORS!
THEY ARE ALL GATHERED FOR THE GREAT DONNER!
THE ULTIMATE ARMY OF THE FINEST WARRIORS!
IT IS MY DESTINY AND MY GREATEST HONOR TO ACCOMPANY THEM IN THE WAIT FOR THE GREAT HOLY WAR!
QUITE RIGHT, KRAL. YOU WILL BE ONE OF THEM SOON...
BUT NOT NOW! WE HAVE TO STOP THE HEATHENS!
IT IS TRUE! SHE SLEEPS HERE!
OUR PROPHET AND LIBERATOR! OUR BEGINNING AND END!
OUR MAGNIFICENT MOTHER DONNER!
YOU ARE A GOOD BOY, KRAL, BUT NOW IS NOT THE TIME.
BLIP
WHAT? NO...THE POWER IS ON. WE HAVE TO STOP THEM!
WE HAVE TO SHUT IT DOWN! IT'S NOT TIME!

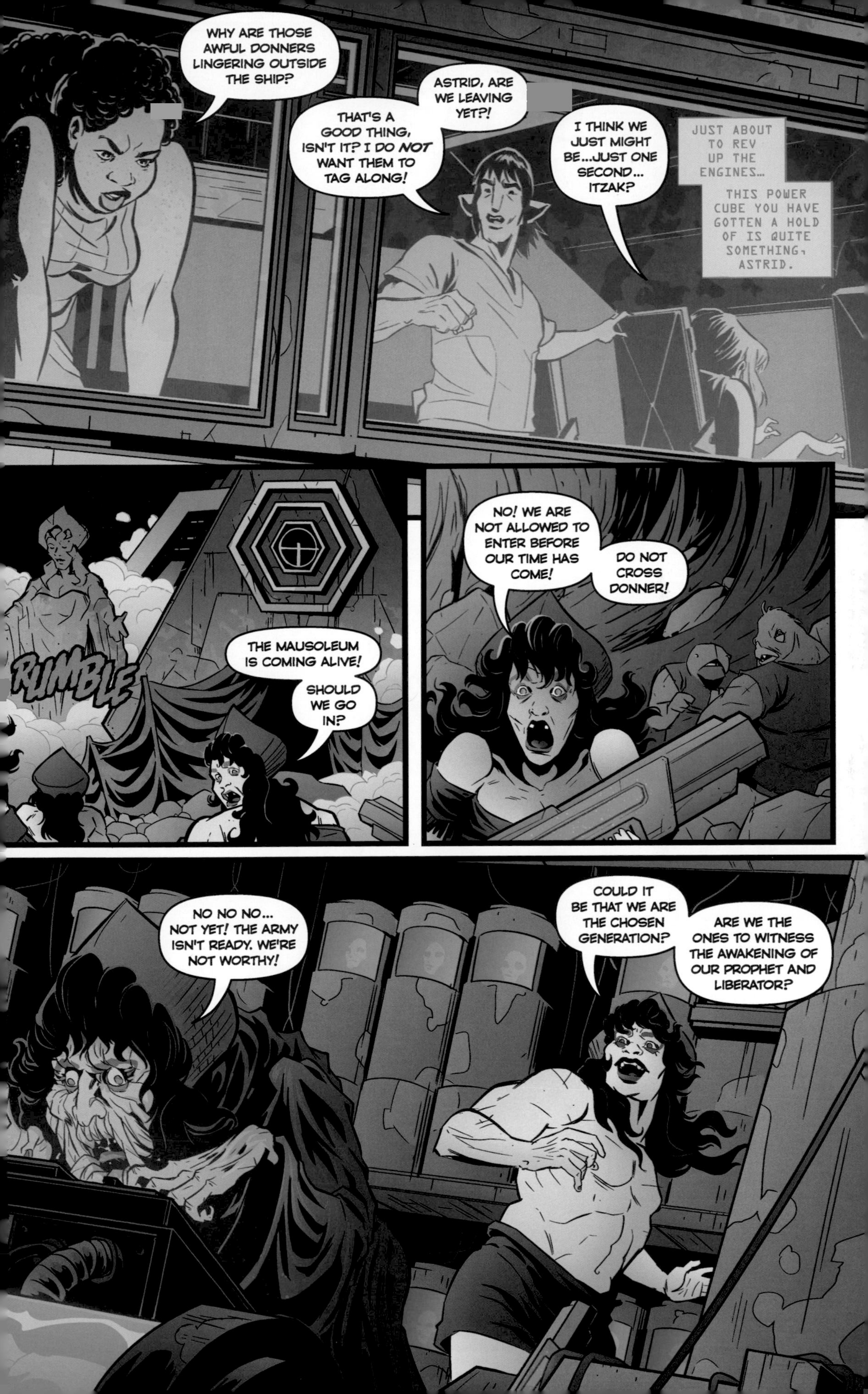
WHY ARE THOSE AWFUL DONNERS LINGERING OUTSIDE THE SHIP?
ASTRID, ARE WE LEAVING YET?!
THAT'S A GOOD THING, ISN'T IT? I DO *NOT* WANT THEM TO TAG ALONG!
I THINK WE JUST MIGHT BE...JUST ONE SECOND... ITZAK?
JUST ABOUT TO REV UP THE ENGINES...
THIS POWER CUBE YOU HAVE GOTTEN A HOLD OF IS QUITE SOMETHING, ASTRID.
RUMBLE
THE MAUSOLEUM IS COMING ALIVE!
SHOULD WE GO IN?
NO! WE ARE NOT ALLOWED TO ENTER BEFORE OUR TIME HAS COME!
DO NOT CROSS DONNER!
NO NO NO... NOT YET! THE ARMY ISN'T READY. WE'RE NOT WORTHY!
COULD IT BE THAT WE ARE THE CHOSEN GENERATION?
ARE WE THE ONES TO WITNESS THE AWAKENING OF OUR PROPHET AND LIBERATOR?

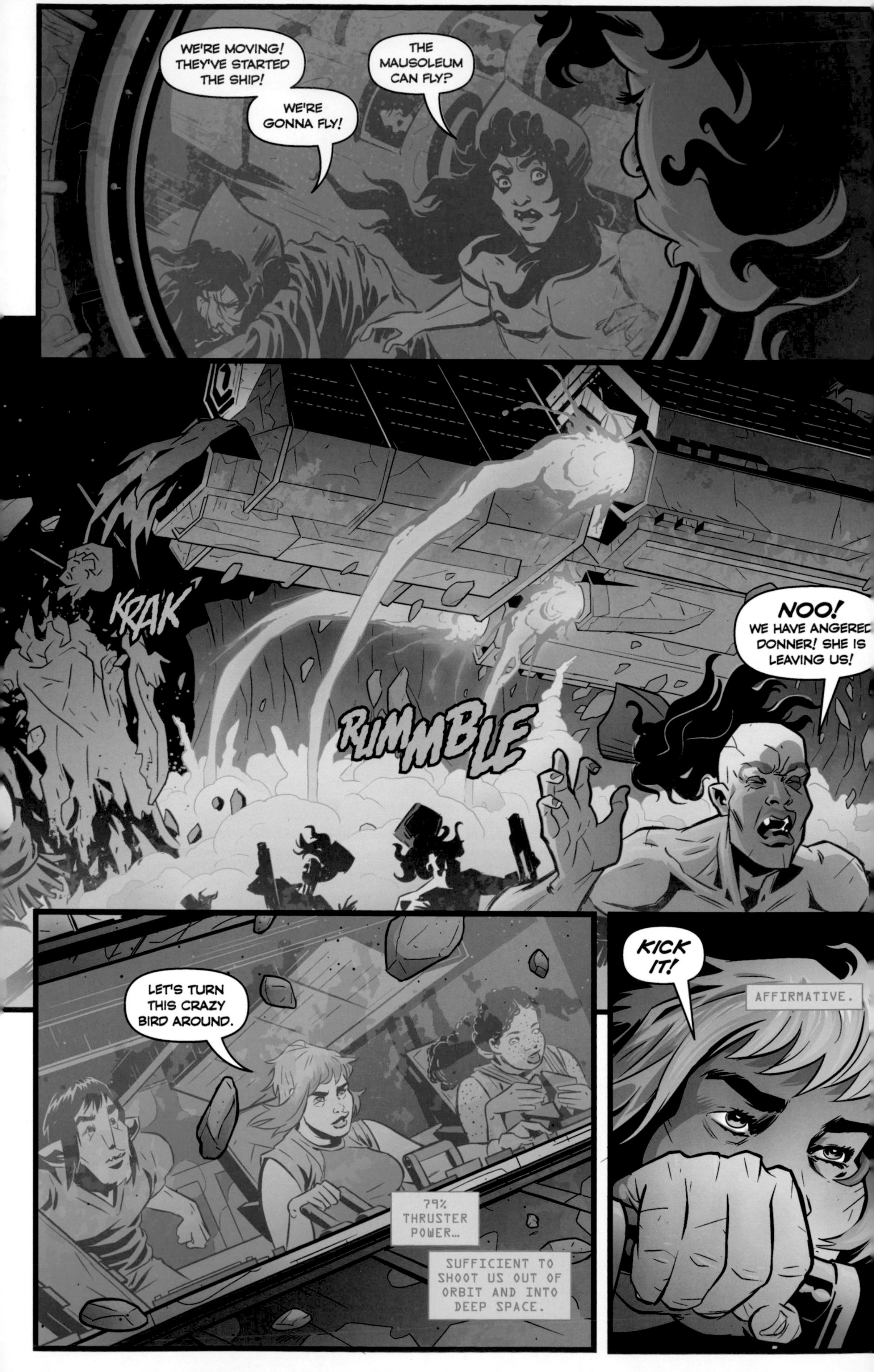
WE'RE MOVING! THEY'VE STARTED THE SHIP!
WE'RE GONNA FLY!
THE MAUSOLEUM CAN FLY?
KRAK
RUMMBLE
NOO! WE HAVE ANGERED DONNER! SHE IS LEAVING US!
LET'S TURN THIS CRAZY BIRD AROUND.
79% THRUSTER POWER...
SUFFICIENT TO SHOOT US OUT OF ORBIT AND INTO DEEP SPACE.
KICK IT!
AFFIRMATIVE.

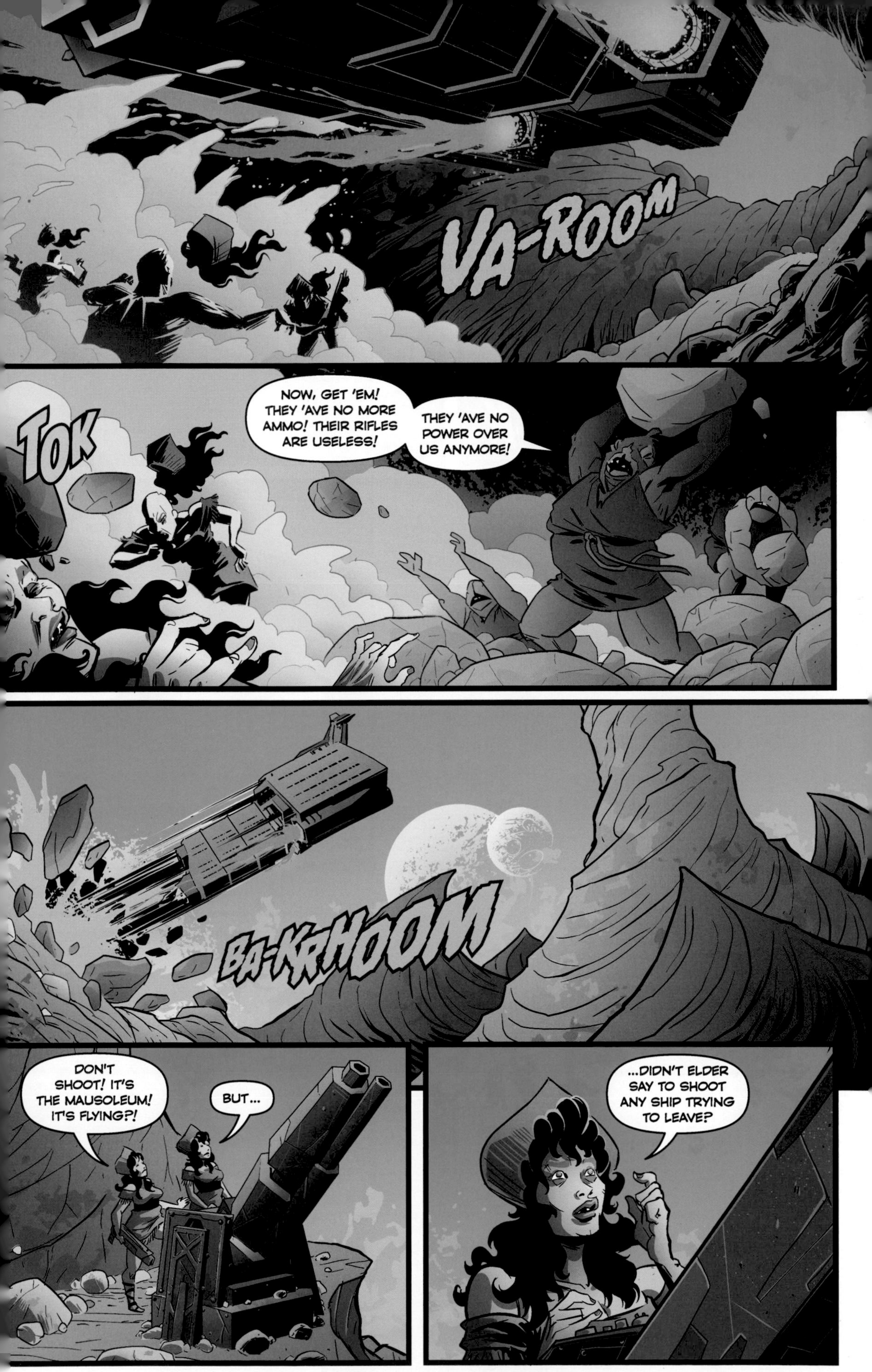
VA-ROOM
TOK
NOW, GET 'EM! THEY 'AVE NO MORE AMMO! THEIR RIFLES ARE USELESS!
THEY 'AVE NO POWER OVER US ANYMORE!
BA-KRHOOM
DON'T SHOOT! IT'S THE MAUSOLEUM! IT'S FLYING?!
BUT...
...DIDN'T ELDER SAY TO SHOOT ANY SHIP TRYING TO LEAVE?

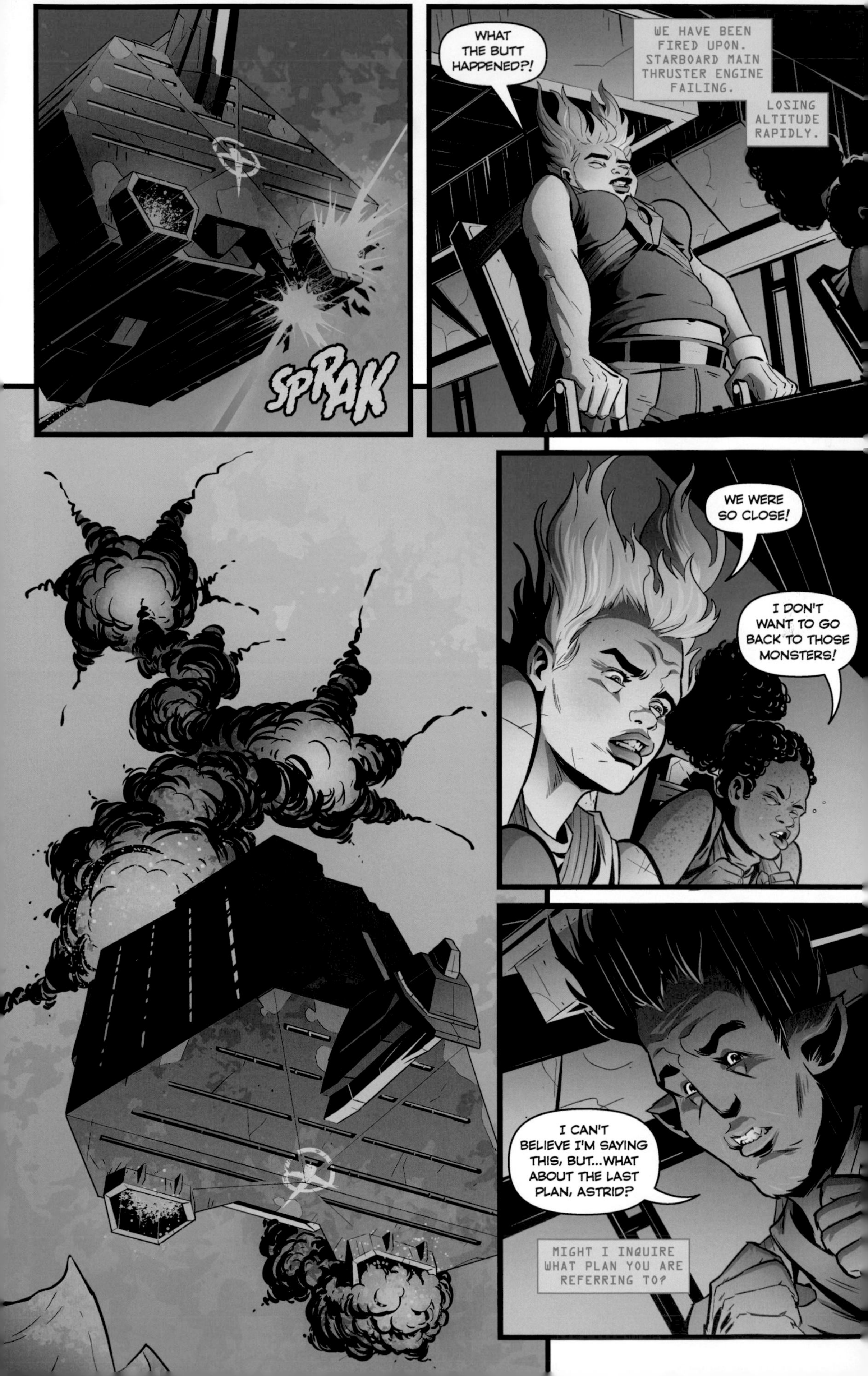
SPRAK
WHAT THE BUTT HAPPENED?!
WE HAVE BEEN FIRED UPON. STARBOARD MAIN THRUSTER ENGINE FAILING.
LOSING ALTITUDE RAPIDLY.
WE WERE SO CLOSE!
I DON'T WANT TO GO BACK TO THOSE MONSTERS!
I CAN'T BELIEVE I'M SAYING THIS, BUT...WHAT ABOUT THE LAST PLAN, ASTRID?
MIGHT I INQUIRE WHAT PLAN YOU ARE REFERRING TO?

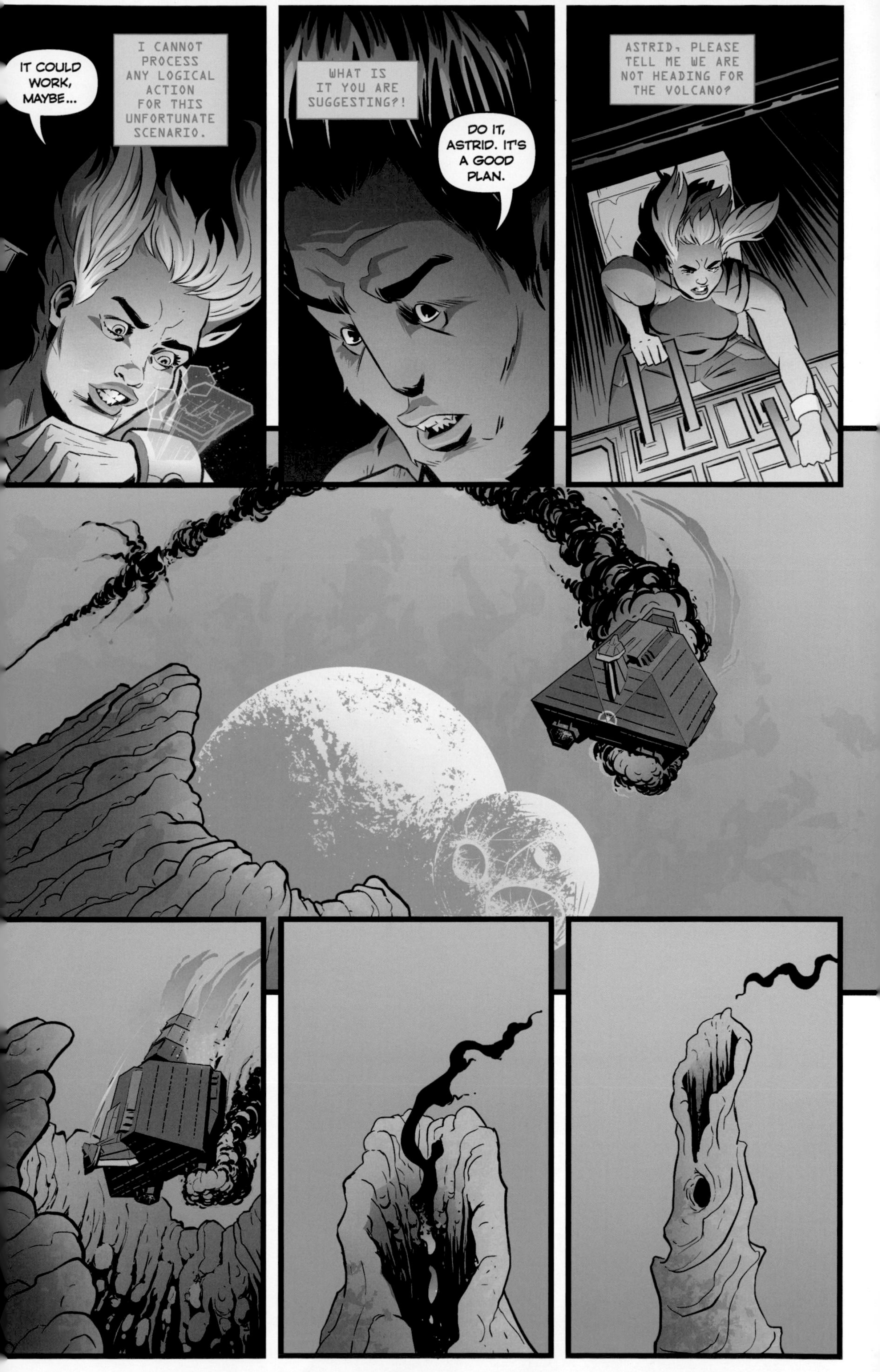
IT COULD WORK, MAYBE...
I CANNOT PROCESS ANY LOGICAL ACTION FOR THIS UNFORTUNATE SCENARIO.
WHAT IS IT YOU ARE SUGGESTING?!
DO IT, ASTRID. IT'S A GOOD PLAN.
ASTRID, PLEASE TELL ME WE ARE NOT HEADING FOR THE VOLCANO?

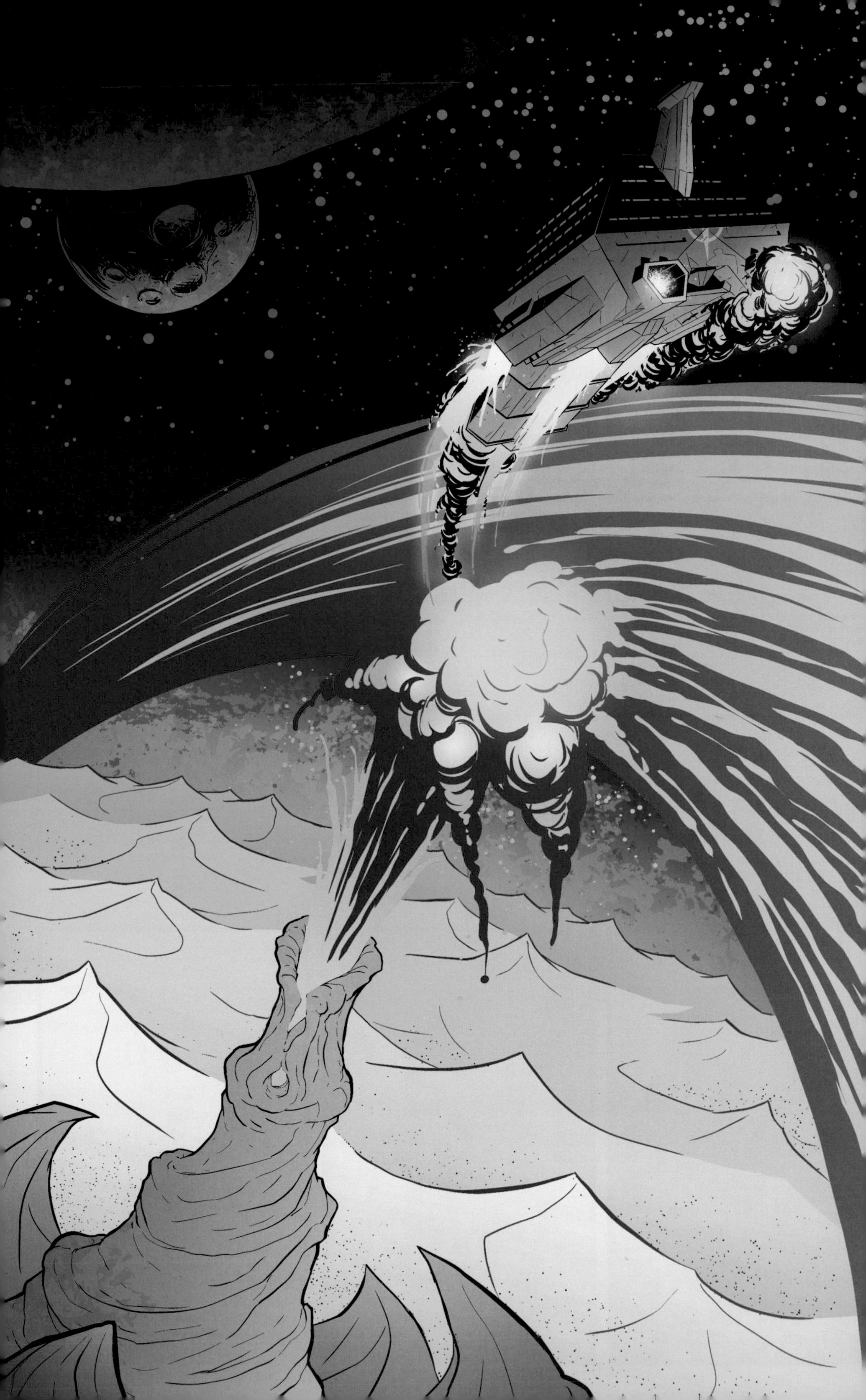

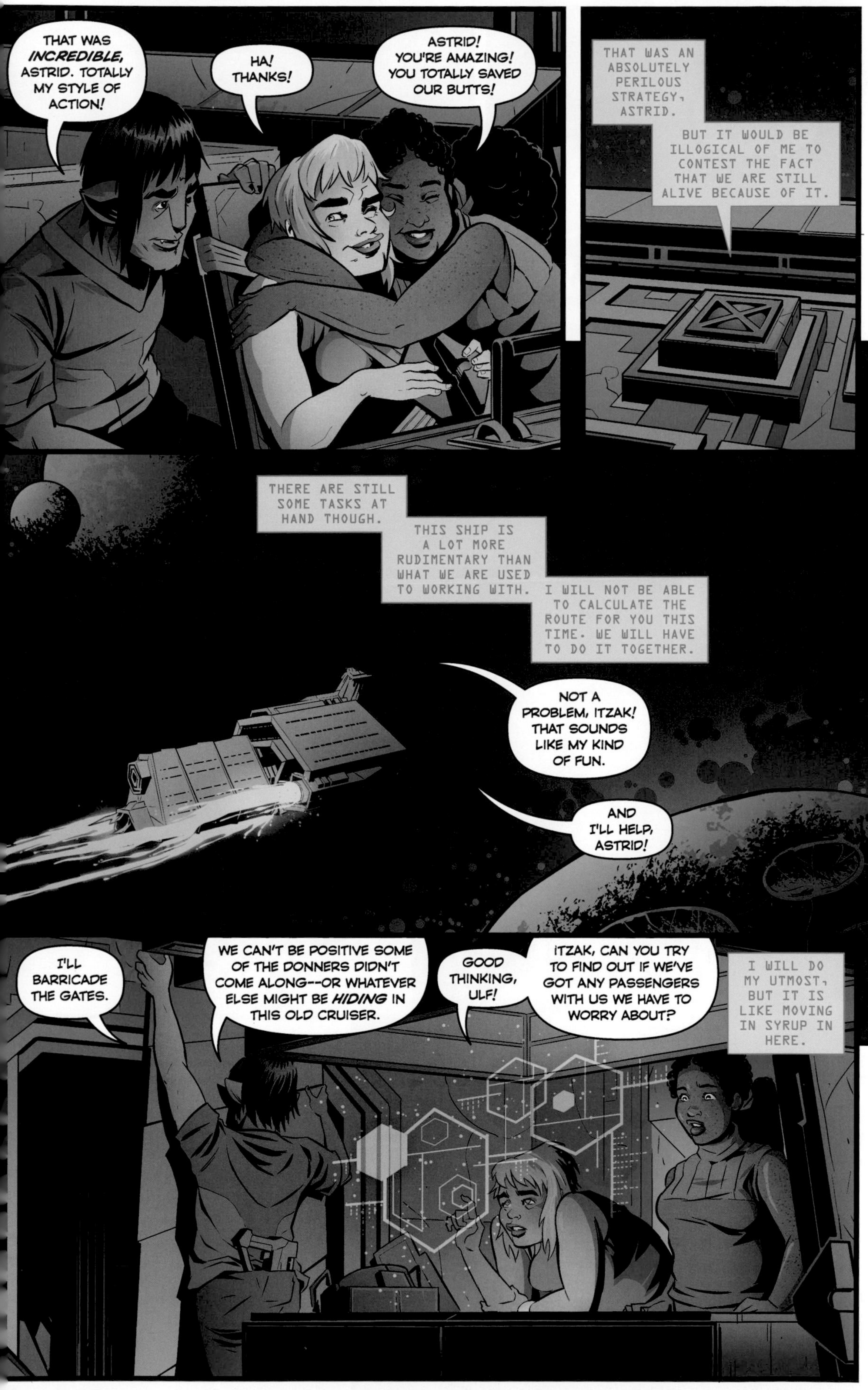
THAT WAS *INCREDIBLE,* ASTRID. TOTALLY MY STYLE OF ACTION!
HA! THANKS!
ASTRID! YOU'RE AMAZING! YOU TOTALLY SAVED OUR BUTTS!
THAT WAS AN ABSOLUTELY PERILOUS STRATEGY, ASTRID.
BUT IT WOULD BE ILLOGICAL OF ME TO CONTEST THE FACT THAT WE ARE STILL ALIVE BECAUSE OF IT.
THERE ARE STILL SOME TASKS AT HAND THOUGH.
THIS SHIP IS A LOT MORE RUDIMENTARY THAN WHAT WE ARE USED TO WORKING WITH.
I WILL NOT BE ABLE TO CALCULATE THE ROUTE FOR YOU THIS TIME. WE WILL HAVE TO DO IT TOGETHER.
NOT A PROBLEM, ITZAK! THAT SOUNDS LIKE MY KIND OF FUN.
AND I'LL HELP, ASTRID!
I'LL BARRICADE THE GATES.
WE CAN'T BE POSITIVE SOME OF THE DONNERS DIDN'T COME ALONG--OR WHATEVER ELSE MIGHT BE *HIDING* IN THIS OLD CRUISER.
GOOD THINKING, ULF!
ITZAK, CAN YOU TRY TO FIND OUT IF WE'VE GOT ANY PASSENGERS WITH US WE HAVE TO WORRY ABOUT?
I WILL DO MY UTMOST, BUT IT IS LIKE MOVING IN SYRUP IN HERE.

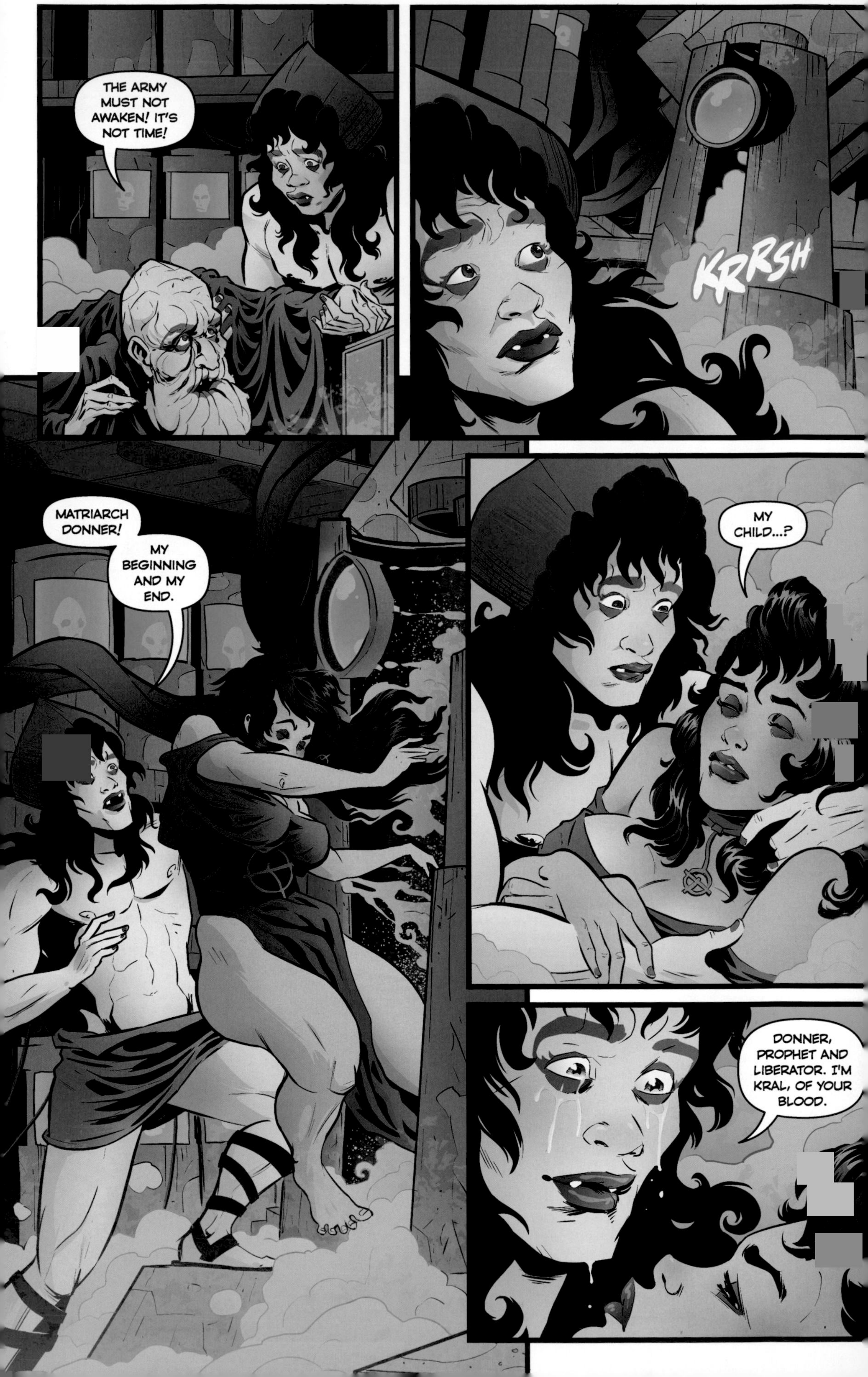
THE ARMY MUST NOT AWAKEN! IT'S NOT TIME!
KRRSH
MATRIARCH DONNER!
MY BEGINNING AND MY END.
MY CHILD...?
DONNER, PROPHET AND LIBERATOR. I'M KRAL, OF YOUR BLOOD.

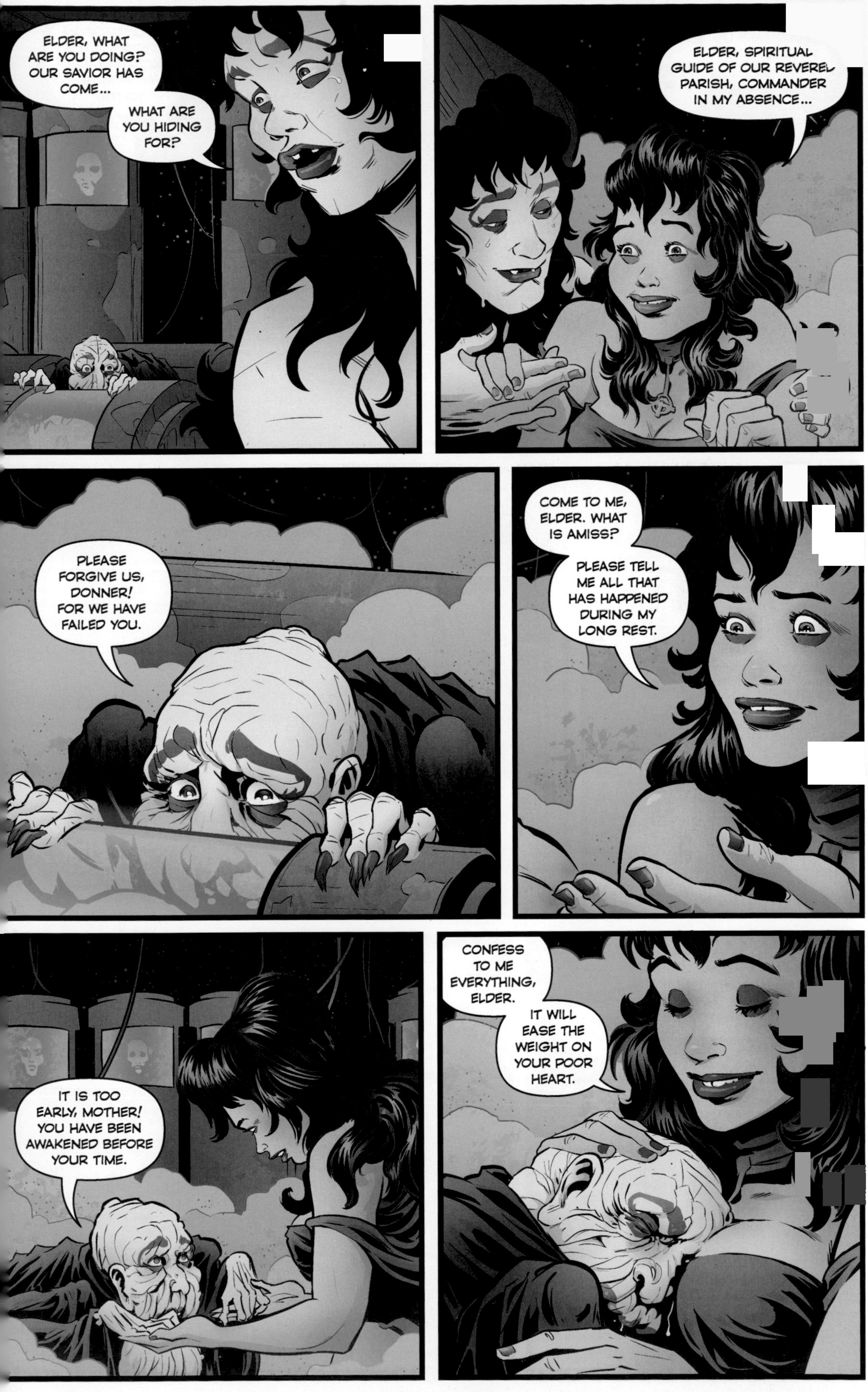
ELDER, WHAT ARE YOU DOING? OUR SAVIOR HAS COME...
WHAT ARE YOU HIDING FOR?
ELDER, SPIRITUAL GUIDE OF OUR REVERE
PARISH, COMMANDER IN MY ABSENCE...
PLEASE FORGIVE US, DONNER! FOR WE HAVE FAILED YOU.
COME TO ME, ELDER. WHAT IS AMISS?
PLEASE TELL ME ALL THAT HAS HAPPENED DURING MY LONG REST.
IT IS TOO EARLY, MOTHER! YOU HAVE BEEN AWAKENED BEFORE YOUR TIME.
CONFESS TO ME EVERYTHING, ELDER.
IT WILL EASE THE WEIGHT ON YOUR POOR HEART.

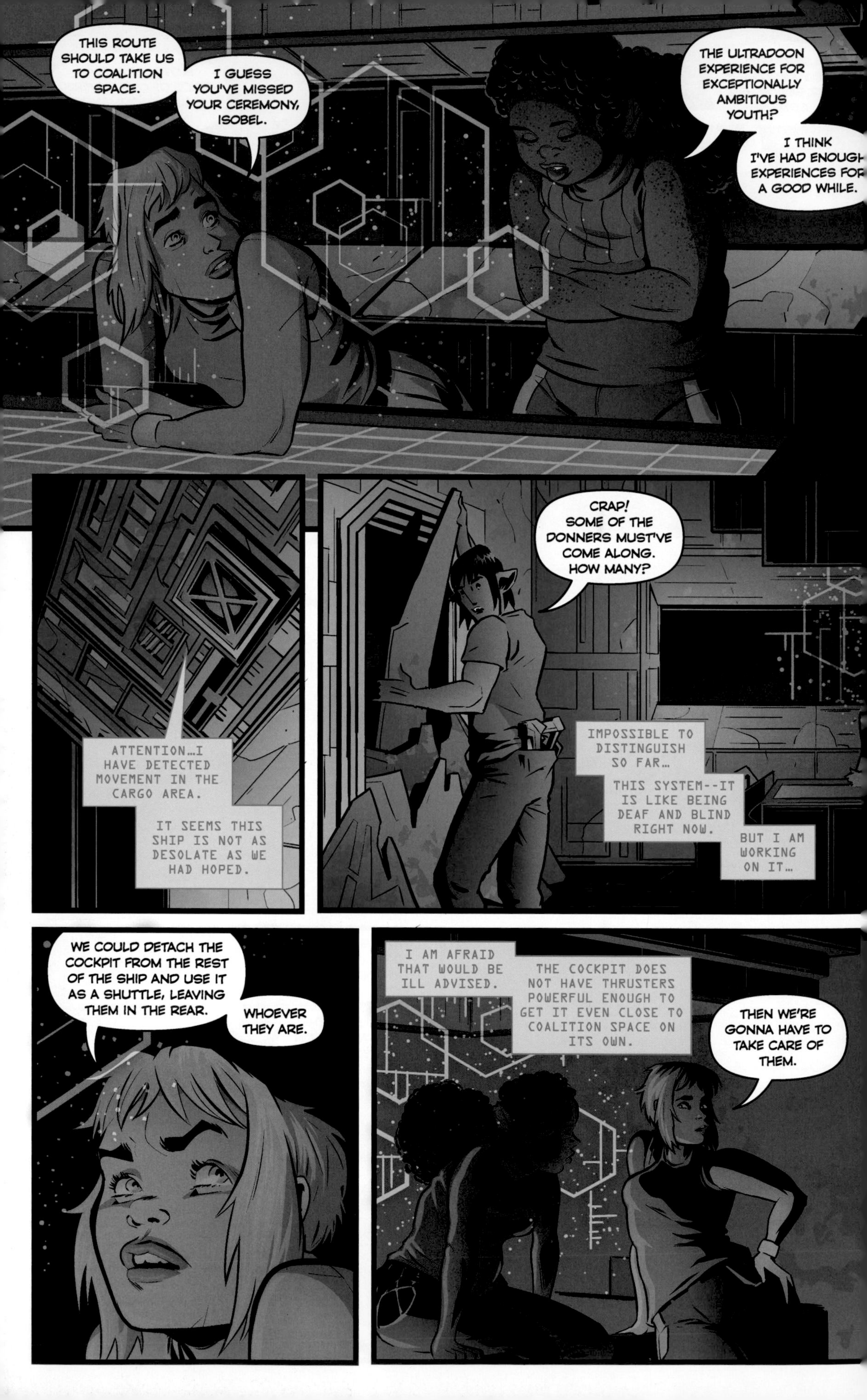
THIS ROUTE SHOULD TAKE US TO COALITION SPACE.
I GUESS YOU'VE MISSED YOUR CEREMONY, ISOBEL.
THE ULTRADOON EXPERIENCE FOR EXCEPTIONALLY AMBITIOUS YOUTH?
I THINK I'VE HAD ENOUGH EXPERIENCES FOR A GOOD WHILE.
ATTENTION...I HAVE DETECTED MOVEMENT IN THE CARGO AREA.
IT SEEMS THIS SHIP IS NOT AS DESOLATE AS WE HAD HOPED.
CRAP! SOME OF THE DONNERS MUST'VE COME ALONG. HOW MANY?
IMPOSSIBLE TO DISTINGUISH SO FAR...
THIS SYSTEM--IT IS LIKE BEING DEAF AND BLIND RIGHT NOW.
BUT I AM WORKING ON IT...
WE COULD DETACH THE COCKPIT FROM THE REST OF THE SHIP AND USE IT AS A SHUTTLE, LEAVING THEM IN THE REAR.
WHOEVER THEY ARE.
I AM AFRAID THAT WOULD BE ILL ADVISED.
THE COCKPIT DOES NOT HAVE THRUSTERS POWERFUL ENOUGH TO GET IT EVEN CLOSE TO COALITION SPACE ON ITS OWN.
THEN WE'RE GONNA HAVE TO TAKE CARE OF THEM.

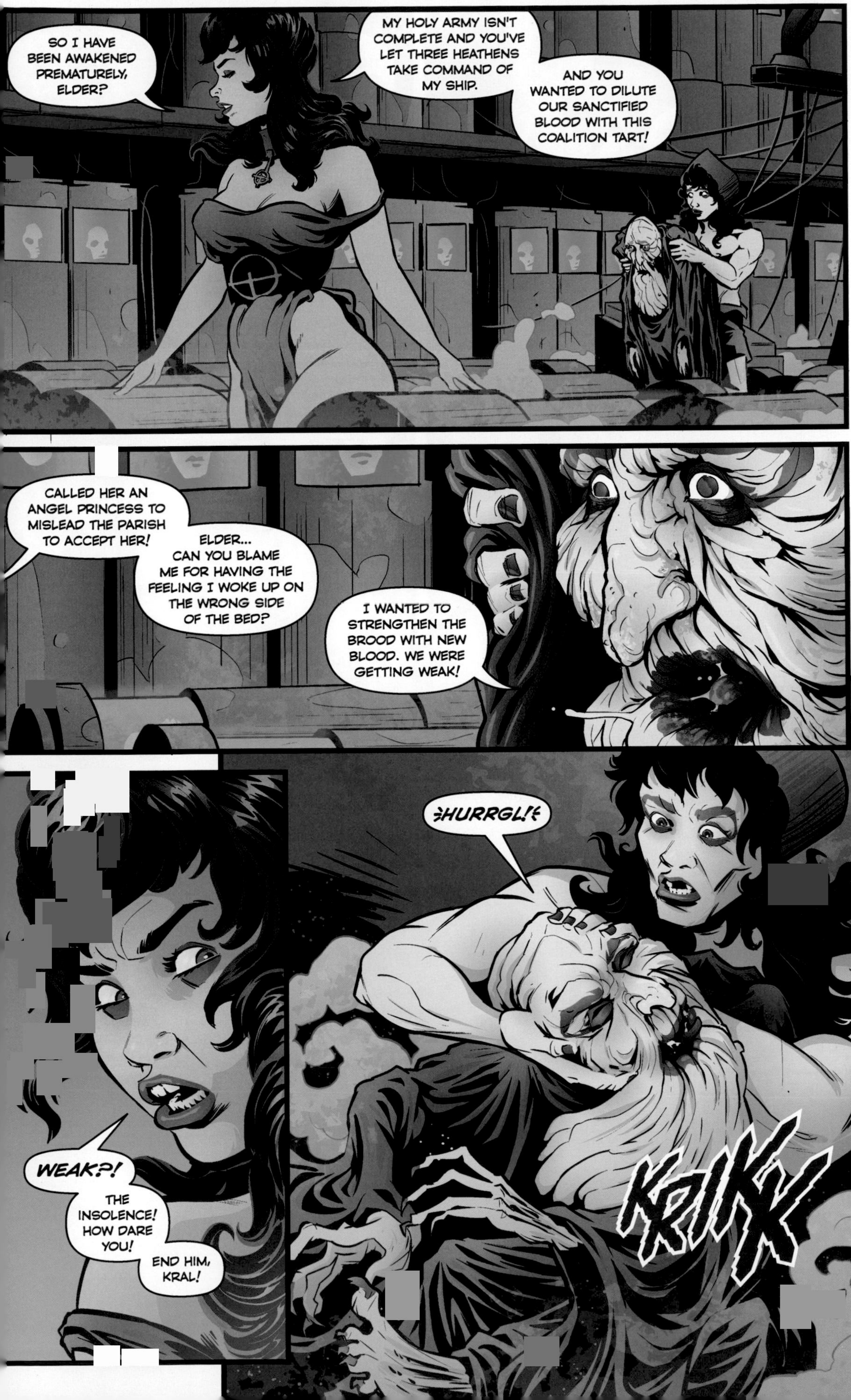
SO I HAVE BEEN AWAKENED PREMATURELY, ELDER?
MY HOLY ARMY ISN'T COMPLETE AND YOU'VE LET THREE HEATHENS TAKE COMMAND OF MY SHIP.
AND YOU WANTED TO DILUTE OUR SANCTIFIED BLOOD WITH THIS COALITION TART!
CALLED HER AN ANGEL PRINCESS TO MISLEAD THE PARISH TO ACCEPT HER!
ELDER... CAN YOU BLAME ME FOR HAVING THE FEELING I WOKE UP ON THE WRONG SIDE OF THE BED?
I WANTED TO STRENGTHEN THE BROOD WITH NEW BLOOD. WE WERE GETTING WEAK!
WEAK?!
THE INSOLENCE! HOW DARE YOU!
END HIM, KRAL!
HURRGL!
KRIK

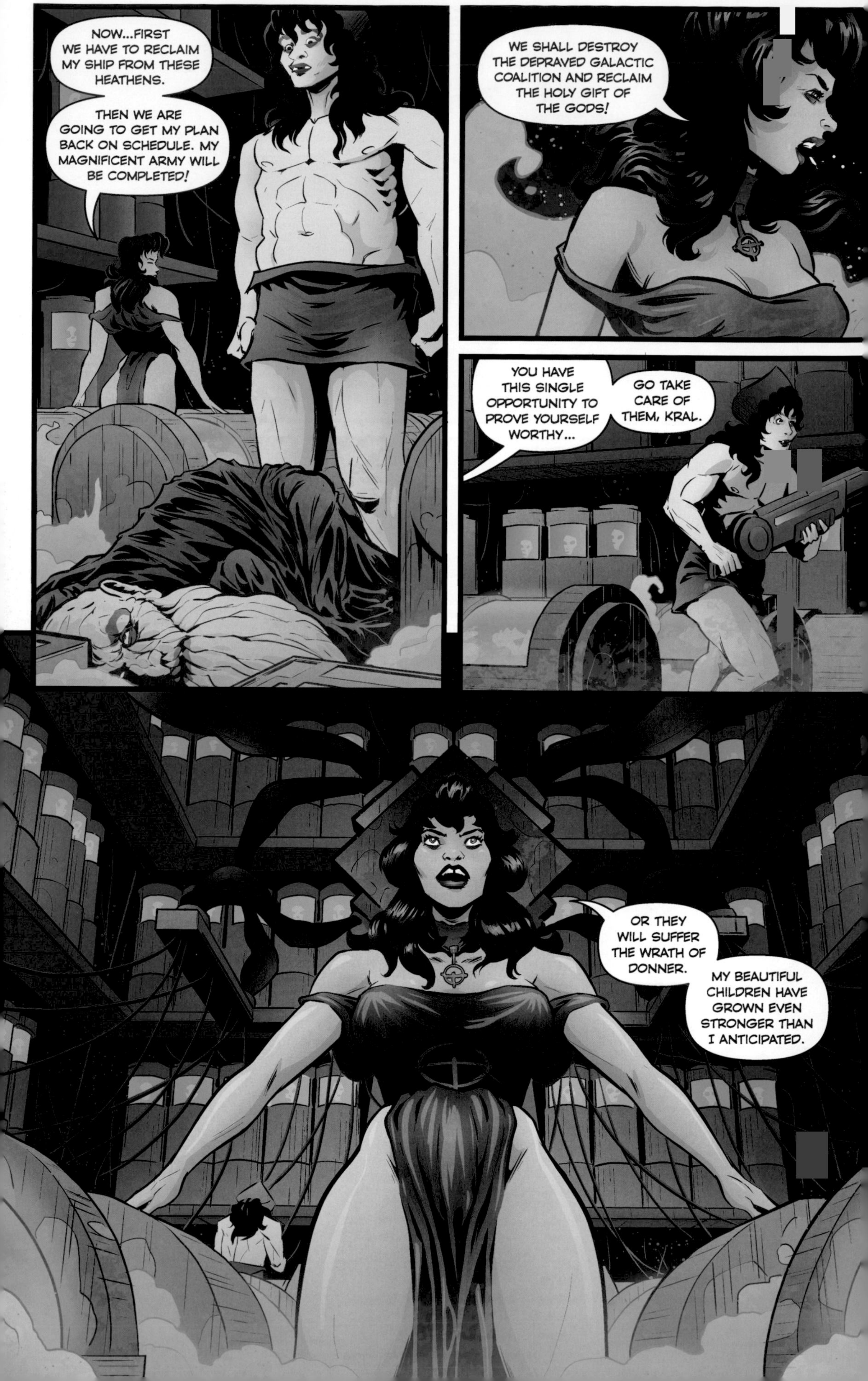
NOW...FIRST WE HAVE TO RECLAIM MY SHIP FROM THESE HEATHENS.
THEN WE ARE GOING TO GET MY PLAN BACK ON SCHEDULE. MY MAGNIFICENT ARMY WILL BE COMPLETED!
WE SHALL DESTROY THE DEPRAVED GALACTIC COALITION AND RECLAIM THE HOLY GIFT OF THE GODS!
YOU HAVE THIS SINGLE OPPORTUNITY TO PROVE YOURSELF WORTHY...
GO TAKE CARE OF THEM, KRAL.
OR THEY WILL SUFFER THE WRATH OF DONNER.
MY BEAUTIFUL CHILDREN HAVE GROWN EVEN STRONGER THAN I ANTICIPATED.

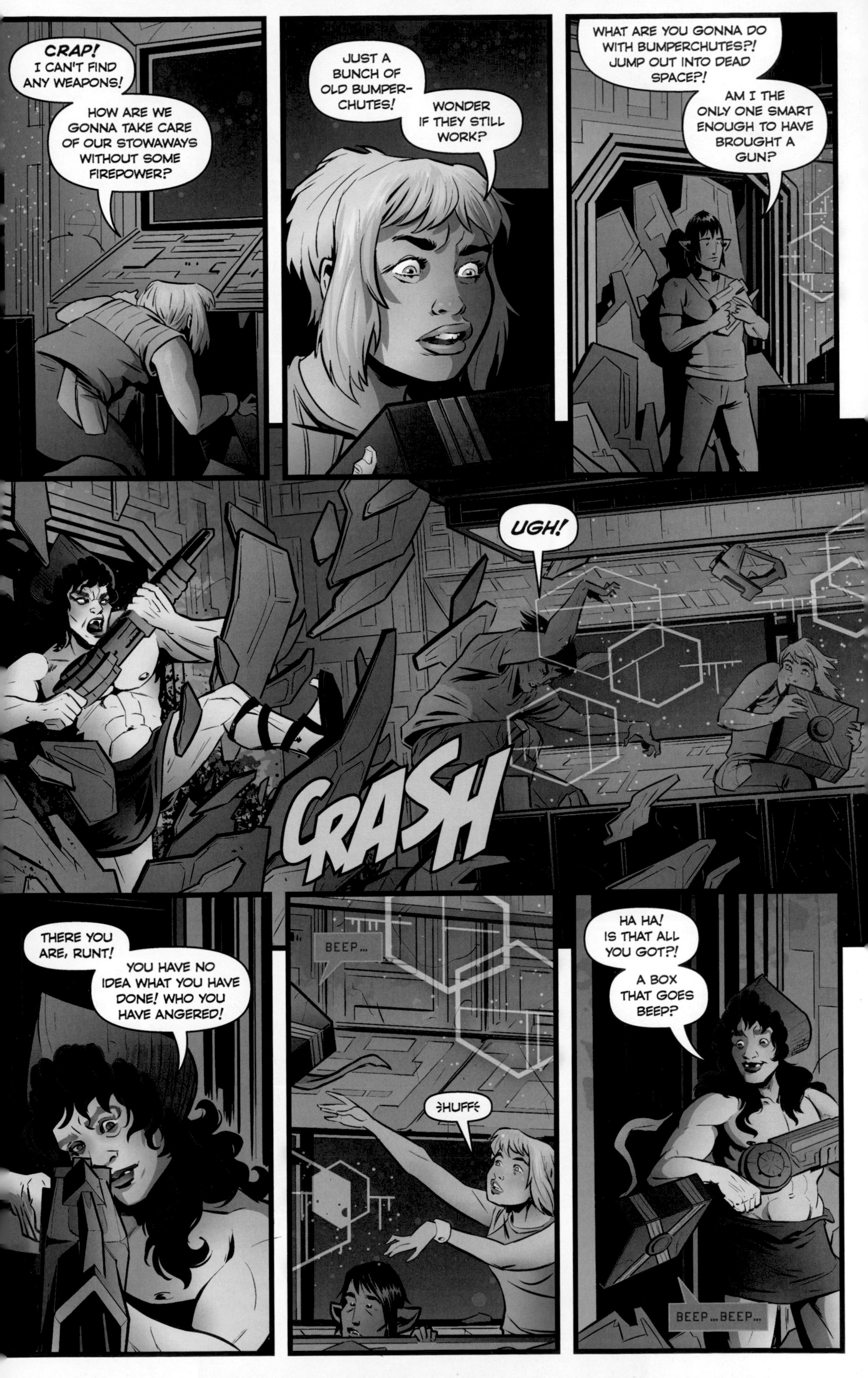
CRAP!
I CAN'T FIND ANY WEAPONS!
HOW ARE WE GONNA TAKE CARE OF OUR STOWAWAYS WITHOUT SOME FIREPOWER?
JUST A BUNCH OF OLD BUMPER-CHUTES!
WONDER IF THEY STILL WORK?
WHAT ARE YOU GONNA DO WITH BUMPERCHUTES?! JUMP OUT INTO DEAD SPACE?!
AM I THE ONLY ONE SMART ENOUGH TO HAVE BROUGHT A GUN?
UGH!
CRASH
THERE YOU ARE, RUNT!
YOU HAVE NO IDEA WHAT YOU HAVE DONE! WHO YOU HAVE ANGERED!
BEEP...
HUFF
HA HA! IS THAT ALL YOU GOT?!
A BOX THAT GOES BEEP?
BEEP...BEEP...

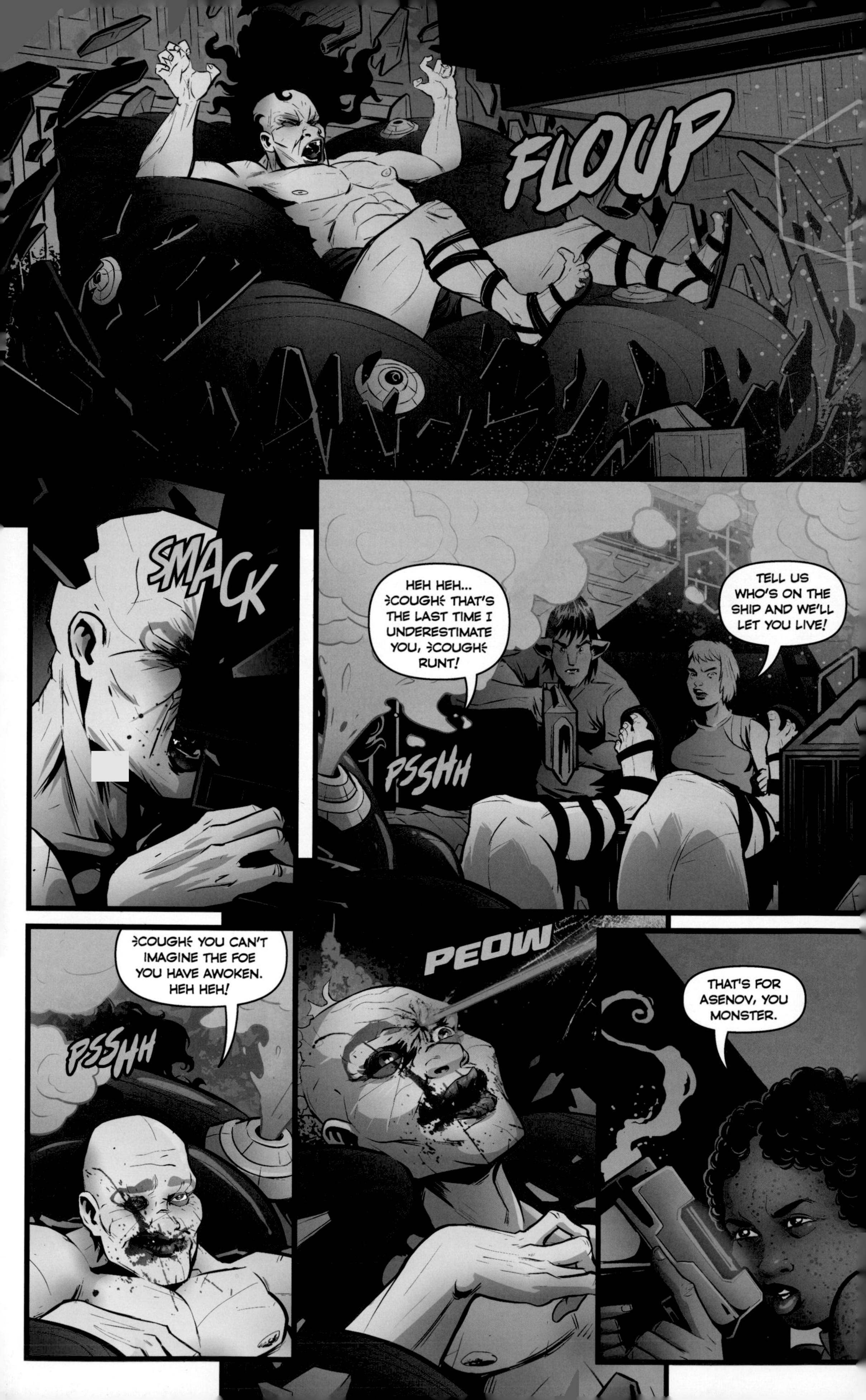
FLOUP
SMACK
HEH HEH... ≯COUGH≮ THAT'S THE LAST TIME I UNDERESTIMATE YOU, ≯COUGH≮ RUNT!
PSSHH
TELL US WHO'S ON THE SHIP AND WE'LL LET YOU LIVE!
≯COUGH≮ YOU CAN'T IMAGINE THE FOE YOU HAVE AWOKEN. HEH HEH!
PSSHH
PEOW
THAT'S FOR ASENOV, YOU MONSTER.

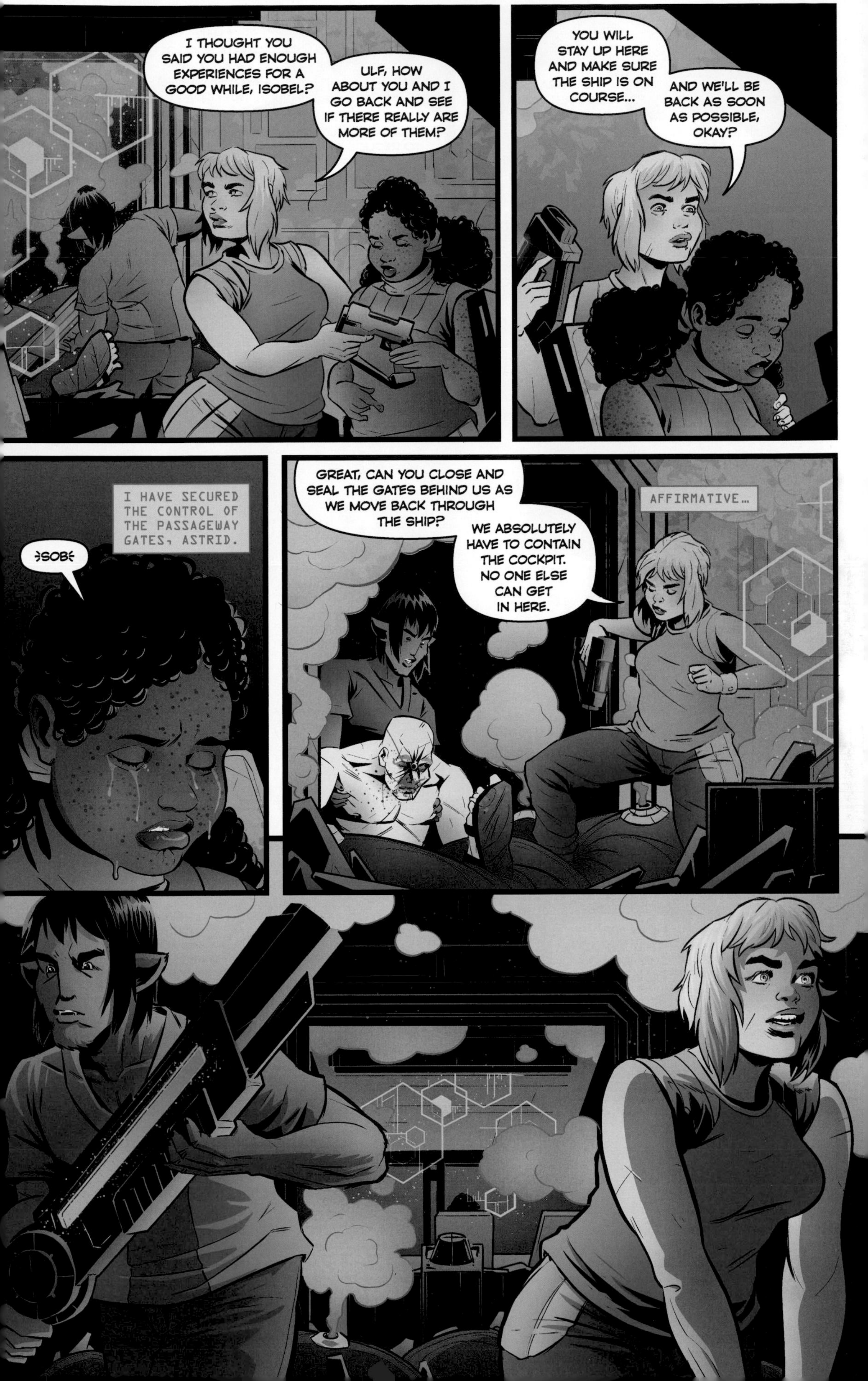
I THOUGHT YOU SAID YOU HAD ENOUGH EXPERIENCES FOR A GOOD WHILE, ISOBEL?
ULF, HOW ABOUT YOU AND I GO BACK AND SEE IF THERE REALLY ARE MORE OF THEM?
YOU WILL STAY UP HERE AND MAKE SURE THE SHIP IS ON COURSE...
AND WE'LL BE BACK AS SOON AS POSSIBLE, OKAY?
I HAVE SECURED THE CONTROL OF THE PASSAGEWAY GATES, ASTRID.
SOB
GREAT, CAN YOU CLOSE AND SEAL THE GATES BEHIND US AS WE MOVE BACK THROUGH THE SHIP?
WE ABSOLUTELY HAVE TO CONTAIN THE COCKPIT. NO ONE ELSE CAN GET IN HERE.
AFFIRMATIVE...

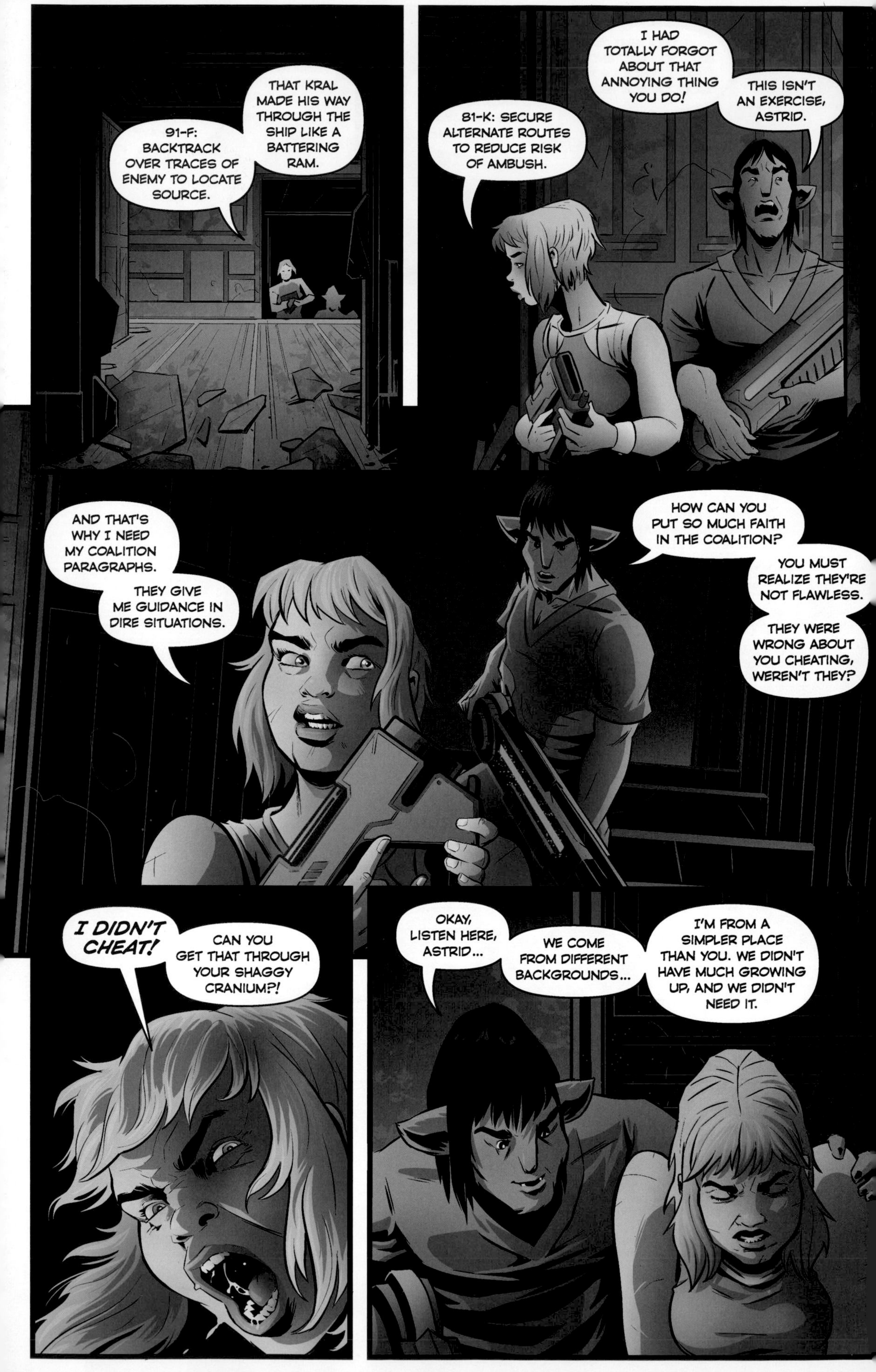
91-F: BACKTRACK OVER TRACES OF ENEMY TO LOCATE SOURCE.
THAT KRAL MADE HIS WAY THROUGH THE SHIP LIKE A BATTERING RAM.
81-K: SECURE ALTERNATE ROUTES TO REDUCE RISK OF AMBUSH.
I HAD TOTALLY FORGOT ABOUT THAT ANNOYING THING YOU DO!
THIS ISN'T AN EXERCISE, ASTRID.
AND THAT'S WHY I NEED MY COALITION PARAGRAPHS.
THEY GIVE ME GUIDANCE IN DIRE SITUATIONS.
HOW CAN YOU PUT SO MUCH FAITH IN THE COALITION?
YOU MUST REALIZE THEY'RE NOT FLAWLESS.
THEY WERE WRONG ABOUT YOU CHEATING, WEREN'T THEY?
I DIDN'T CHEAT!
CAN YOU GET THAT THROUGH YOUR SHAGGY CRANIUM?!
OKAY, LISTEN HERE, ASTRID...
WE COME FROM DIFFERENT BACKGROUNDS...
I'M FROM A SIMPLER PLACE THAN YOU. WE DIDN'T HAVE MUCH GROWING UP, AND WE DIDN'T NEED IT.

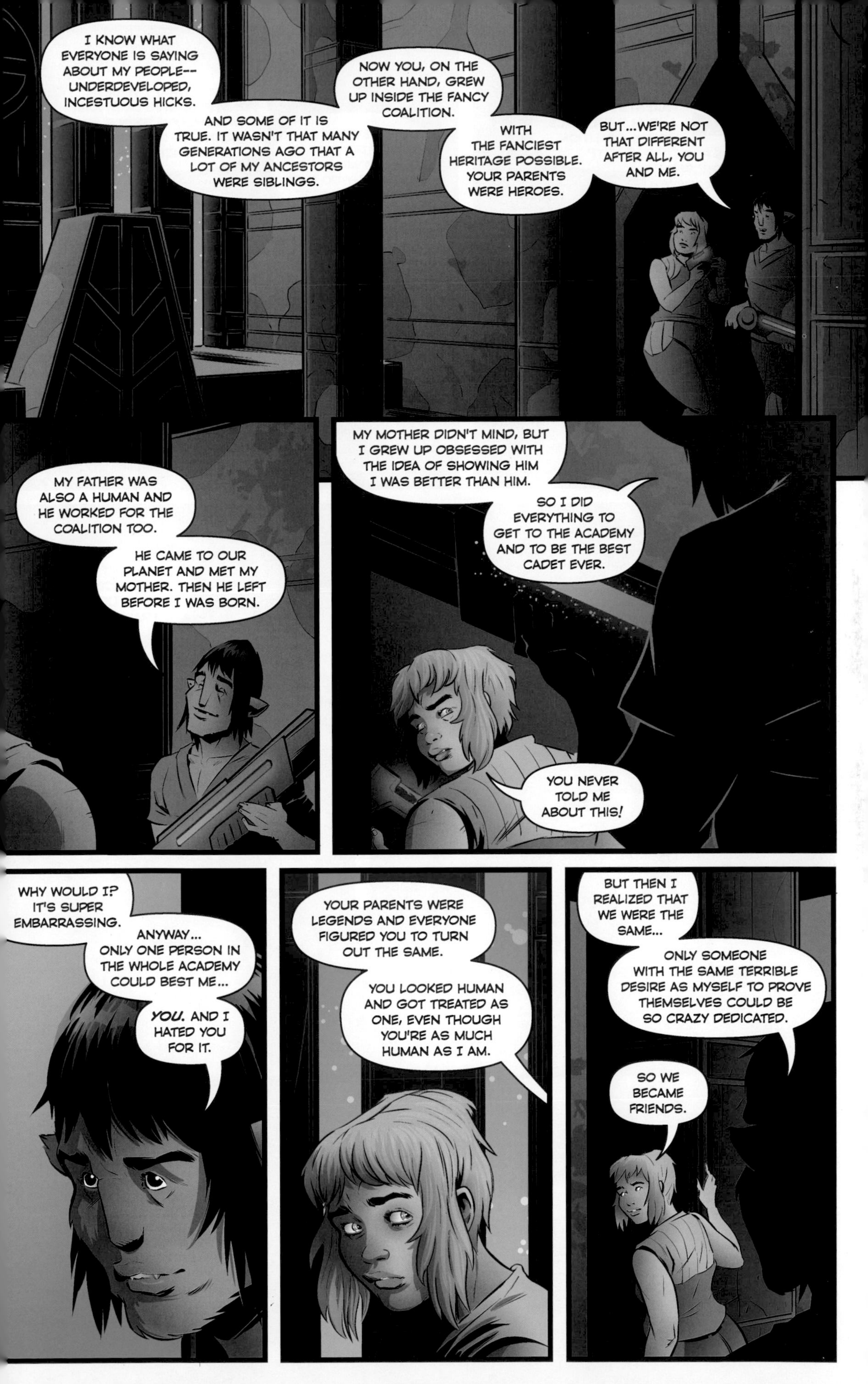
I KNOW WHAT EVERYONE IS SAYING ABOUT MY PEOPLE-- UNDERDEVELOPED, INCESTUOUS HICKS.
AND SOME OF IT IS TRUE. IT WASN'T THAT MANY GENERATIONS AGO THAT A LOT OF MY ANCESTORS WERE SIBLINGS.
NOW YOU, ON THE OTHER HAND, GREW UP INSIDE THE FANCY COALITION.
WITH THE FANCIEST HERITAGE POSSIBLE. YOUR PARENTS WERE HEROES.
BUT...WE'RE NOT THAT DIFFERENT AFTER ALL, YOU AND ME.
MY FATHER WAS ALSO A HUMAN AND HE WORKED FOR THE COALITION TOO.
HE CAME TO OUR PLANET AND MET MY MOTHER. THEN HE LEFT BEFORE I WAS BORN.
MY MOTHER DIDN'T MIND, BUT I GREW UP OBSESSED WITH THE IDEA OF SHOWING HIM I WAS BETTER THAN HIM.
SO I DID EVERYTHING TO GET TO THE ACADEMY AND TO BE THE BEST CADET EVER.
YOU NEVER TOLD ME ABOUT THIS!
WHY WOULD I? IT'S SUPER EMBARRASSING.
ANYWAY... ONLY ONE PERSON IN THE WHOLE ACADEMY COULD BEST ME...
*YOU.* AND I HATED YOU FOR IT.
YOUR PARENTS WERE LEGENDS AND EVERYONE FIGURED YOU TO TURN OUT THE SAME.
YOU LOOKED HUMAN AND GOT TREATED AS ONE, EVEN THOUGH YOU'RE AS MUCH HUMAN AS I AM.
BUT THEN I REALIZED THAT WE WERE THE SAME...
ONLY SOMEONE WITH THE SAME TERRIBLE DESIRE AS MYSELF TO PROVE THEMSELVES COULD BE SO CRAZY DEDICATED.
SO WE BECAME FRIENDS.

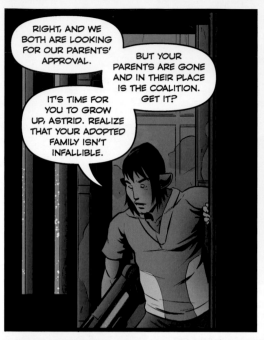

RIGHT, AND WE BOTH ARE LOOKING FOR OUR PARENTS' APPROVAL.

BUT YOUR PARENTS ARE GONE AND IN THEIR PLACE IS THE COALITION. GET IT?

IT'S TIME FOR YOU TO GROW UP, ASTRID. REALIZE THAT YOUR ADOPTED FAMILY ISN'T INFALLIBLE.

BUT EVEN IF I WOULD DO THAT, IT DOESN'T MAKE ANY SENSE. WHY DO THEY THINK I CHEATED?

THAT'S WHAT I'VE BEEN PONDERING THIS LAST YEAR. WHILE YOU'VE BEEN BUSY TRYING TO IMPRESS THE PRINCIPAL--

--WHO, AS LONG AS YOU ARE DISGRACED, IS NEVER GONNA GIVE YOU A SECOND CHANCE.

WHATEVER, GET TO THE POINT.

YOU HAVE TO FIGURE OUT WHO WOULD BENEFIT FROM YOU FAILING THE TEST AND NEVER BECOMING A PEACEKEEPER.

OKAY... WHO?

I DON'T KNOW! BUT WHOEVER IT IS SET YOU UP. YOU WERE FRAMED, GET IT?

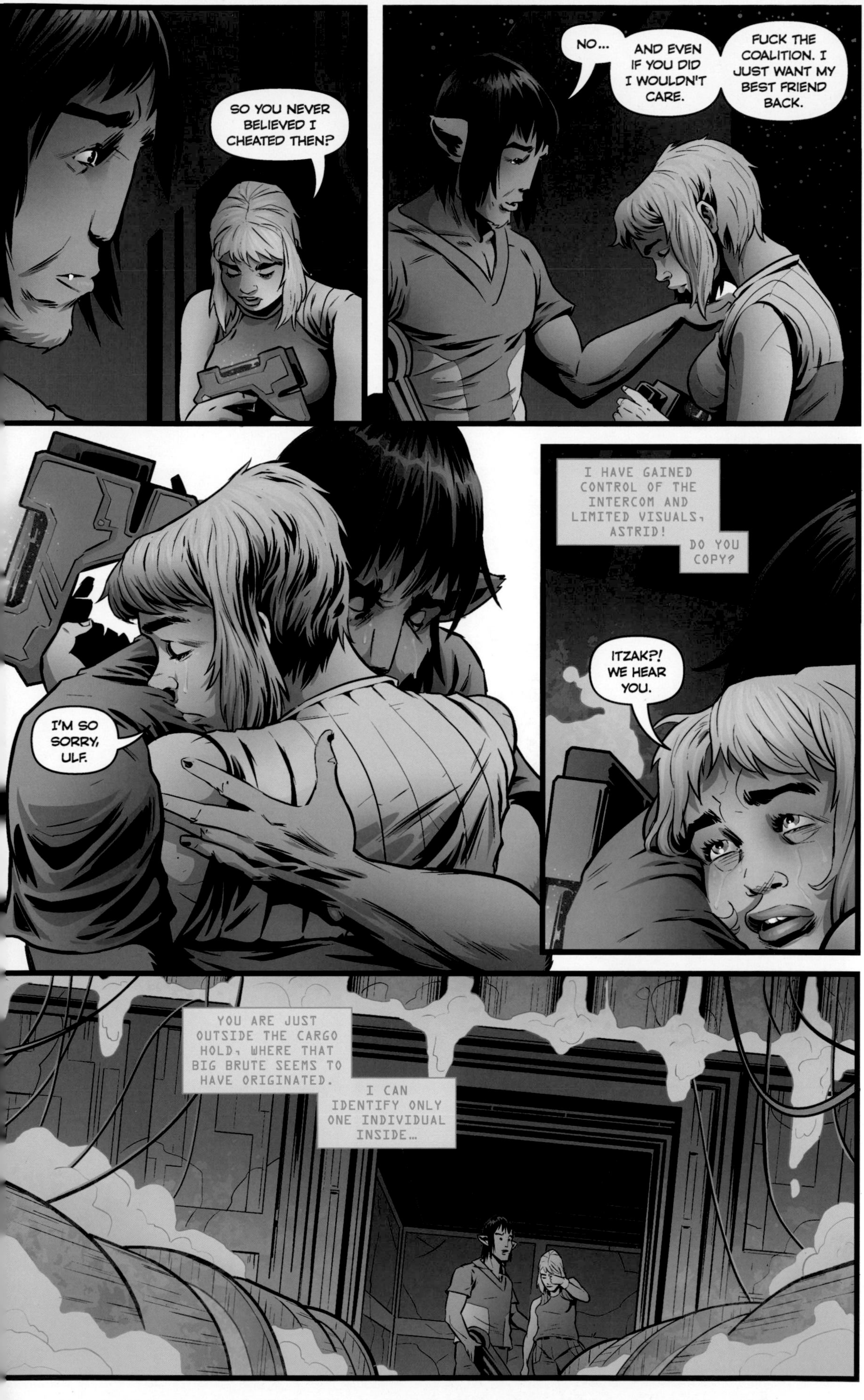
SO YOU NEVER BELIEVED I CHEATED THEN?
NO...
AND EVEN IF YOU DID I WOULDN'T CARE.
FUCK THE COALITION. I JUST WANT MY BEST FRIEND BACK.
I'M SO SORRY, ULF.
I HAVE GAINED CONTROL OF THE INTERCOM AND LIMITED VISUALS, ASTRID!
DO YOU COPY?
ITZAK?! WE HEAR YOU.
YOU ARE JUST OUTSIDE THE CARGO HOLD, WHERE THAT BIG BRUTE SEEMS TO HAVE ORIGINATED.
I CAN IDENTIFY ONLY ONE INDIVIDUAL INSIDE...

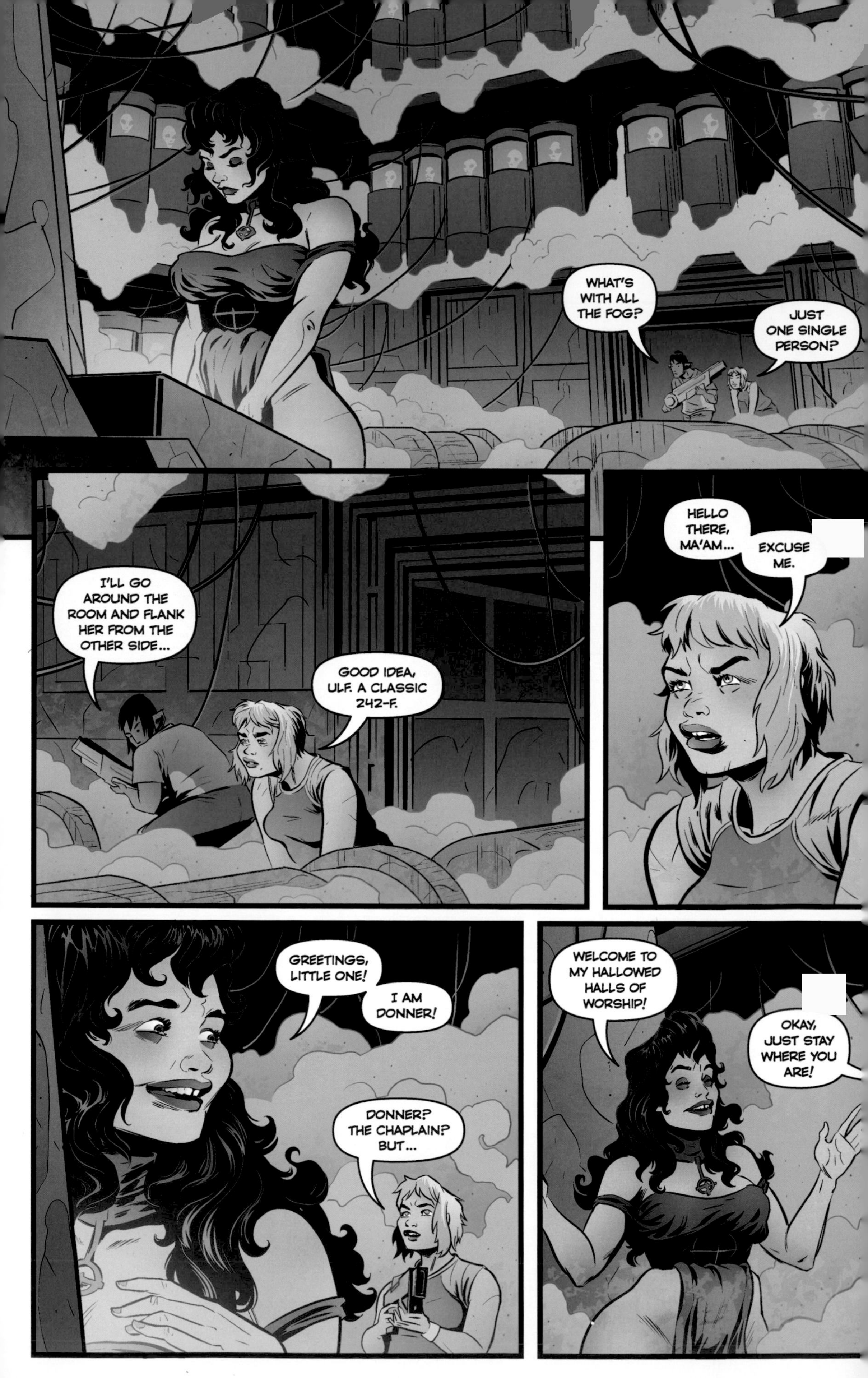
WHAT'S WITH ALL THE FOG?
JUST ONE SINGLE PERSON?
I'LL GO AROUND THE ROOM AND FLANK HER FROM THE OTHER SIDE...
GOOD IDEA, ULF. A CLASSIC 242-F.
HELLO THERE, MA'AM...
EXCUSE ME.
GREETINGS, LITTLE ONE!
I AM DONNER!
DONNER? THE CHAPLAIN? BUT...
WELCOME TO MY HALLOWED HALLS OF WORSHIP!
OKAY, JUST STAY WHERE YOU ARE!

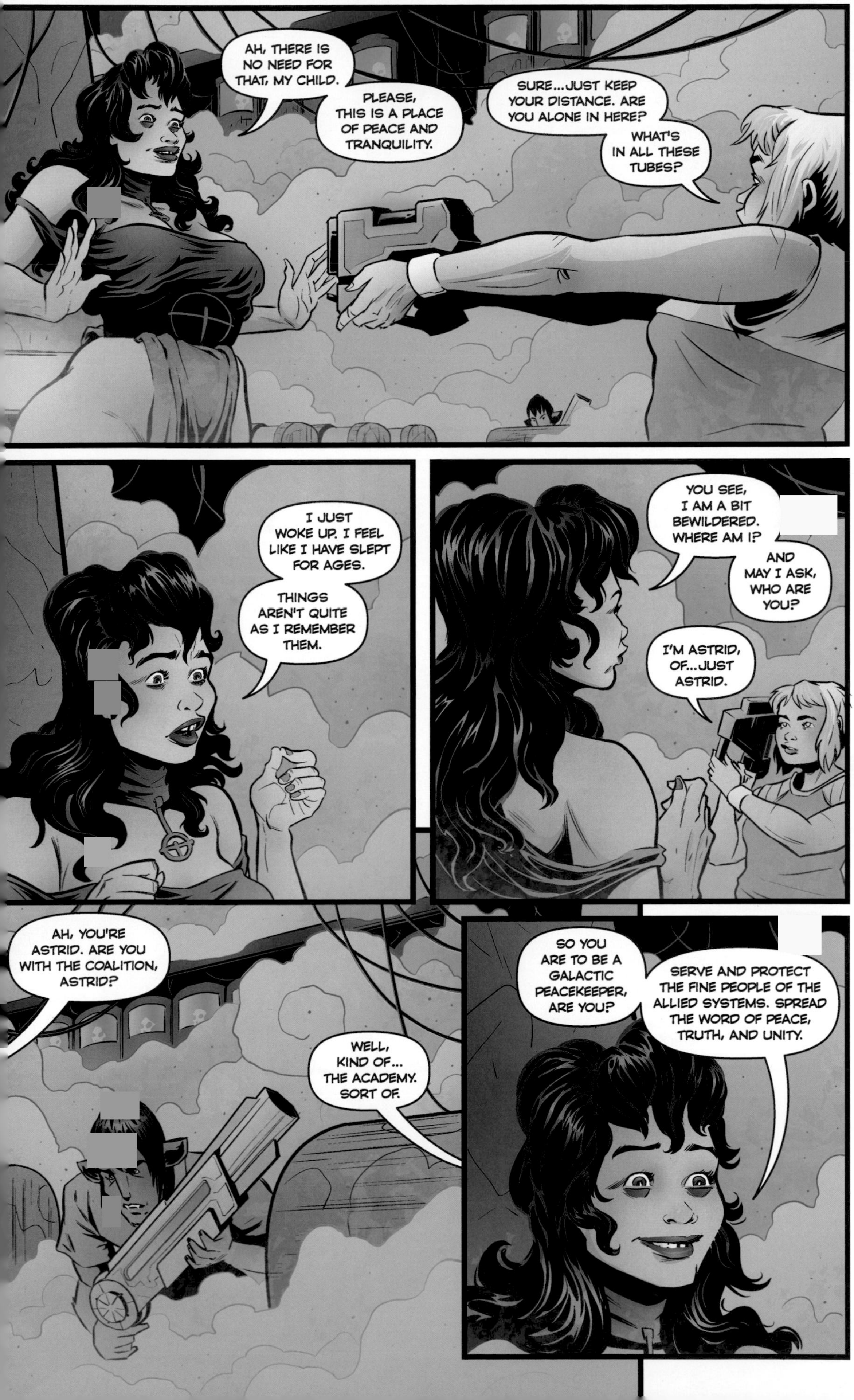
AH, THERE IS NO NEED FOR THAT, MY CHILD.
PLEASE, THIS IS A PLACE OF PEACE AND TRANQUILITY.
SURE...JUST KEEP YOUR DISTANCE. ARE YOU ALONE IN HERE?
WHAT'S IN ALL THESE TUBES?
I JUST WOKE UP. I FEEL LIKE I HAVE SLEPT FOR AGES.
THINGS AREN'T QUITE AS I REMEMBER THEM.
YOU SEE, I AM A BIT BEWILDERED. WHERE AM I?
AND MAY I ASK, WHO ARE YOU?
I'M ASTRID, OF...JUST ASTRID.
AH, YOU'RE ASTRID. ARE YOU WITH THE COALITION, ASTRID?
WELL, KIND OF... THE ACADEMY. SORT OF.
SO YOU ARE TO BE A GALACTIC PEACEKEEPER, ARE YOU?
SERVE AND PROTECT THE FINE PEOPLE OF THE ALLIED SYSTEMS. SPREAD THE WORD OF PEACE, TRUTH, AND UNITY.

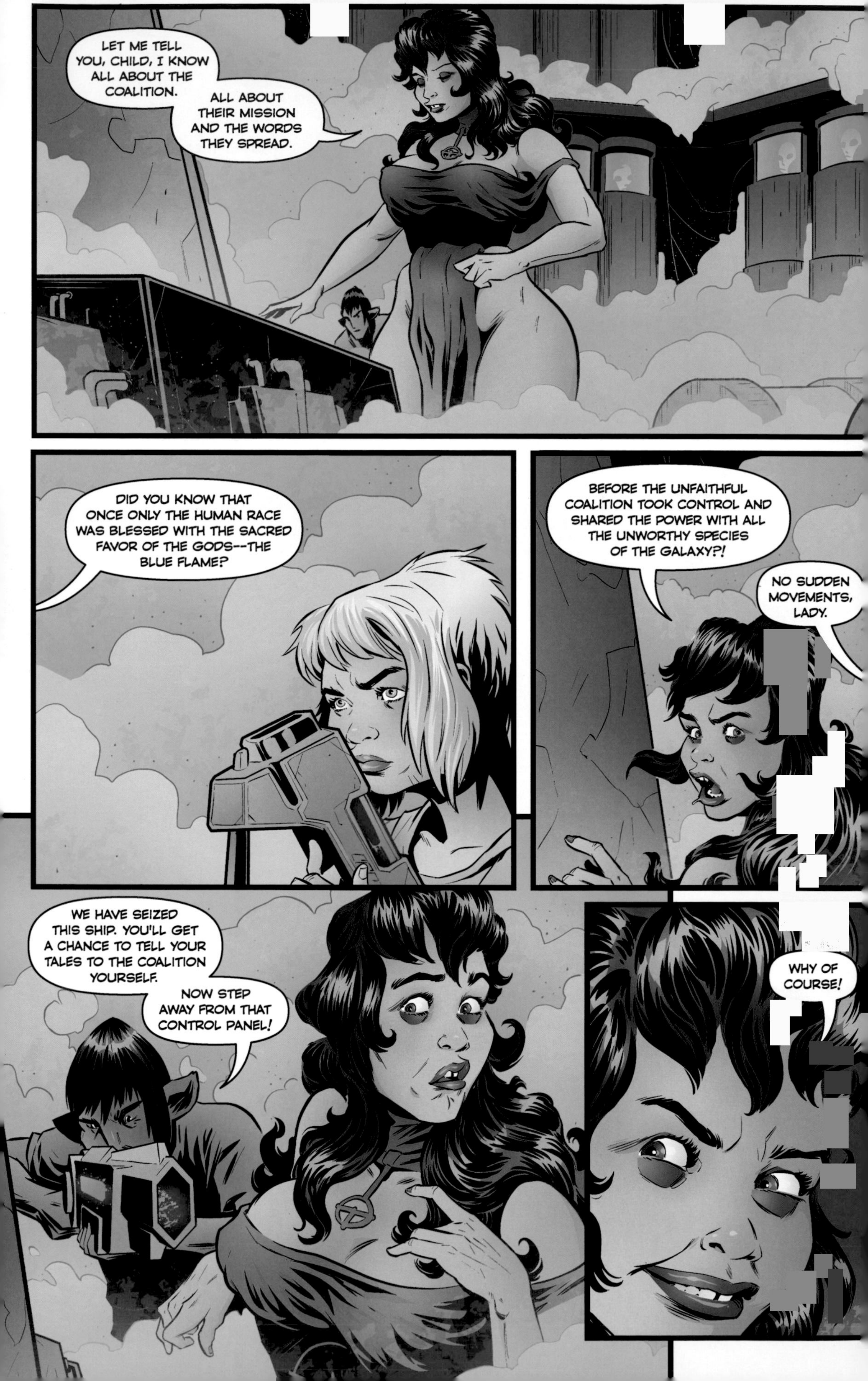
LET ME TELL YOU, CHILD, I KNOW ALL ABOUT THE COALITION.
ALL ABOUT THEIR MISSION AND THE WORDS THEY SPREAD.
DID YOU KNOW THAT ONCE ONLY THE HUMAN RACE WAS BLESSED WITH THE SACRED FAVOR OF THE GODS--THE BLUE FLAME?
BEFORE THE UNFAITHFUL COALITION TOOK CONTROL AND SHARED THE POWER WITH ALL THE UNWORTHY SPECIES OF THE GALAXY?!
NO SUDDEN MOVEMENTS, LADY.
WE HAVE SEIZED THIS SHIP. YOU'LL GET A CHANCE TO TELL YOUR TALES TO THE COALITION YOURSELF.
NOW STEP AWAY FROM THAT CONTROL PANEL!
WHY OF COURSE!

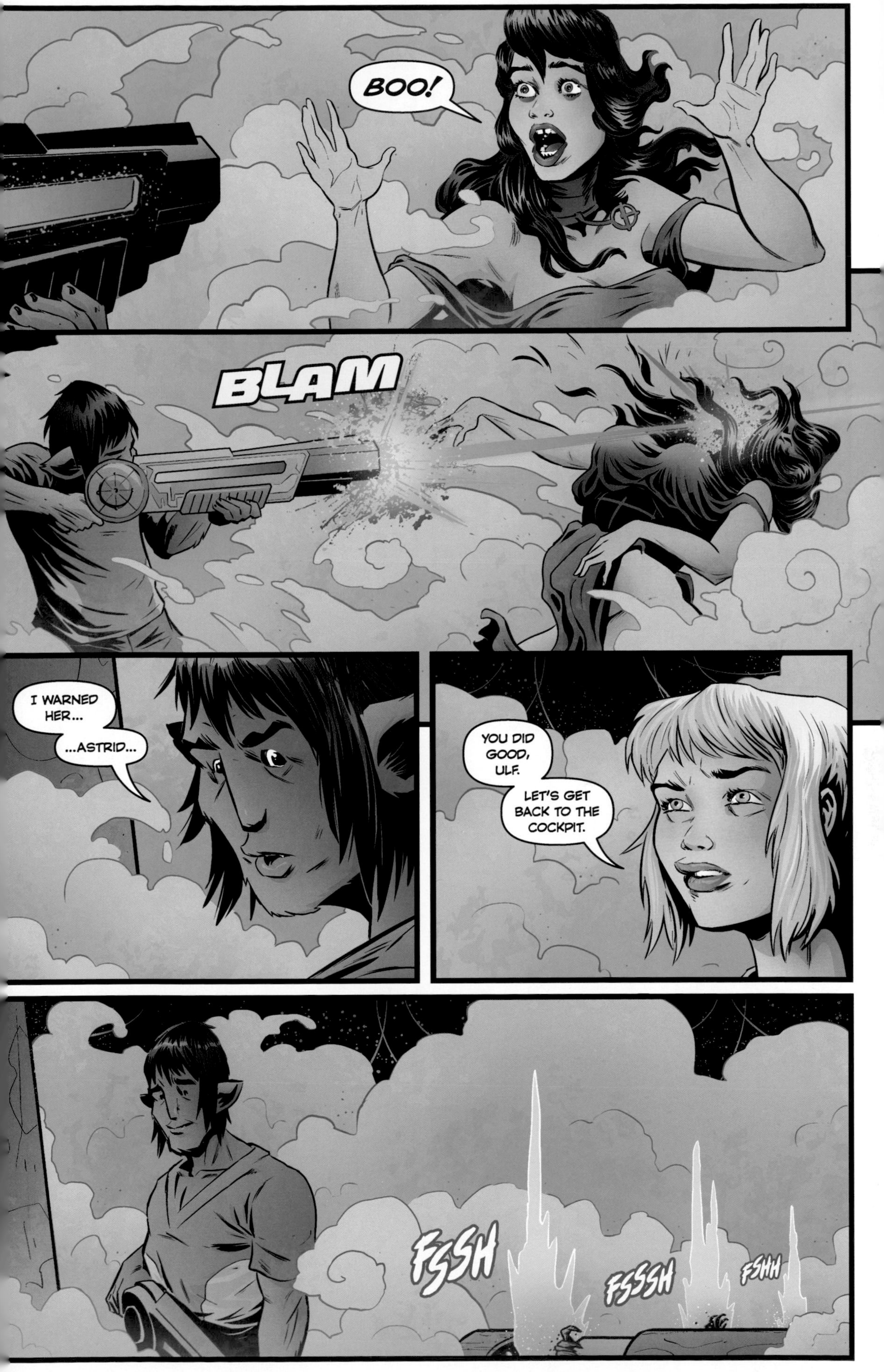
BOO!
BLAM
I WARNED HER...
...ASTRID...
YOU DID GOOD, ULF.
LET'S GET BACK TO THE COCKPIT.
FSSH
FSSSH
FSHH

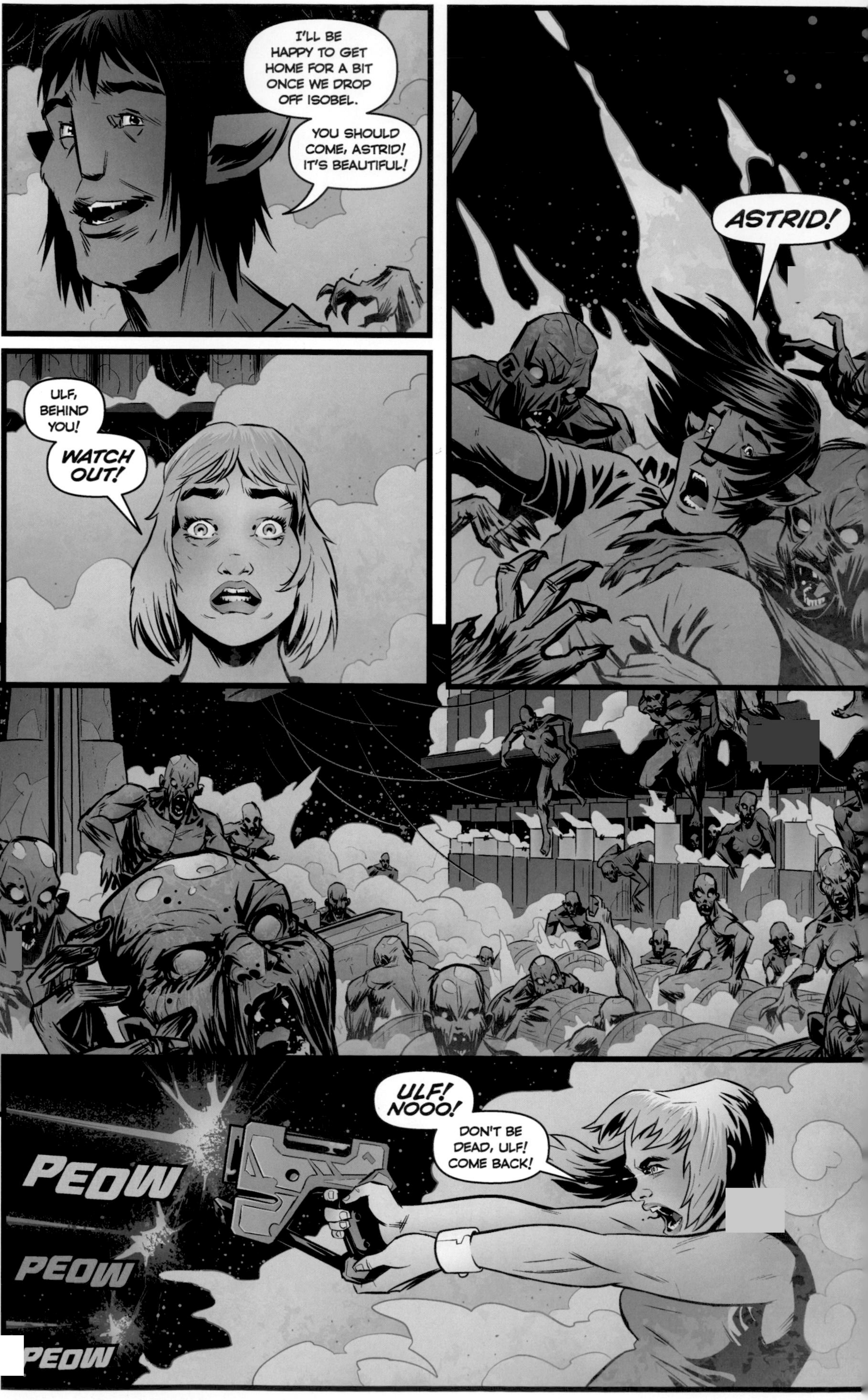
I'LL BE HAPPY TO GET HOME FOR A BIT ONCE WE DROP OFF ISOBEL.
YOU SHOULD COME, ASTRID! IT'S BEAUTIFUL!
ASTRID!
ULF, BEHIND YOU!
WATCH OUT!
ULF! NOOO!
DON'T BE DEAD, ULF! COME BACK!
PEOW
PEOW
PEOW

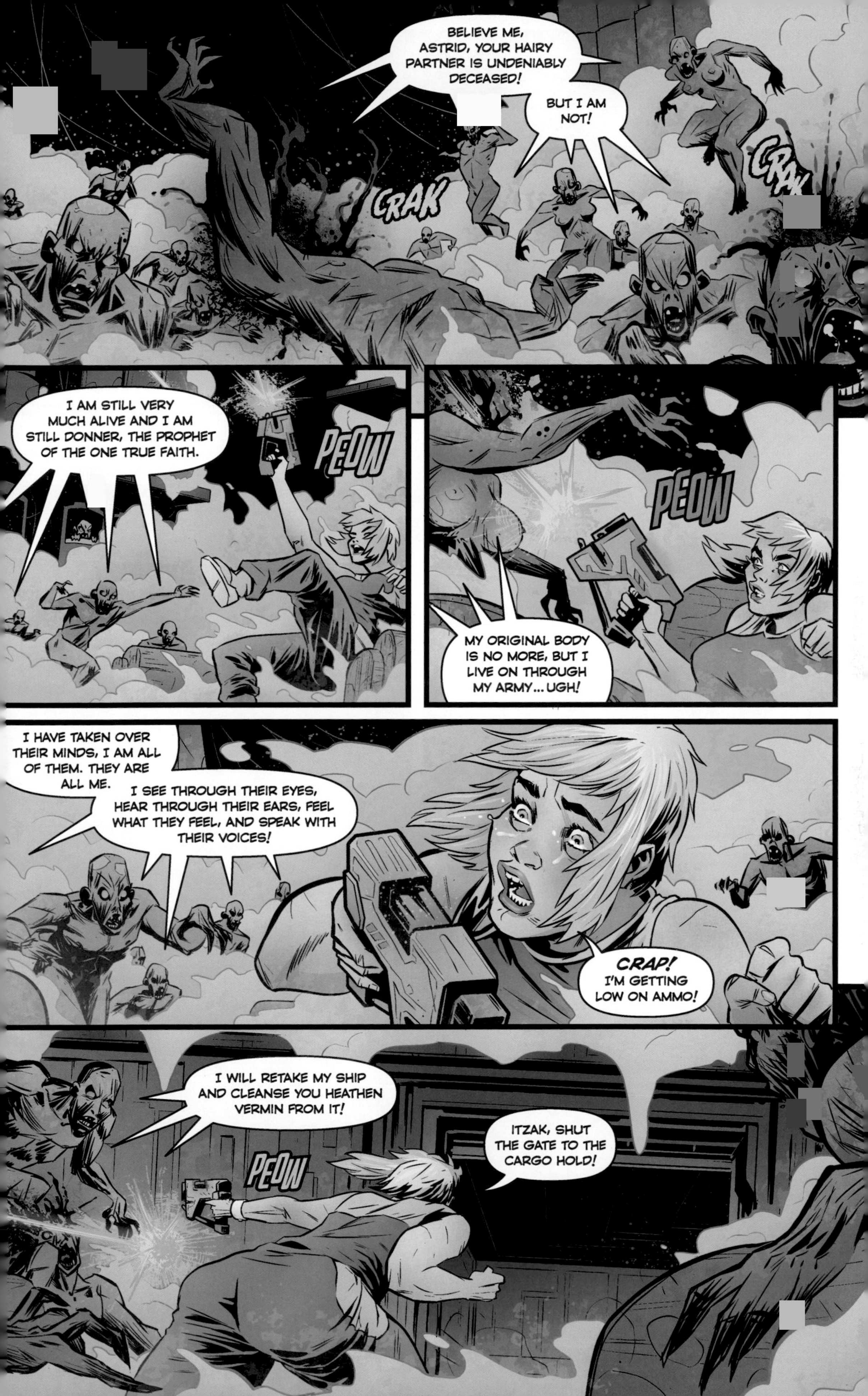
BELIEVE ME, ASTRID, YOUR HAIRY PARTNER IS UNDENIABLY DECEASED!
BUT I AM NOT!
CRAK
CRAK
I AM STILL VERY MUCH ALIVE AND I AM STILL DONNER, THE PROPHET OF THE ONE TRUE FAITH.
PEOW
PEOW
MY ORIGINAL BODY IS NO MORE, BUT I LIVE ON THROUGH MY ARMY... UGH!
I HAVE TAKEN OVER THEIR MINDS, I AM ALL OF THEM. THEY ARE ALL ME.
I SEE THROUGH THEIR EYES, HEAR THROUGH THEIR EARS, FEEL WHAT THEY FEEL, AND SPEAK WITH THEIR VOICES!
CRAP! I'M GETTING LOW ON AMMO!
I WILL RETAKE MY SHIP AND CLEANSE YOU HEATHEN VERMIN FROM IT!
PEOW
ITZAK, SHUT THE GATE TO THE CARGO HOLD!

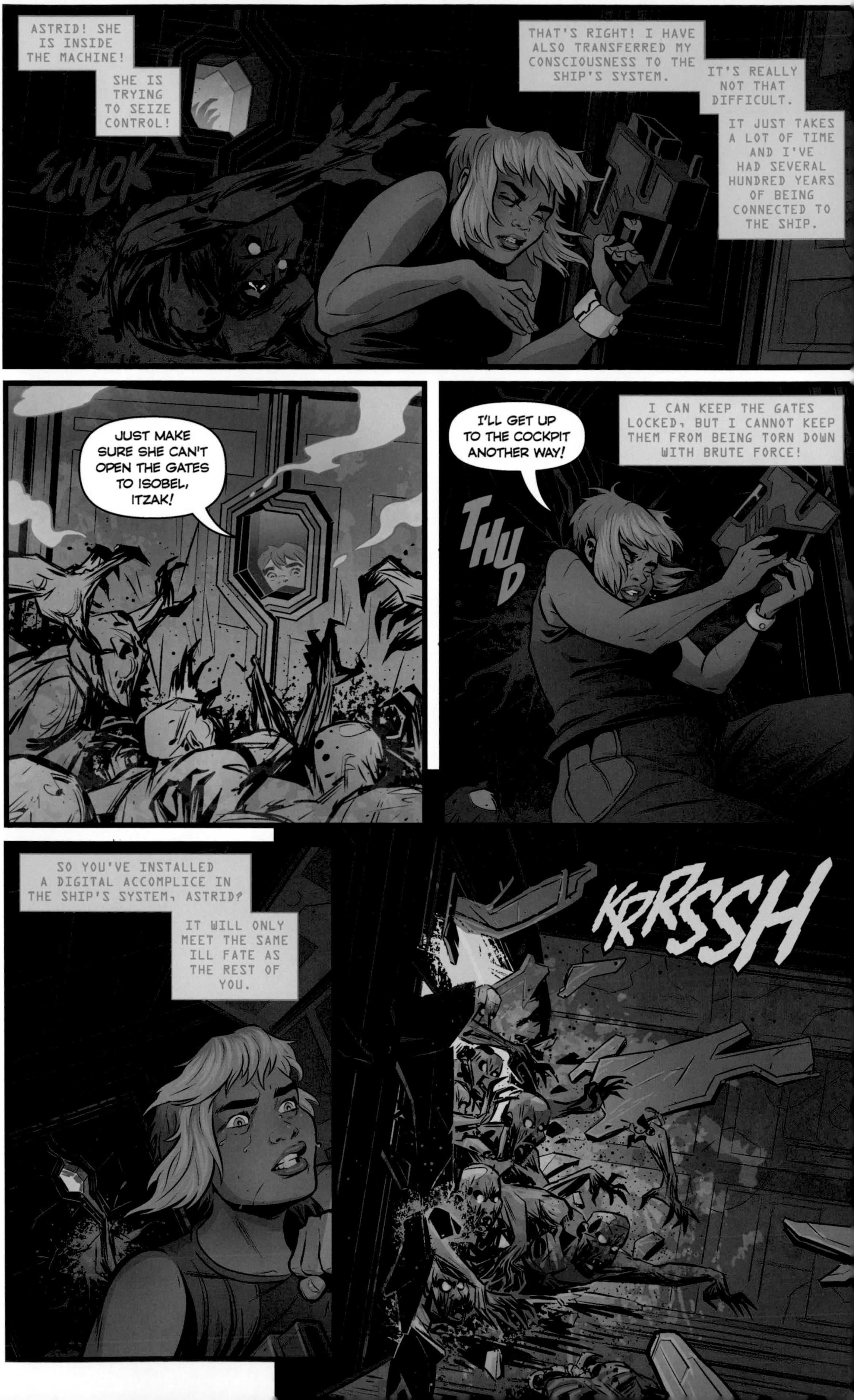

ASTRID! SHE IS INSIDE THE MACHINE!
SHE IS TRYING TO SEIZE CONTROL!
SCHLOK
THAT'S RIGHT! I HAVE ALSO TRANSFERRED MY CONSCIOUSNESS TO THE SHIP'S SYSTEM.
IT'S REALLY NOT THAT DIFFICULT.
IT JUST TAKES A LOT OF TIME AND I'VE HAD SEVERAL HUNDRED YEARS OF BEING CONNECTED TO THE SHIP.
JUST MAKE SURE SHE CAN'T OPEN THE GATES TO ISOBEL, ITZAK!
I'LL GET UP TO THE COCKPIT ANOTHER WAY!
THUD
I CAN KEEP THE GATES LOCKED, BUT I CANNOT KEEP THEM FROM BEING TORN DOWN WITH BRUTE FORCE!
SO YOU'VE INSTALLED A DIGITAL ACCOMPLICE IN THE SHIP'S SYSTEM, ASTRID?
IT WILL ONLY MEET THE SAME ILL FATE AS THE REST OF YOU.
KRRSSH

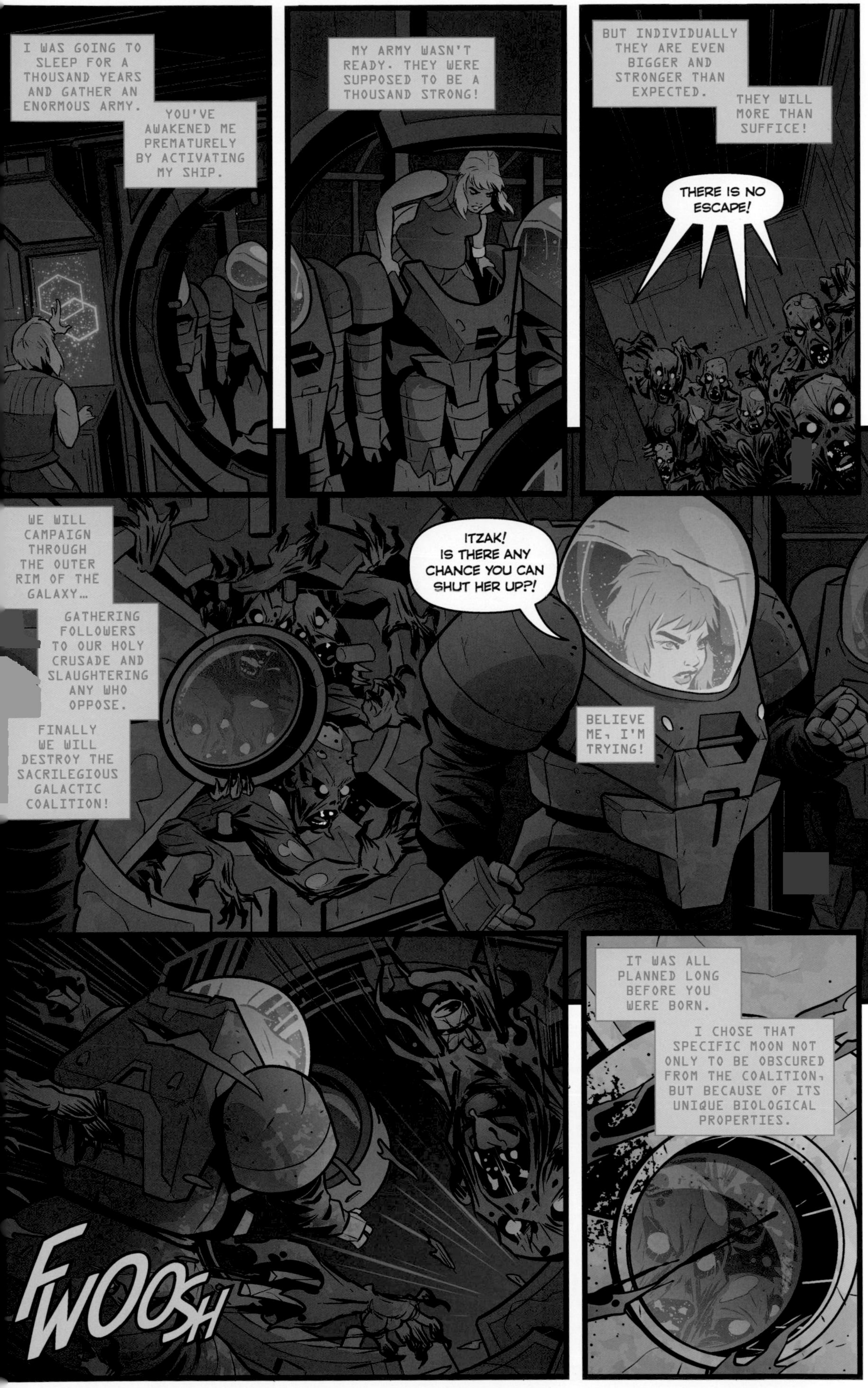

I WAS GOING TO SLEEP FOR A THOUSAND YEARS AND GATHER AN ENORMOUS ARMY.
YOU'VE AWAKENED ME PREMATURELY BY ACTIVATING MY SHIP.
MY ARMY WASN'T READY. THEY WERE SUPPOSED TO BE A THOUSAND STRONG!
BUT INDIVIDUALLY THEY ARE EVEN BIGGER AND STRONGER THAN EXPECTED.
THEY WILL MORE THAN SUFFICE!
THERE IS NO ESCAPE!
WE WILL CAMPAIGN THROUGH THE OUTER RIM OF THE GALAXY…
GATHERING FOLLOWERS TO OUR HOLY CRUSADE AND SLAUGHTERING ANY WHO OPPOSE.
FINALLY WE WILL DESTROY THE SACRILEGIOUS GALACTIC COALITION!
ITZAK! IS THERE ANY CHANCE YOU CAN SHUT HER UP?!
BELIEVE ME, I'M TRYING!
FWOOSH
IT WAS ALL PLANNED LONG BEFORE YOU WERE BORN.
I CHOSE THAT SPECIFIC MOON NOT ONLY TO BE OBSCURED FROM THE COALITION, BUT BECAUSE OF ITS UNIQUE BIOLOGICAL PROPERTIES.

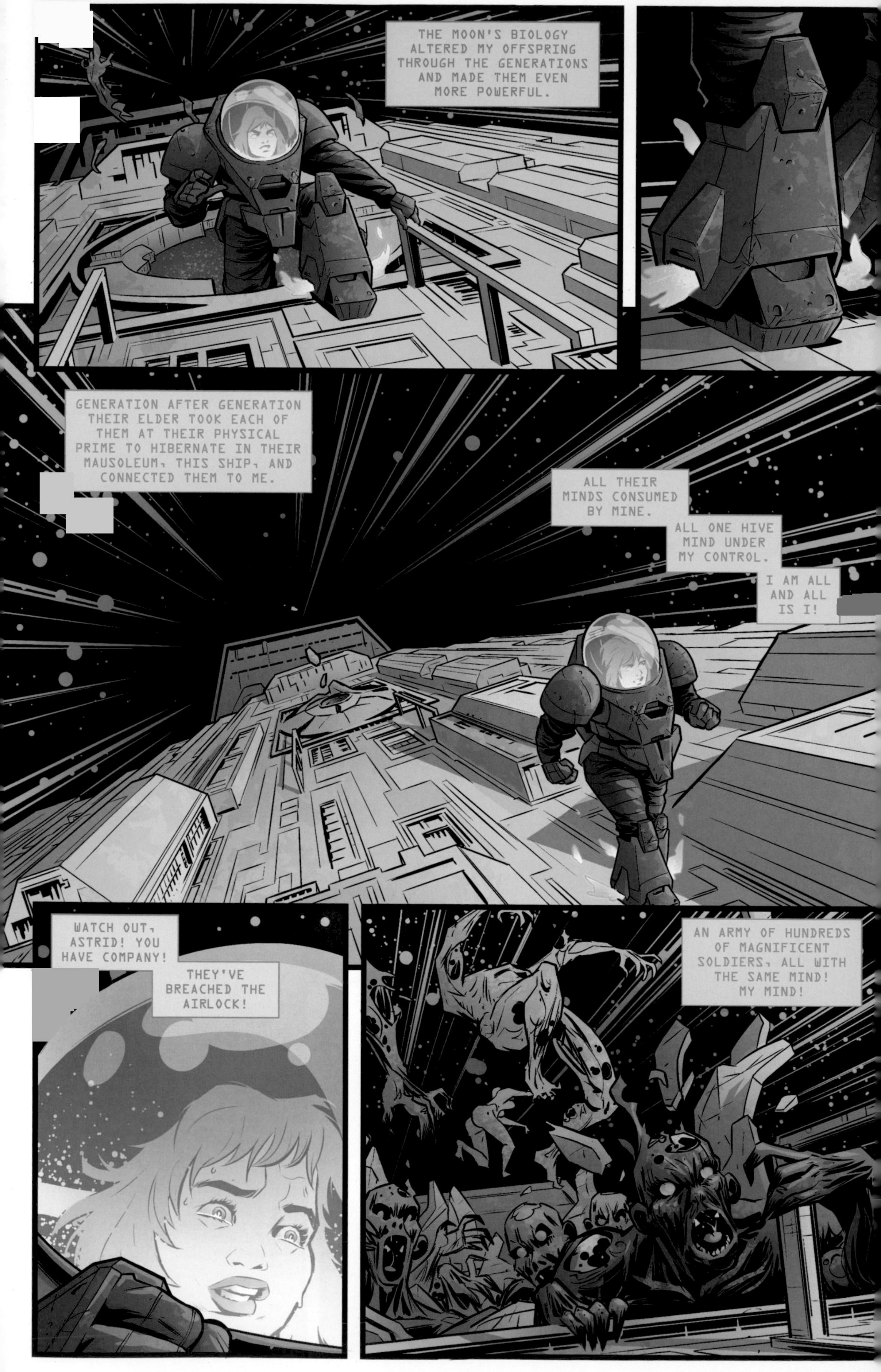
THE MOON'S BIOLOGY ALTERED MY OFFSPRING THROUGH THE GENERATIONS AND MADE THEM EVEN MORE POWERFUL.
GENERATION AFTER GENERATION THEIR ELDER TOOK EACH OF THEM AT THEIR PHYSICAL PRIME TO HIBERNATE IN THEIR MAUSOLEUM, THIS SHIP, AND CONNECTED THEM TO ME.
ALL THEIR MINDS CONSUMED BY MINE.
ALL ONE HIVE MIND UNDER MY CONTROL.
I AM ALL AND ALL IS I!
WATCH OUT, ASTRID! YOU HAVE COMPANY!
THEY'VE BREACHED THE AIRLOCK!
AN ARMY OF HUNDREDS OF MAGNIFICENT SOLDIERS, ALL WITH THE SAME MIND! MY MIND!

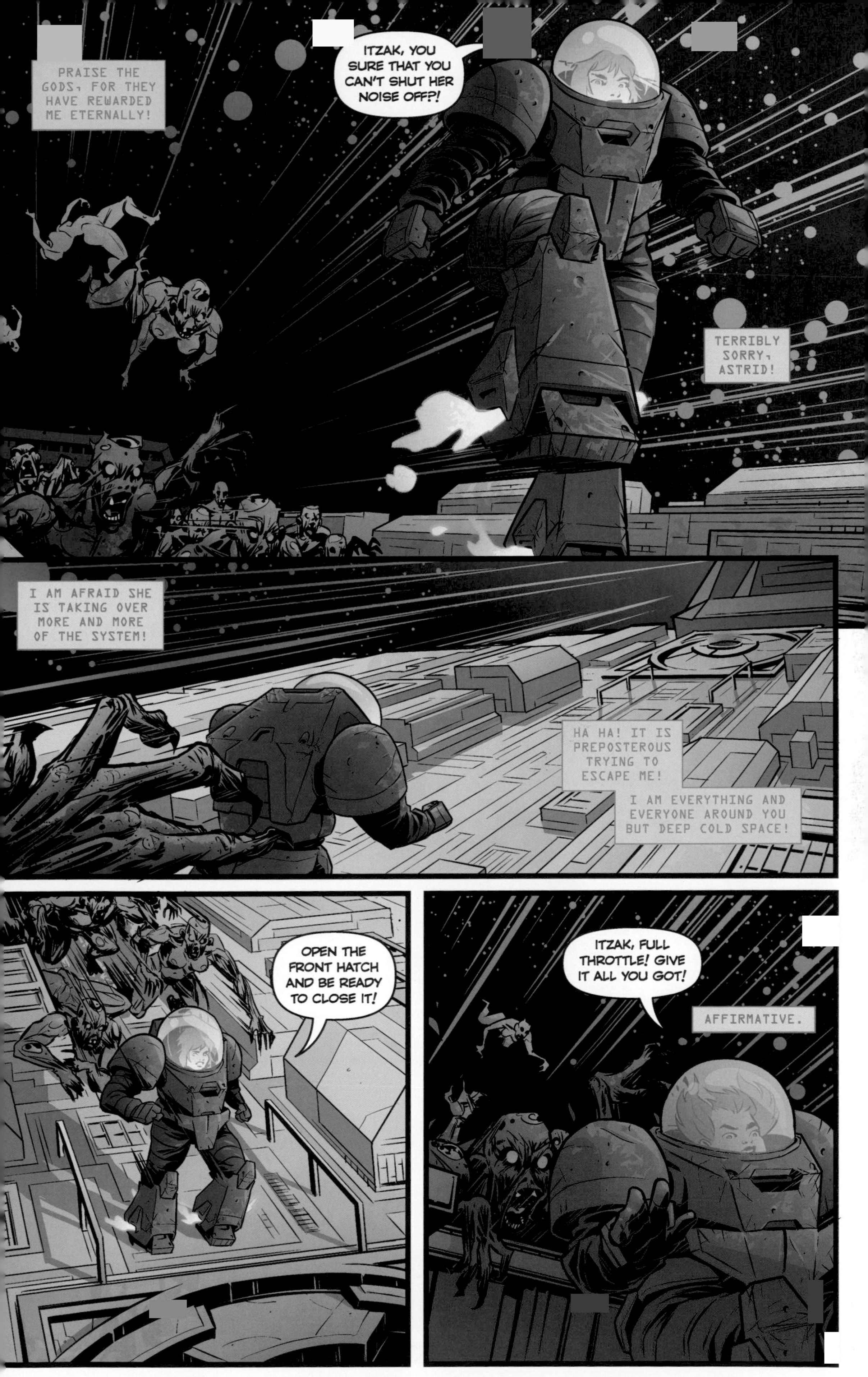

PRAISE THE GODS, FOR THEY HAVE REWARDED ME ETERNALLY!
ITZAK, YOU SURE THAT YOU CAN'T SHUT HER NOISE OFF?!
TERRIBLY SORRY, ASTRID!
I AM AFRAID SHE IS TAKING OVER MORE AND MORE OF THE SYSTEM!
HA HA! IT IS PREPOSTEROUS TRYING TO ESCAPE ME!
I AM EVERYTHING AND EVERYONE AROUND YOU BUT DEEP COLD SPACE!
OPEN THE FRONT HATCH AND BE READY TO CLOSE IT!
ITZAK, FULL THROTTLE! GIVE IT ALL YOU GOT!
AFFIRMATIVE.

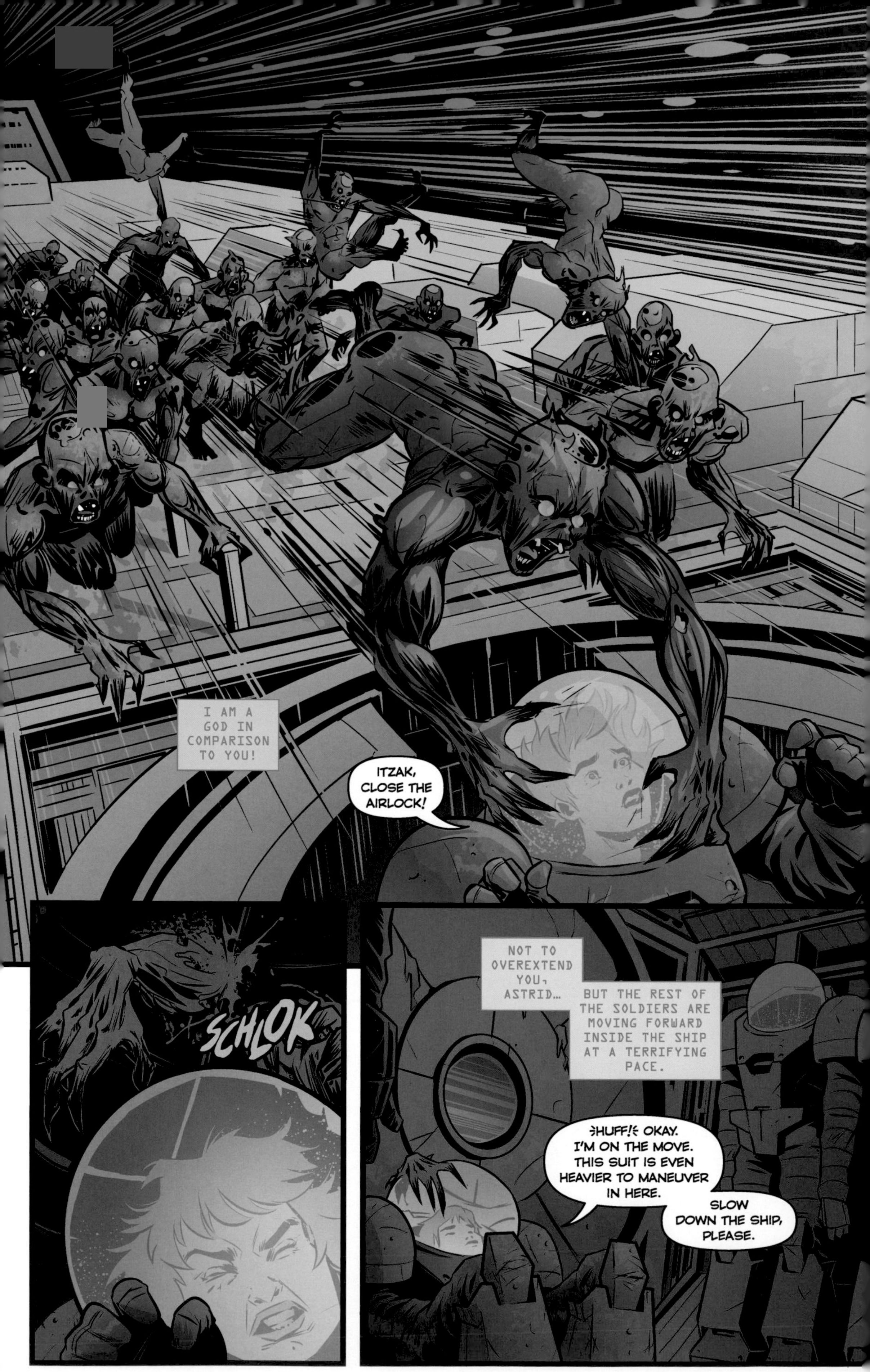

I AM A GOD IN COMPARISON TO YOU!
ITZAK, CLOSE THE AIRLOCK!
SCHLOK
NOT TO OVEREXTEND YOU, ASTRID...
BUT THE REST OF THE SOLDIERS ARE MOVING FORWARD INSIDE THE SHIP AT A TERRIFYING PACE.
HUFF! OKAY. I'M ON THE MOVE. THIS SUIT IS EVEN HEAVIER TO MANEUVER IN HERE.
SLOW DOWN THE SHIP, PLEASE.

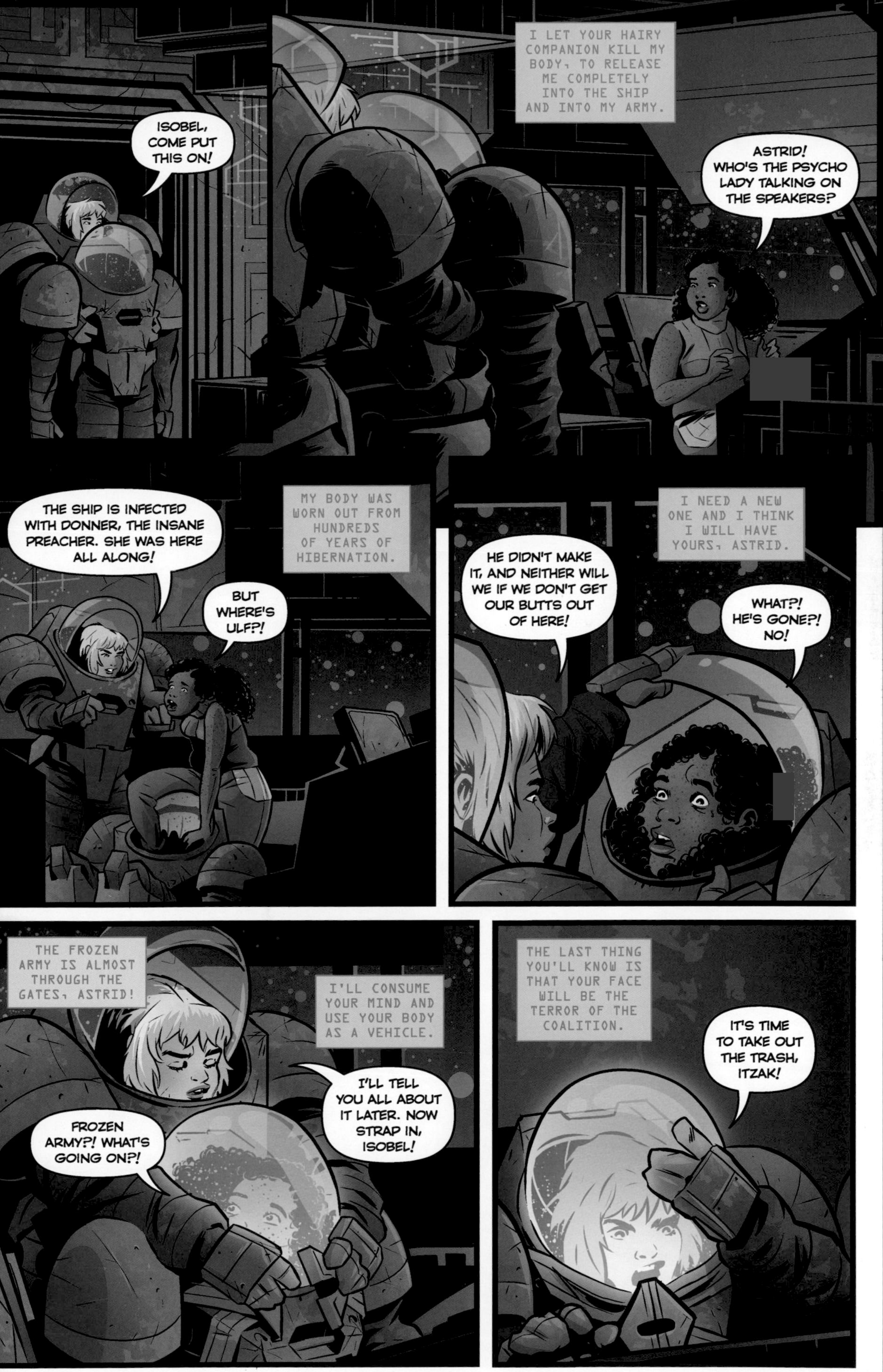
ISOBEL, COME PUT THIS ON!
I LET YOUR HAIRY COMPANION KILL MY BODY, TO RELEASE ME COMPLETELY INTO THE SHIP AND INTO MY ARMY.
ASTRID! WHO'S THE PSYCHO LADY TALKING ON THE SPEAKERS?
THE SHIP IS INFECTED WITH DONNER, THE INSANE PREACHER. SHE WAS HERE ALL ALONG!
MY BODY WAS WORN OUT FROM HUNDREDS OF YEARS OF HIBERNATION.
BUT WHERE'S ULF?!
I NEED A NEW ONE AND I THINK I WILL HAVE YOURS, ASTRID.
HE DIDN'T MAKE IT, AND NEITHER WILL WE IF WE DON'T GET OUR BUTTS OUT OF HERE!
WHAT?! HE'S GONE?! NO!
THE FROZEN ARMY IS ALMOST THROUGH THE GATES, ASTRID!
I'LL CONSUME YOUR MIND AND USE YOUR BODY AS A VEHICLE.
FROZEN ARMY?! WHAT'S GOING ON?!
I'LL TELL YOU ALL ABOUT IT LATER. NOW STRAP IN, ISOBEL!
THE LAST THING YOU'LL KNOW IS THAT YOUR FACE WILL BE THE TERROR OF THE COALITION.
IT'S TIME TO TAKE OUT THE TRASH, ITZAK!

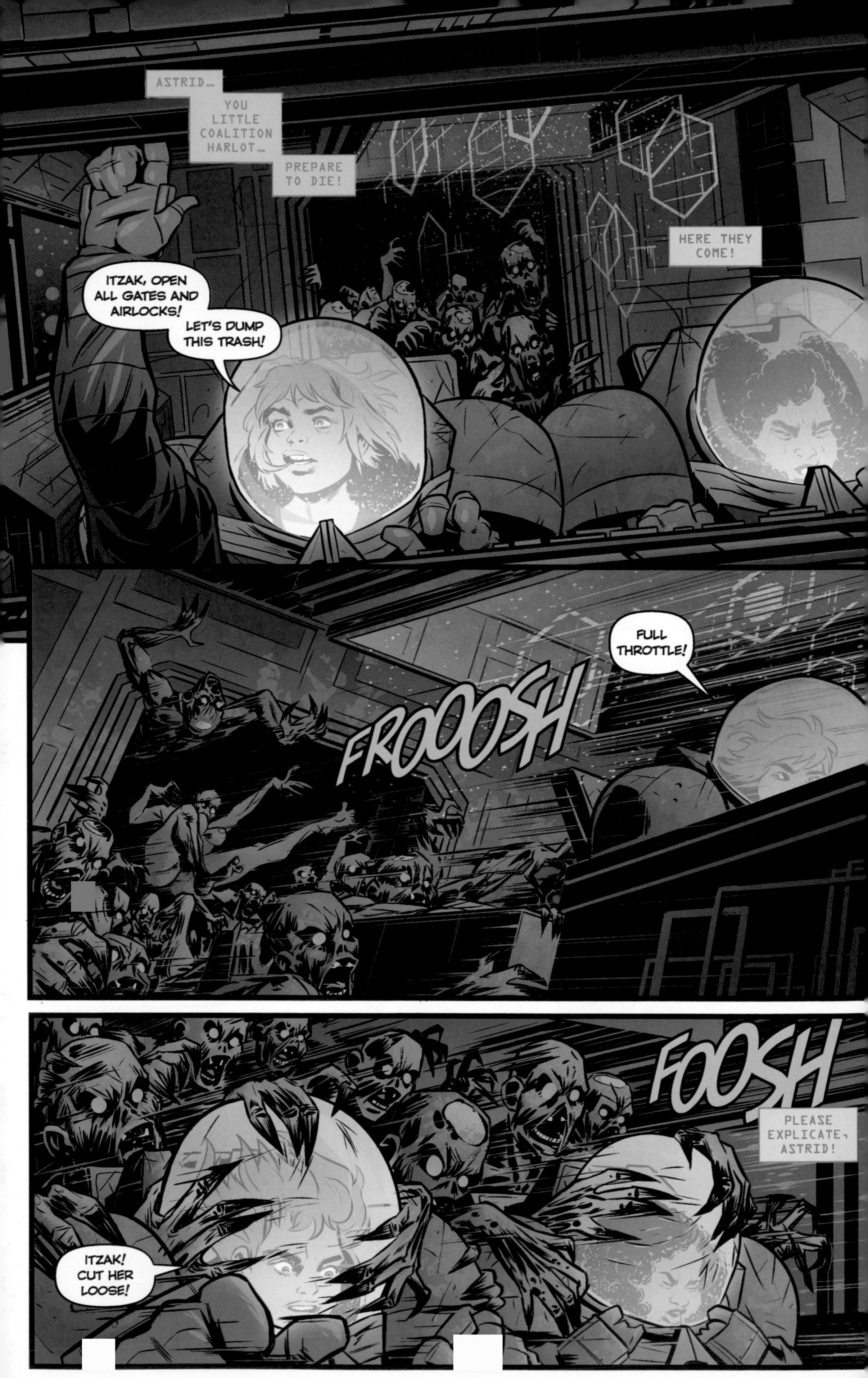
ASTRID...
YOU LITTLE COALITION HARLOT...
PREPARE TO DIE!
HERE THEY COME!
ITZAK, OPEN ALL GATES AND AIRLOCKS!
LET'S DUMP THIS TRASH!
FULL THROTTLE!
FROOOSH
FOOSH
PLEASE EXPLICATE, ASTRID!
ITZAK! CUT HER LOOSE!

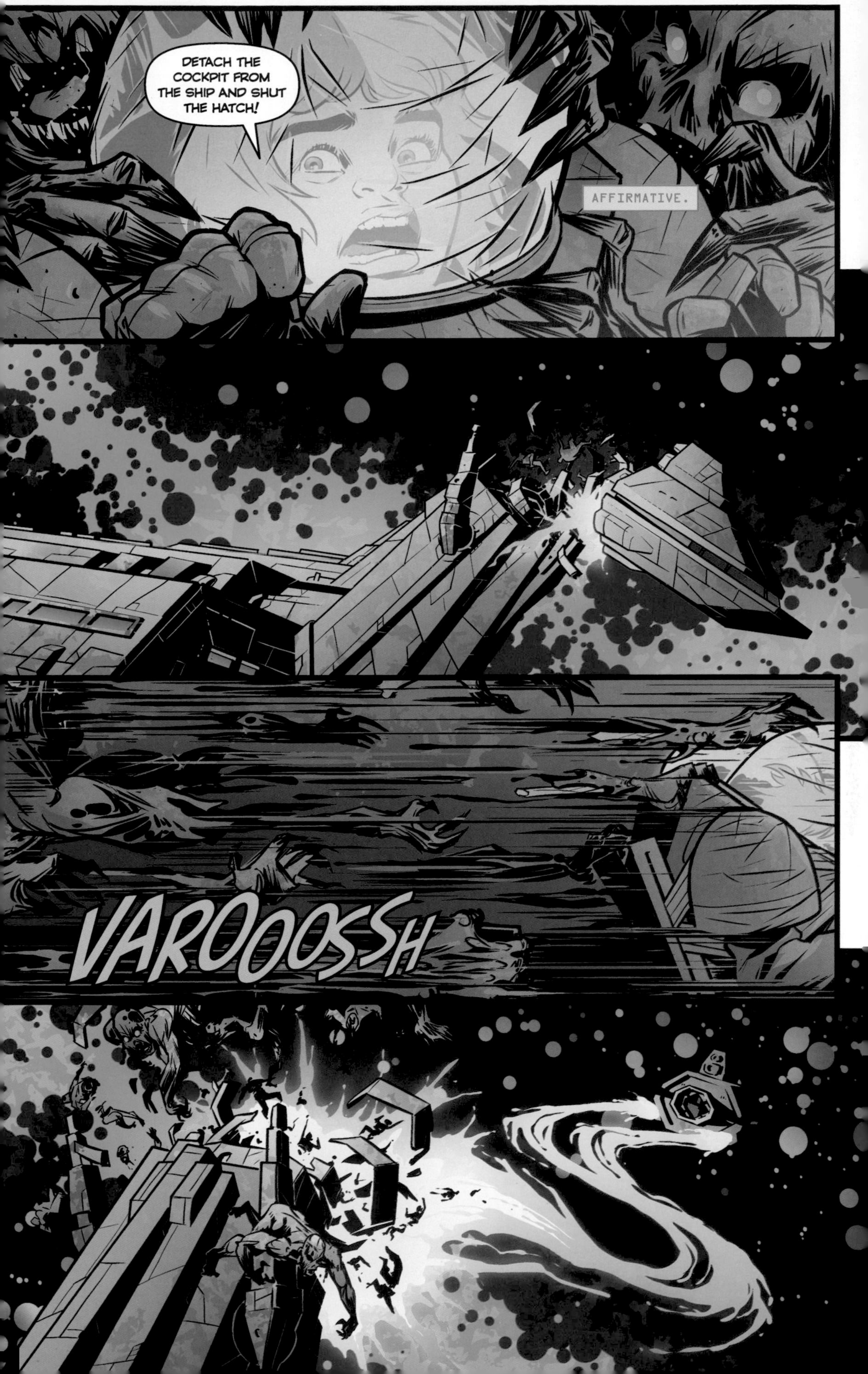
DETACH THE COCKPIT FROM THE SHIP AND SHUT THE HATCH!
AFFIRMATIVE.
VAROOOSSH

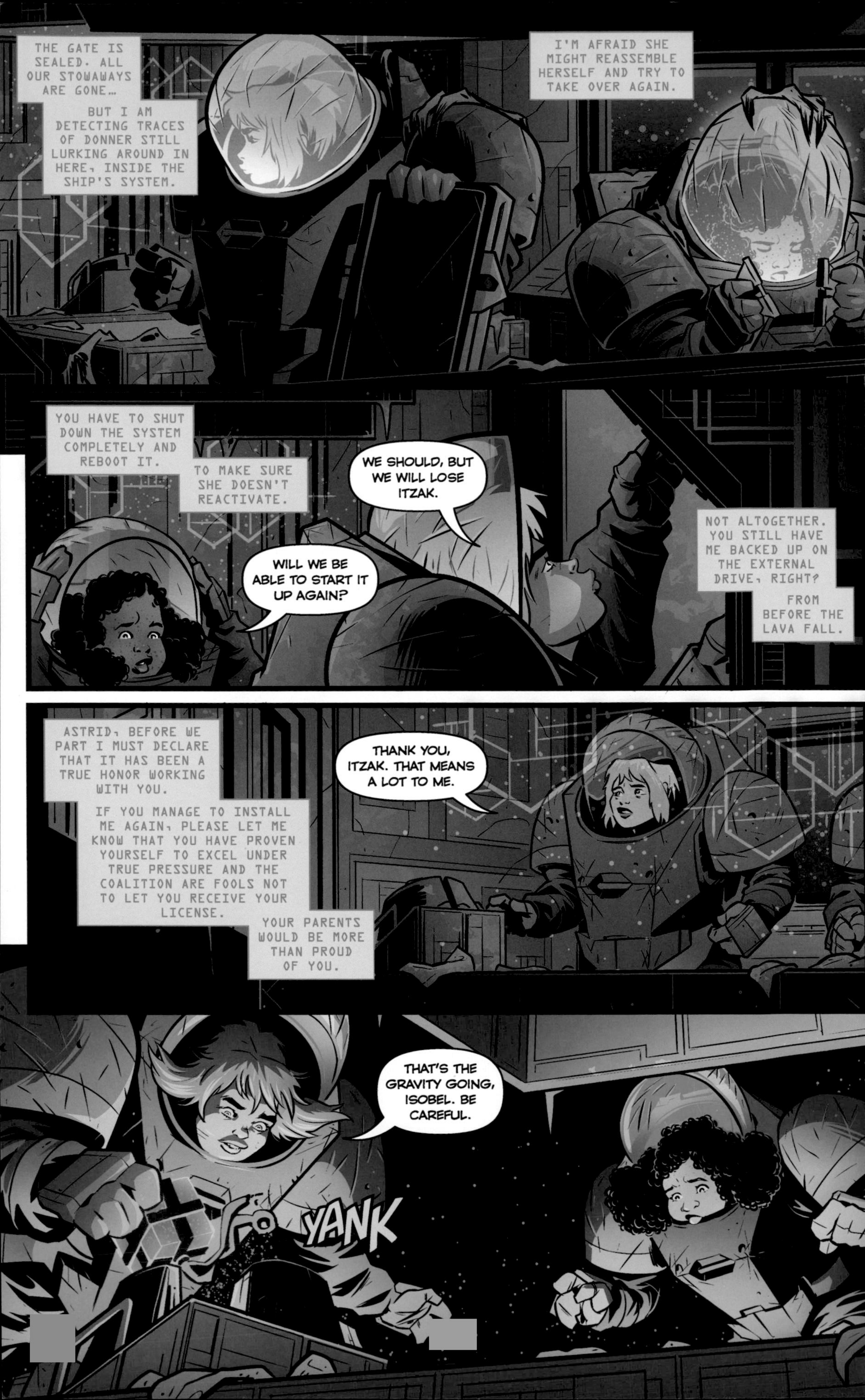
THE GATE IS SEALED. ALL OUR STOWAWAYS ARE GONE…
BUT I AM DETECTING TRACES OF DONNER STILL LURKING AROUND IN HERE, INSIDE THE SHIP'S SYSTEM.
I'M AFRAID SHE MIGHT REASSEMBLE HERSELF AND TRY TO TAKE OVER AGAIN.
YOU HAVE TO SHUT DOWN THE SYSTEM COMPLETELY AND REBOOT IT.
TO MAKE SURE SHE DOESN'T REACTIVATE.
WE SHOULD, BUT WE WILL LOSE ITZAK.
WILL WE BE ABLE TO START IT UP AGAIN?
NOT ALTOGETHER. YOU STILL HAVE ME BACKED UP ON THE EXTERNAL DRIVE, RIGHT?
FROM BEFORE THE LAVA FALL.
ASTRID, BEFORE WE PART I MUST DECLARE THAT IT HAS BEEN A TRUE HONOR WORKING WITH YOU.
IF YOU MANAGE TO INSTALL ME AGAIN, PLEASE LET ME KNOW THAT YOU HAVE PROVEN YOURSELF TO EXCEL UNDER TRUE PRESSURE AND THE COALITION ARE FOOLS NOT TO LET YOU RECEIVE YOUR LICENSE.
YOUR PARENTS WOULD BE MORE THAN PROUD OF YOU.
THANK YOU, ITZAK. THAT MEANS A LOT TO ME.
THAT'S THE GRAVITY GOING, ISOBEL. BE CAREFUL.
YANK

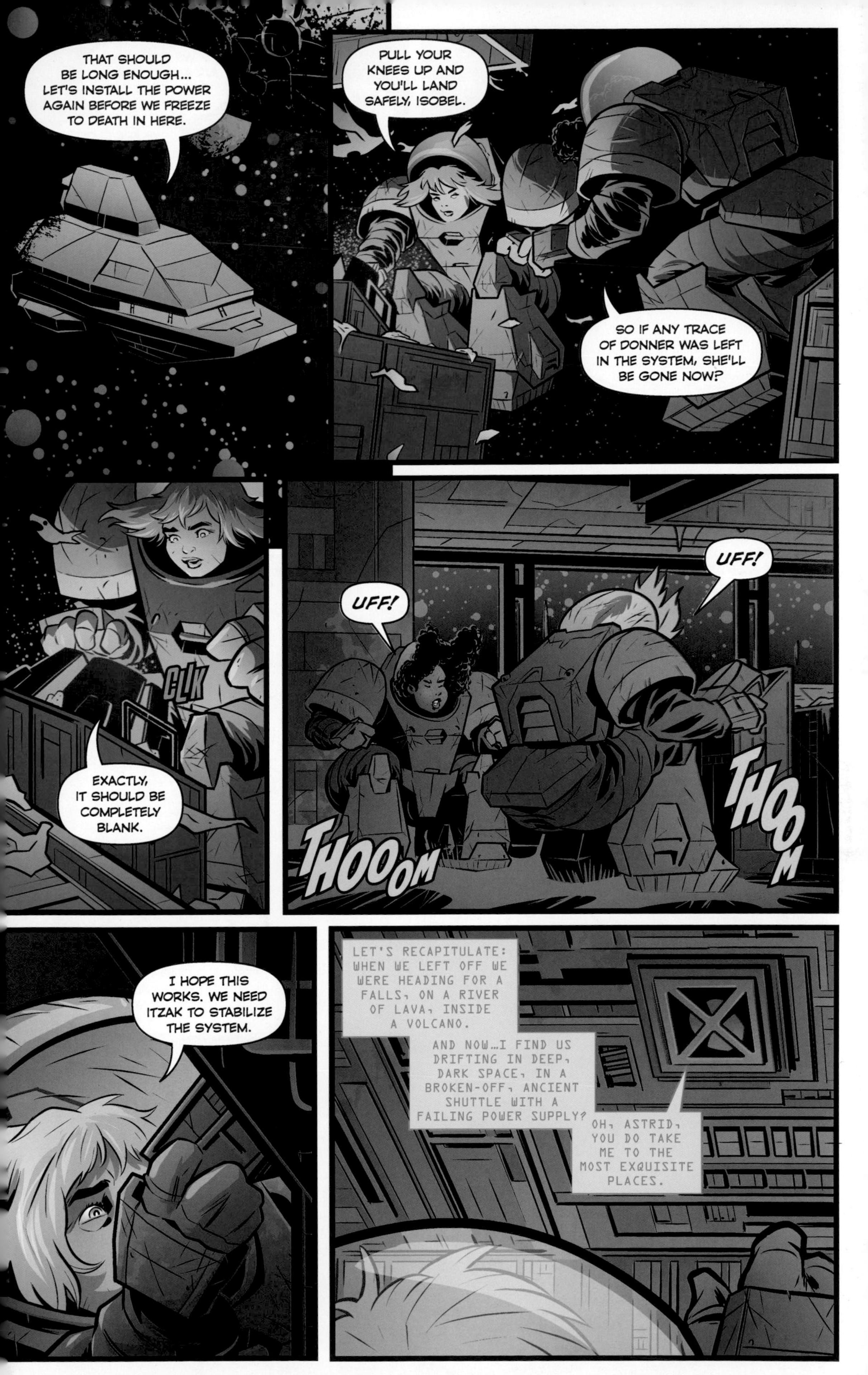
THAT SHOULD BE LONG ENOUGH... LET'S INSTALL THE POWER AGAIN BEFORE WE FREEZE TO DEATH IN HERE.
PULL YOUR KNEES UP AND YOU'LL LAND SAFELY, ISOBEL.
SO IF ANY TRACE OF DONNER WAS LEFT IN THE SYSTEM, SHE'LL BE GONE NOW?
CLIK
EXACTLY, IT SHOULD BE COMPLETELY BLANK.
UFF!
UFF!
THOOOOM
THOOOM
I HOPE THIS WORKS. WE NEED ITZAK TO STABILIZE THE SYSTEM.
LET'S RECAPITULATE: WHEN WE LEFT OFF WE WERE HEADING FOR A FALLS, ON A RIVER OF LAVA, INSIDE A VOLCANO.
AND NOW...I FIND US DRIFTING IN DEEP, DARK SPACE, IN A BROKEN-OFF, ANCIENT SHUTTLE WITH A FAILING POWER SUPPLY?
OH, ASTRID, YOU DO TAKE ME TO THE MOST EXQUISITE PLACES.

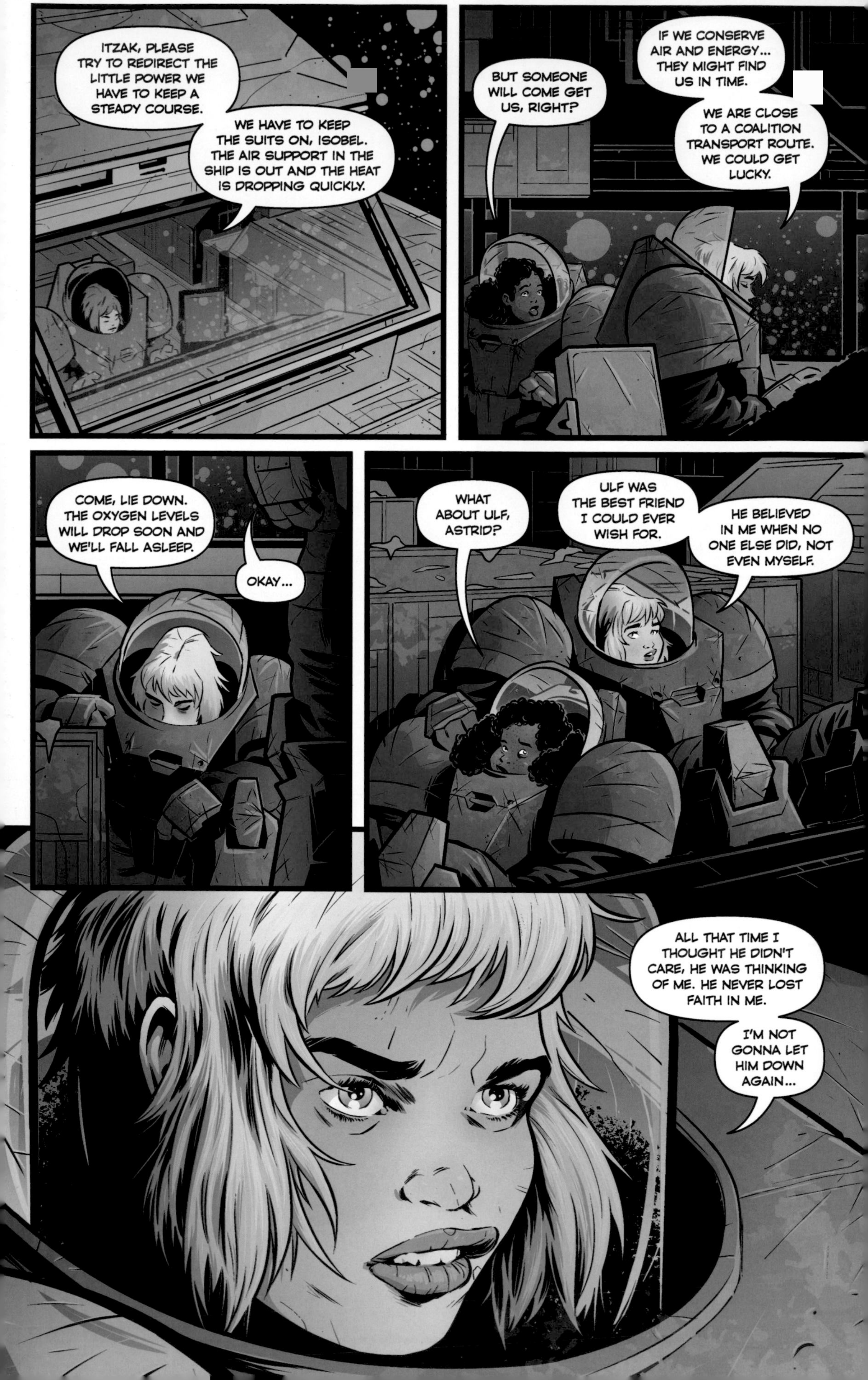
ITZAK, PLEASE TRY TO REDIRECT THE LITTLE POWER WE HAVE TO KEEP A STEADY COURSE.
WE HAVE TO KEEP THE SUITS ON, ISOBEL. THE AIR SUPPORT IN THE SHIP IS OUT AND THE HEAT IS DROPPING QUICKLY.
BUT SOMEONE WILL COME GET US, RIGHT?
IF WE CONSERVE AIR AND ENERGY... THEY MIGHT FIND US IN TIME.
WE ARE CLOSE TO A COALITION TRANSPORT ROUTE. WE COULD GET LUCKY.
COME, LIE DOWN. THE OXYGEN LEVELS WILL DROP SOON AND WE'LL FALL ASLEEP.
OKAY...
WHAT ABOUT ULF, ASTRID?
ULF WAS THE BEST FRIEND I COULD EVER WISH FOR.
HE BELIEVED IN ME WHEN NO ONE ELSE DID, NOT EVEN MYSELF.
ALL THAT TIME I THOUGHT HE DIDN'T CARE, HE WAS THINKING OF ME. HE NEVER LOST FAITH IN ME.
I'M NOT GONNA LET HIM DOWN AGAIN...

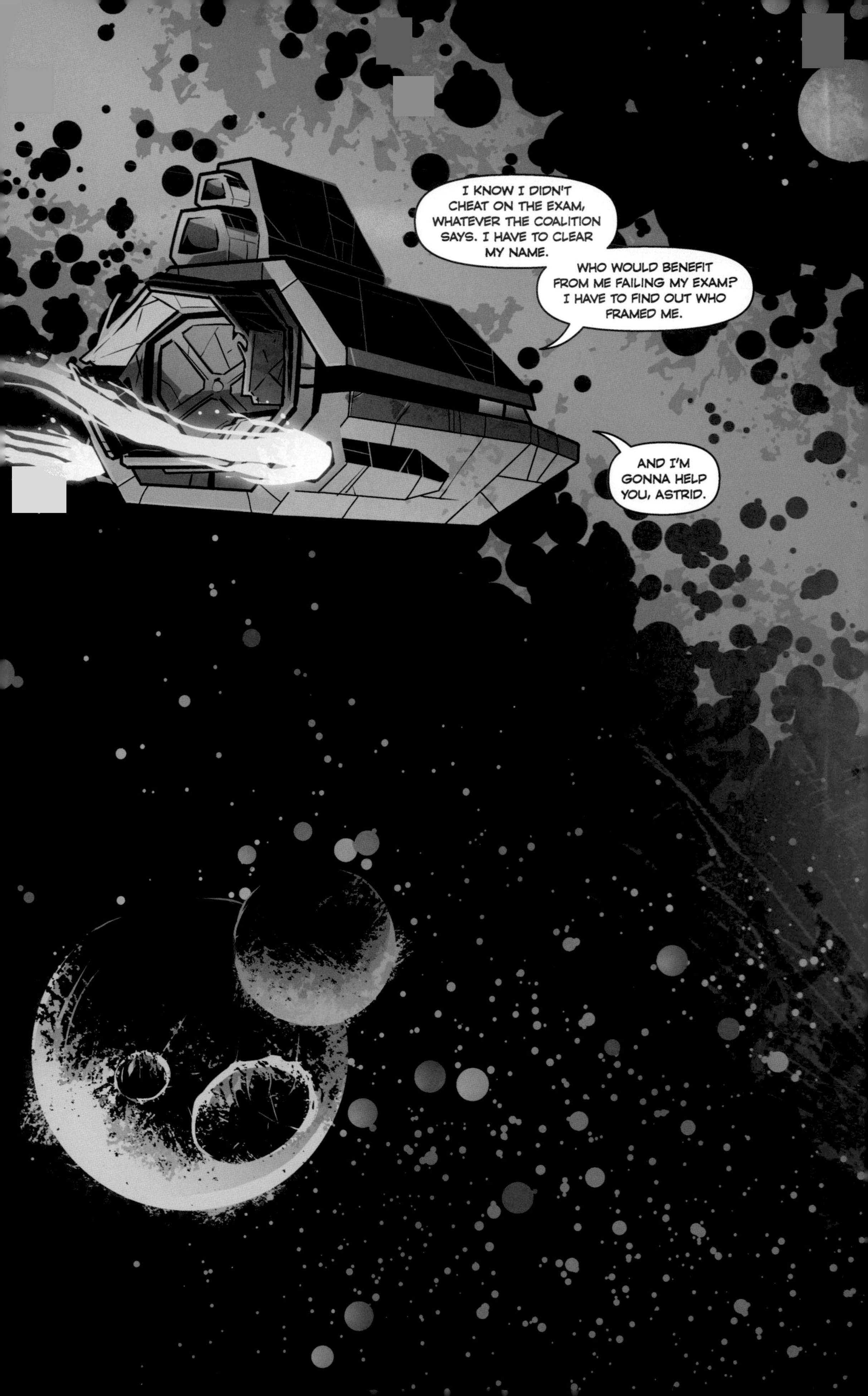
I KNOW I DIDN'T CHEAT ON THE EXAM, WHATEVER THE COALITION SAYS. I HAVE TO CLEAR MY NAME.
WHO WOULD BENEFIT FROM ME FAILING MY EXAM? I HAVE TO FIND OUT WHO FRAMED ME.
AND I'M GONNA HELP YOU, ASTRID.

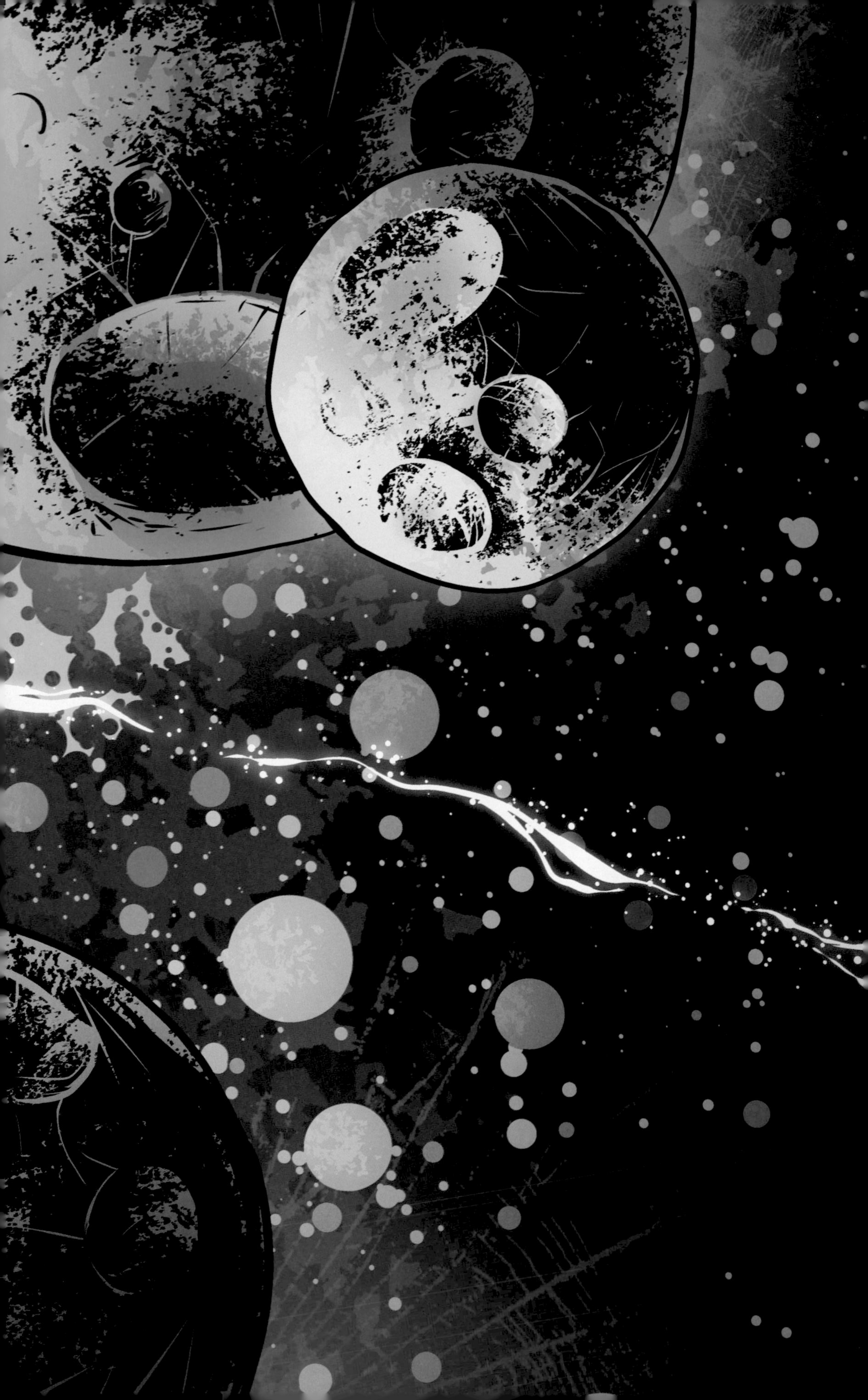

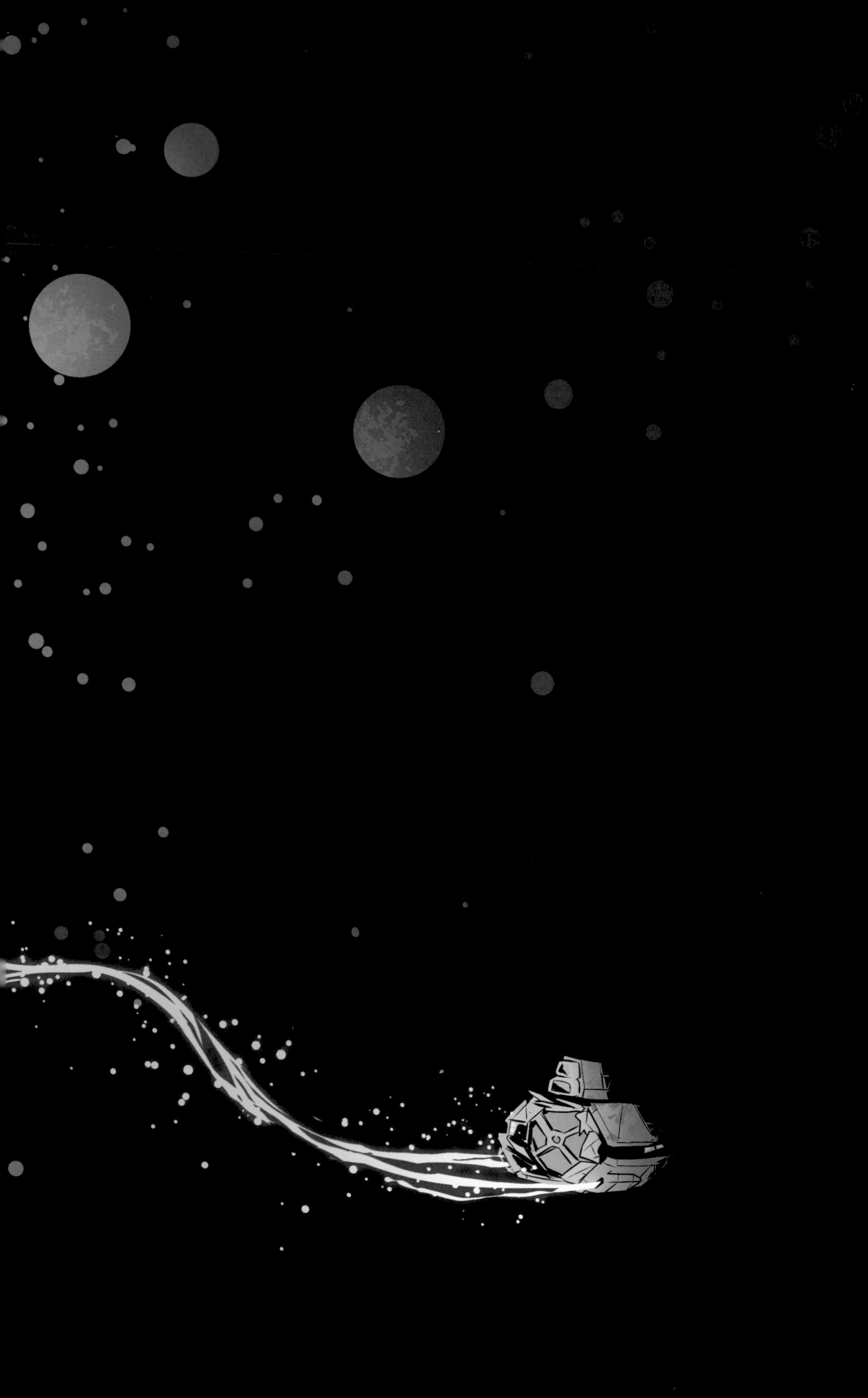

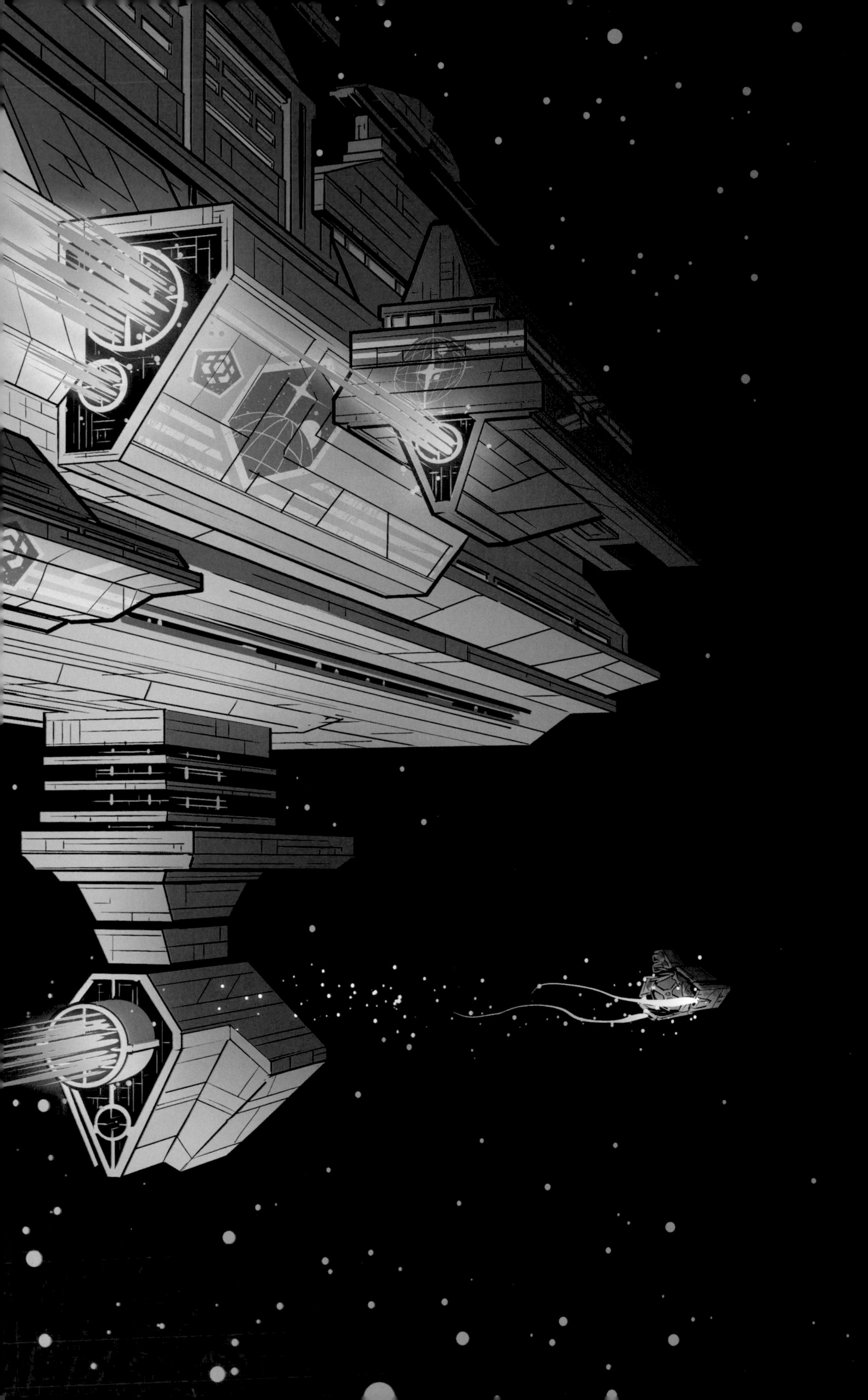

# KIM W. ANDERSSON

## "WICKED FUN FOR THE RIGHT AUDIENCE."—BOOKLIST

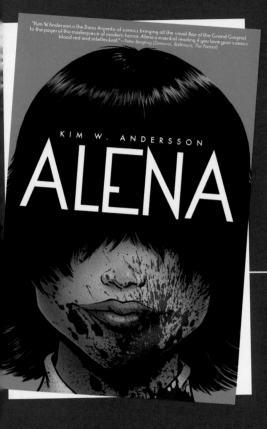

"Kim W Andersson is the Dario Argento of comics, bringing all the visual flair of the Grand Guignol to the pages of this masterpiece of modern horror. *Alena* is essential reading if you love your comics blood red and intellectual."—Peter Bergting (*Domovoi, Baltimore, The Portent*)
KIM W. ANDERSSON
ALENA

### ALENA

**NOW A MAJOR MOTION PICTURE!**

Alena's life is a living hell. Since she arrived at a snobbish boarding school, she's been harassed every day by Philippa and the girls on the lacrosse team. But Alena's best friend Josephine is not going to accept that anymore. Not from the counselor or the principal, not from Philippa, and not from anyone else at that horrid school. If Alena doesn't fight back, then Josephine will take matters into her own hands. There's just one problem . . . Josephine has been dead for a year . . .

978-1-50670-215-5 | $17.99

Love
HURTS

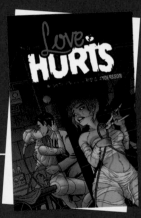

### THE COMPLETE LOVE HURTS

A shocking series of short stories about love gone horribly wrong—romance comics with brutal, terrible twists which show that, no matter who you are or what you do, love can be one deadly bitch!

978-1-61655-859-8 | $19.99

ASTRID
KIM W. ANDERSSON

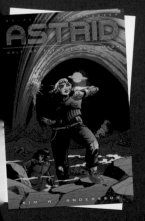

### ASTRID VOLUME 1:

### CULT OF THE VOLCANIC MOON

A comedic sci-fi epic for fans of *Firefly* and *Mass Effect*! Formerly the Galactic Coalition's top recruit, the now-disgraced Astrid is offered a special mission from her old commander. She'll prove herself worthy of another chance at becoming a Galactic Peacekeeper . . . if she can survive the ancient evil of an uncharted moon, of course!

978-1-61655-690-7 | $19.99

DARK HORSE BOOKS

DARKHORSE.COM

AVAILABLE AT YOUR LOCAL COMICS SHOP OR BOOKSTORE
TO FIND A COMICS SHOP IN YOUR AREA, CALL 1-888-266-4226



FOR MORE INFORMATION OR TO ORDER DIRECT:
ON THE WEB: DARKHORSE.COM
EMAIL: MAILORDER@DARKHORSE.COM
PHONE: 1-800-862-0052 MON.–FRI.
9 AM TO 5 PM PACIFIC TIME.